**MEMOIRS OF A CAPTIVITY
AMONG THE INDIANS
OF NORTH AMERICA**

JOHN D. HUNTER.

MEMOIRS OF A CAPTIVITY AMONG THE INDIANS OF NORTH AMERICA

JOHN DUNN HUNTER

Edited by Richard Drinnon

SCHOCKEN BOOKS · NEW YORK

This edition is based on the third and most complete English edition of the *Memoirs of a Captivity* . . . , published in London in 1824.

Copyright © 1973 by Richard Drinnon
Library of Congress Catalog Card No. 73-79053
Manufactured in the United States of America

Frontispiece: The drawing of John Dunn Hunter is by Charles R. Leslie and appeared as the frontispiece of the 1824 London edition of *Memoirs of a Captivity* . . . . (Reproduced courtesy of the American History Division, The New York Public Library, Astor, Lenox and Tilden Foundations.)

Contents

Introduction by Richard Drinnon   xi

Preface   1

PART ONE: **MEMOIRS OF A CAPTIVITY AMONG THE INDIANS OF NORTH AMERICA, FROM THE AUTHOR'S EARLIEST RECOLLECTION TO HIS ASSUMPTION OF THE HABITS OF CIVILIZED LIFE**   5

PART TWO: **MANNERS AND CUSTOMS OF SEVERAL INDIAN TRIBES LOCATED WEST OF THE MISSISSIPPI; INCLUDING SOME OBSERVATIONS ON THE EXTENT, ASPECT, AND NATURAL PRODUCTIONS AND CIRCUMSTANCES OF THE COUNTRY THEY INHABIT**

1   Considerations on the Physical and Moral Condition of the Indians   83

2   Views of Theocracy, Religion, Agency of Good and Bad Spirits; of the Soul and Its Migration; Religious Rites; Prophets, Priests, and Physicians; Dreams, &c.   101

3   Courtship, Marriage, Widowhood, Polygamy, Divorcements, Continuance of Families, Adoption of Children, Indian Names, Disposition of the Infirm and Poor   111

4	Family Government, Occupation, and Economy; Birth, Nursing, and Education of Infants; Education and Amusements of Youth; Games of Chance; Modes of Salutation; Treatment of Strangers; Forms of Visits, Feasts, Festivals, &c.	123
5	Hunting, Fishing, Agriculture, Manufactures, Currency, and Trade	136
6	Crimes and Modes of Punishment	148
7	Policy, Councils, Transaction of Public Business Generally, Election of Chiefs, Reception of Ambassadors, Peace-runners, &c.	152
8	Patriotism, Martial Character and Propensity, War Implements, Preparations for, and Management and Termination of War, &c.	157
9	Residence, Dress, Painting, Disposal of the Dead, Mournings, &c.	165
10	Indian Anecdotes	171
11	Indian Diseases	180
12	Observations on the Materia Medica of the Indians	188
13	Observations on the Indian Practice of Surgery and Medicine	208
14	Observations on Civilizing the American Indians	212
	Reflections on the Different States and Conditions of Society; with the Outlines of a Plan to Ameliorate the Circumstances of the Indians of North America	220
	Notes	230

OSAGE SONGS OF THE CLOUDS

Mysterious are those that stand upright,
  Four among them are greatest in mystery.

Look at the beauty of the moving black clouds.
Look at the beauty of the moving gray clouds.
Look at the beauty of the moving white clouds.
Look at the beauty of the moving blue sky.

STAND ASLEEP OR VIGIL SONG

I make myself sleep. I make myself sleep.
I bring myself to dream. I bring myself to dream.
Come here dreams. Come here dreams.
Teach me dreams. Teach me dreams.
In the light of the house I stand with browned hands.
  (Browned with the soil of the earth.)
In the light of the house I stand with darkened face.
  (Darkened with the sacred soil of the earth.)
In the light of the mystery I see the down of the eagle.

RITUAL OF THE SYMBOLIC PAINTING

When they adorn their bodies
  With the crimson shed by the God of Day,
Then shall the Little Ones make themselves
  Free from death,
As they travel the path of life.

Truly, at that time and place,
  It has been said in this house,
They said to one another: What shall
  The people place upon his wrists?
It is a bond spoken of as a captive's bond,
  That they shall place upon his wrists.

Truly, it is not a captive's bond,
  That is spoken of.
But it is a soul,
  That they shall place upon his wrists.

*Based on the literal translations
of Francis La Flesche,
"Osage Tribe: The Rite of Vigil"*

Introduction

For that moment imagined by F. Scott Fitzgerald, the first Europeans may have stood in wonder before the green vastness of North America. For those who had eyes to see, the continent must have been truly enchanting, from the shadowed lushness of southern swamps to the dancing lights of clear-running northern streams. There the land lay, uncharted and unconquered, watched over reverentially by the savages in residence. Still, if this moment ever existed, it lasted no longer than the flicker of an eyelash.

"Here," said Cotton Mather, "hath arisen light in darkness." The light, of course Christian, shone down on a great moral drama, the completion of the Protestant Reformation in the New World. It was a celestial light, however, not earthy, spiritual rather than physical. It was not of the eyes but of the head, a reversed head-light: it commenced to shine with its peculiar brilliance only when the Puritans closed their eyes to natural beauties.

These sightless eyes beheld "a hideous and desolate Wilderness." By way of ultimate paradox, their eyes, as organs of the body, had become organs of darkness, the darkness of a fallen and corrupt world where "Life's a very Death": "This World's a Wilderness," said Michael Wiggelsworth, "To God's afflicted Saints." It was an affliction unto death: The World = Wilderness = Darkness = Death. Not even the nuclear technicians of Almagordo's peculiar flash—Mather's light updated to our own day—were more alienated from themselves and their surroundings. Shut up in their heads, unhappy sojourners in a world of "Woes and Wants," the Saints could not conceive of themselves as integral parts of nature—insofar as they lived in their own bodies—nor could they conceive of themselves as residents of our Mother Earth.

Hold on to this uncuttable connection between their own "lower nature" and the rest of the physical world for a second: when these first Europeans launched their war against nature in the New World, they were crusading against both the wildness in their environment and the never-to-be-completely repressed wildness in themselves. Nature had to be explored, mapped, surveyed, parceled out, fenced in, and later, bulldozed, and paved over. As we know too well, the end result turned green forests into lighted parking lots. In like fashion, natural man had to be fenced in, paved over, as it were, and bulldozed into proper subjection to the Kingdom of God. The enemy was anything or anyone unknown and unordered, an uncut forest, an undammed river, unleashed impulse, spontaneity, tumescent desire, irrational coupling. And it was Jesus himself, according to another seventeenth-century settler, who worked through the faithful to turn "one of the most hideous, boundless and unknown wildernesses in the world . . . to a well-ordered Commonwealth."

By definition the Indians were not well-ordered. But did the Saints see them as a race apart or merely, as has been insisted recently, as men living in a state of sin? This posing of the question is in truth fatuous, for the answer is that the Puritans saw them as both insofar as the Indians resisted becoming tawny Calvinists. Of course, congregations could urge the erection of churches among the pagans, though few were built, and they could call on one another to bring them "out of that woeful state and condition they are now in." That state, as I have implied, was an intimate communion with nature and faith in an indwelling Great Spirit that made the very stones sacred. The Puritans ordered them out of it, with the command that they share their own faith in a disembodied Deity who remained, most of the time, completely *outside* nature. If religious in origin, their demand hit with racist impact. It was no less than that the Indians agree to their own negation: they had to stop being Indians.

"If thy right eye offend thee, pluck it out and cast it from thee." Christians willing to carry the war against nature that far and that close had to hate the Indians for living in the wilderness and being at home in it. To the Puritans they were offending eyes, organs out of control, running wild, so to speak, and most hateful of all, eyes that offended without even a winking acknowledgment of their offenses. They lived in glades reminiscent of the groves condemned in the Bible and no doubt therein carried out their own wanton and licentious rites. Thus the Indians too were named "idolatrous canaanites." They were, said John White, "men transformed into beasts." Their long hair was especially repulsive, for it seemed ungroomed, filthy and sexual, suggestive of the unmentionable, of flesh, mortality, and beastliness.

In 1649 there was even a campaign to Clean up the Bay Colony or, as Thomas Hutchinson called it, "an association against long hair." Among the documents later collected by the governor, one bears that date and the signatures of the doughty John Endicott, Richard Saltonstall, and other magistrates. It reads:

> For as much as the wearing of long hair, after the manner of ruffians and barbarous Indians, has begun to invade New England, contrary to the rule of God's word, which says it is a shame for a man to wear long hair, as also the commendable custom generally of all the Godly of our nation until within these few years, we, the Magistrates who have subscribed to this paper (for the showing of our *own innocency* in this behalf), do declare and manifest our dislike and detestation against the wearing of such long hair, as a thing uncivil and unmanly, whereby men do deform themselves and offend sober and modest men.

The elders were instructed to manifest their zeal in insuring that members of their "respective Churches be not defiled therewith." Hard on themselves, to be sure, these sober and modest men were merciless when it came to native long hairs.

Recalcitrance brought down a shower of epithets: "skulking heathens," "wild beasts," "ravening wolves." The least show of resistance was sign sufficient that they were "devil-driven." Indians, said John White, were "bond-slaves of Sathan." Or consider Cotton Mather's account of how Metacom, or King Philip, as the English called him, brought down God's vengeance for scorning the missionary attentions of John Eliot:

> our Elliot [sic] made a tender of *everlasting salvation* unto that king but the monster entertained it with contempt and anger, and after the *Indian* mode of joining signs with words, he took a button upon the coat of the reverend man, adding, that *he cared for his gospel as much as he cared for that button*. The world has heard what terrible ruins soon came upon that monarch and upon all his people. It was not long before the hand that now writes, upon a certain occasion, took off the jaw from the exposed *skull* of that *blasphemous leviathan*.

Even Roger Williams, no Mather he, decades earlier had asserted that the Pequots dared defy the Puritan armies because they counted on the support of Satan.

It followed that for whites to fall into red hands during hostilities was for them to fall out of Christian light into primal darkness. They fell into a blackness as impenetrable as that said to exist before God created light and divided night from day. "Now away we must go with those barbarous creatures," sighed Mrs. Mary Rowlandson in her *Soveraignty and Goodness of God* (1682). The victory celebrations of her captors suitably took place in the dark: "This was the dolefullest night that ever my eyes saw," she recounted. "Oh the roaring and singing and dancing and yelling of those black creatures in the night. . . ." Other still more doleful nights of singing and dancing came to pass during the following century. In her narrative of 1797 Maria Kittle related how she lost members of her family to the tomahawk and fire, had the forehead of her infant son dashed against the stone—an apple tree was usually preferred for this purpose—and had been carried away into captivity there to suffer other heaven-defying cruelties: "O barbarous! surpassing devils in wickedness! so may a tenfold night of misery enwrap your black souls as you have deprived the babe of my bosom, the comfort of my cares, my blessed cherub, of light and life—O hell! are not thy flames impatient to cleave the center and engulph these wretches in thy ever burning waves?"

Readers were impatient, if the flames were not, for such combustibles: From Mrs. Rowlandson's pamphlet of 1682 to the mid-1820s they consumed almost a hundred captivity tales, along with fifteen novels which had captivity episodes or themes in their plots.* At once penny dreadfuls and shilling horrors, they were the equivalent of the modern mystery and detective story and no doubt served some of the same psychological needs. They made fine repositories for the urges to cruelty of repressed whites: *O barbarous! so may a tenfold night of misery enwrap your black souls!* Most satisfying of all in this respect was Mrs. Hannah Duston's account, preserved in Mather's *Magnalia* (1702), of joining her two companions one dark night in chopping up their captors with hatchets and returning triumphantly with scalps for which they received fifty pounds from the General Assembly. Prohibited any explicitly salacious reading, the colonists had to settle for such violence pornography and feed on its tortures, gore, and bloodshed. Fantasies of real orgies were always there, to be sure, rustlings of raw sex just beyond the forest's edge, but they never quite surfaced in the narratives. The leading reason, apart from the "puritanism" that survived the Saints, was the reluctance of red captors to fulfill their fantasy roles as sex maniacs —cases of rape were so rare as to be nonexistent. On the public level, however, the narratives provided sure and steady political income. They channeled hatred against particular tribes and individual leaders, such as Metacom, and depending on the point in time, depicted the Indians as devil-inspired, French-inspired, or later still, final irony, English-inspired. Their sensationalism mounted

---

*Notes for this introduction and the text which follows, indicated by asterisks (*), commence below on p. 230. Hunter had some footnotes, and I have added a few of an explanatory nature. These are identified by his initials (JDH) or by mine (RD).

and their format calcified, but all along the hatred they preached served to justify the extermination they furthered. The title of Archibald Loudon's early nineteenth-century anthology neatly summed up their uses on both levels, psychological and political: *A Selection of Some of the Most Interesting Narratives of Outrages Committed by the Indians in Their Wars, with the White People* (1808).

More interesting still, however, were the narratives that were never written. Not a few "captives" refused to return from their voyages into darkness. In his *History of the Five Indian Nations* (1727), Cadwallader Colden was at a loss to account for why so many white prisoners of the wars of 1699 and 1700 could not be persuaded to go back to the clearings; try as he would, he was unable to think of a single comparable instance of an Indian choosing to remain with the English. And decades later, in a well-known passage, Crèvecoeur wondered why out loud. Why was it "thousands of Europeans are Indians, and we have no example of even one of those aborigines having from choice become European"? Could there really be "something superior in Indian society"?* Unthinkable as it was, the thought had occurred to the English. In his *Danger of Apostacy* (1679), Increase Mather had come perilously close to letting the whole cat out of the bag: "People are ready to run wild into the woods again and to be as Heathenish as ever, if you do not prevent it." Every "captive" who chose to stay with the Indians strengthened this temptation to wildness and had a story to tell that undermined the orthodoxies of the published narratives. Or better, every "unredeemed" white threatened to topple the myth of civilized light and savage darkness. Unhappily, apart from some fading memories back in the settlements, these stories were merely written on the wind, as we say, and not heard beyond the sentinel pines of the deep forest.

Yet there was another threat to the prevailing view of the savages as those "animals, vulgarly called Indians," and it too had existed from the outset: A "restored captive" could conceivably contend the Indians were human beings. The bearer of such tidings could clearly expect no warm welcome from white America, but this is to anticipate our own story.

2

In early 1823 John Dunn Hunter burst upon transatlantic readers with his singular narrative. After it first appeared in Philadelphia, it was retitled, enlarged, and published in London as *Memoirs of a Captivity among the Indians of North America*, two editions of which were printed in 1823, followed by a third in 1824. As Hunter's fame spread to the Continent, Dutch and German editions were published in 1824 and a Swedish edition in 1826.*

With his first sentence Hunter pulled the reader into an oddly attractive tension between style and content. He was very nearly unique among the writers of this genre in not straining for sensationalism. No bestial savages, hordes of which ran through the pages of other narratives, committed acts of unspeakable cruelty that could then be described in prurient detail. No one was invited to sumptuous repasts of blood and gore. No cries rose to the heavens for the hand of God (and man) to descend on the writer's heartless captors. Instead Hunter's tone was modest and quiet. Pleading an imperfect acquaintance with the language and total ignorance of "book-making," he besought indulgence for his inability to do his subject justice. He half apologized for intruding on the reader at all, for he had wanted to exclude himself entirely, but friends had persuaded him to include his own story—indeed, his wish was partly reflected in the *Manners and Customs* title of the Philadelphia edition, to which the history of the author's life was merely "prefixed" in the words of the subtitle. It is true that his tone became anxious, even agitated, in his discussion of the impending annihilation of the Indians, but this—though stunningly unusual—hardly made his work sensational.

The sobriety of Hunter's manner stood in sharp contrast to the high romance of his adventures. Here was a man who had been kidnapped by Indians around the turn of the century, as an infant of two or three, who had lived for most of his youth and young manhood with the Kansas and Osage tribes across the Mississippi, who had learned to read and write after his return to white society in 1816, but who was now the author, a scant seven years later, of this account of his strange life. His story evoked the faraway wilderness and her people almost as if the unknown West had found voice. Take, as a lone illustration, his reaction to the drowning of his Kansas mother during a flood. He experienced deep grief, he related, for his adopted mother had earned his love with her tender and affectionate care during this early "helpless period of my life." Then, obviously anticipating white incredulity that a red woman could have been capable of such goodness, Hunter asked the reader to try to understand his feelings, to make a special effort of the imagination:

> If, however, the imagination be allowed scope, and a lad of ten or twelve years of age, without kindred or name, or any knowledge by which he could arrive at an acquaintance with any of the circumstances connected with his being, be supposed in the central wilds

of North America, nearly a thousand miles from any white settlement, a prisoner or sojourner among a people on whom he had not the slightest claim, and with whose language, habits, and character he was wholly unacquainted; but who, nevertheless, treated him kindly; it will appear not only natural but rational, that he should return such kindness with gratitude and affection. Such nearly was my situation, and such in fact were my feelings at that time; and however my circumstances have since changed, or however they may change in the future, I have no hope of seeing happier days than I experienced at this early period of my life, while sojourning with the Kansas nation, on the Kansas River, some hundred miles above its confluence with the Missouri.

Reviewers were naturally enthusiastic about having word so directly from within tribal life. Though much had been heard about the Indians "and the wild regions they inhabit—the country rude as the savage, and the savage rude as the country," remarked a writer in the London *Monthly Review*—little or nothing had been heard from the Indians themselves. Yet here was an account "from the pen of an individual who has been for years one of themselves, and, in everything but his actual birth and parentage, an Indian, imbibing their feelings, practicing their manners, and living their life."

So extraordinary was Hunter's story some English reviewers paused in their enthusiasm to wonder if he might not be an "ingenious impostor." But after meeting him, one critic found it "impossible but to entertain a deep interest" in his life. "None who have passed a single afternoon in his company, whatever might have been their previous impressions, have any longer had the slightest doubt that he is exactly what he represents himself to be," reported another former skeptic. "Or that his story, recorded as it is entirely from memory, the savages among whom he lived having no written language, is perfectly faithful." Yet another concluded that "the internal marks of authenticity are so strong, that we entertain no suspicion whatever of its substantial genuineness and accuracy."

Hunter's appearance and poise were equally reassuring. "In person he is rather short, with a swarthy complexion," wrote one English witness, "not handsome, but with eyes full of intelligence; and his countenance lights up unusually in conversation, in which he takes great delight, though . . . he is silent unless particularly addressed." Cyrus Redding, the working editor of the *New Monthly Magazine*, reported that Hunter was "a strongly built, well-looking man, about the middle size, and of a grave carriage. . . . His manners were perfectly simple, and his temper said to be amiable; his garb plain, with not a shadow of ostentation, intelligent as to all that he noted." Another observer was impressed by his perspicuity and by his balanced view of the Indians, whose virtues he did not magnify and whose vices he did not exaggerate.

So did Hunter become, in the winter of 1823–24, "the *Lion* of the fashionable world in London." He was presented at court and in great demand at social occasions. Thomas William Coke, the great agriculturist, became his friend and patron, as did the Duke of Sussex, the libertarian brother of the king, and Robert Owen, the industrialist and social critic. The New England Company for the Propagation of the Gospel persuaded him to put on paper his views on the best means of "civilizing" the Indians. These "Reflections on the Different States and Conditions of Society" in turn elicited the admiration and support of leading savants. Sir James Smith, the distinguished botanist, for instance, characterized Hunter's plan to help his "Red Friends" as "the noble design of improving them on the wisest and best principles."

As you will observe, Hunter's famous plan still seems noble but not very novel. A century and a half ago, however, the conviction at its core was breathtakingly radical: "The title of the Indians to the distinctive character of human beings, from their moral and physical endowments, is as good, considering the circumstances in which they are found, as that of any other race of men on the face of the earth."* And if the Indians were human beings, as Hunter so firmly maintained, it followed that it was of the utmost consequence to save them from destruction. Unreconciled to the thought they might soon become extinct, he hoped to wean them away from their dependence on hunting and to help them establish farming settlements of their own. He hoped to persuade them through personal example and proposed to start on some land he owned in Arkansas near the Quapaw villages. Once he had demonstrated that it was possible to combine their ancient love of hunting, which he would have them continue for pleasure, with successful cultivation of the soil, they would themselves take up the plow not to be outdone. Or so argued Hunter in his "Reflections," republished herein for the first time since they appeared in the 1820s (see pp. 220 ff.). The modern reader can thus turn directly to them for the details of how he proposed to preserve "a high-minded, noble race of the human family, who have been debased, cheated and slandered. . . ."

In the late spring of 1824 Hunter returned to the United States, carrying with him the best wishes of all his English friends. His project of ameliorating the condition of the Indians had their warm support. As one writer asserted, "no one can be better qualified to promote it." Another expressed similar confidence in his ability to achieve his noble purpose: "And we can vouch from our own observation, that uniting the intrepid and persevering character of the Indian with the intelligence of the educated European, he is eminently fitted to achieve this grand design, and change the face of an important race of mankind."

3

Across the Atlantic the *Cincinnati Literary Gazette* greeted Hunter's narrative as the next best thing to an account written by one of the North American Indians themselves. The reviewer's comments showed that white attitudes toward the natives had changed little since the Saints: "They rank in our esteem but little above the brutes, and we are taught to shudder with horror at the bare mention of their names." From the time of the first settlements they had been "generally represented to us by their enemies"; they had "had no poet and are dead." At long last, however, a voice had spoken for them from a work entitled to more consideration than any "we have hitherto seen upon the subject. It is calculated to remove many prejudices, and to give us a more favorable opinion of the native inhabitants, than any previous accounts of them." But Hunter himself had been a little less confident about the effect of his work, gauging with some precision how stubbornly men cherished their hatreds. After demonstrating the Indian capacity for moral improvement with evidence sufficient "to convince all unprejudiced and reflecting minds," he still anticipated that, "for those who think differently, if volumes were to be written in support of this position, it is probable their opinions would remain unaltered." In the event he was proved sadly right, for his perceptive Cincinnati reviewer stood almost alone in welcoming his good word on the red people.

His countrymen choked on Hunter as though he were gall and wormwood. Imagine what a bitter draft he had to seem: the Indians, he contended, displayed "as great energy of mental powers, and capability of accommodating it to particular exigencies, as any other people ever have." They were deeply religious, following the wishes of the Great Spirit, not "from selfish views, but from principle; to which they in general accommodate their conduct with greater zeal, in my opinion, than any other people on the globe." Red men and women built their relationships on love, and Hunter believed no other society "more exempt from strife and contention between husband and wife, than that of the Indians generally." Ordinarily implacable in their enmities, they were also prompt and steady friends, and for "a friendly stranger, they have no measure for their kindness and hospitality." Their economics reflected this spirit of fellowship, for "no one of respectable standing will be allowed to experience want or sufferings of any kind, while it is in the power of others of the same community to prevent it." Concern for each other led naturally to this communism of goods that Hunter so imprudently celebrated: "In this equality of condition and privilege enjoined by natural laws, the Indians, where they understand how differently people in civilized life manage their affairs, feel themselves supremely happy, in being exempted from the evils which avarice, pride, and folly entail on them."

Indian politics were no less subversive of the practices of "well-ordered" republics. From the standpoint of natural rights' theory, Hunter argued, native political institutions were very nearly ideal: individuals acknowledged no superior and subordinated themselves to no government save that which experience had taught them to be necessary for their own preservation and well-being. Even then they could withhold their obedience at any time, for the root principle of their politics was a functional voluntarism—what a twentieth-century writer would call "ordered anarchy." Some chiefs had such extraordinary qualifications, they exercised almost absolute authority, Hunter conceded, but the warriors were generally "exceedingly tenacious of their freedom, and live together in a state of equality, closely approximated to natural rights." The consequent capriciousness and disorder were usually tolerable and more than offset by the gains: majorities could not bind minorities; individuals enjoyed freedoms that other political structures vaguely and frequently vainly promised their citizens. And the end result of the Indian political process was a free man of principle: "He disdains everything little," Hunter remarked proudly, "and despises the mean soul that can stoop to perpetrate an unprincipled action. . . . and all that motley train of vices which are daily practiced behind the counters, and in too many of the walks of refined life; to such a mind how contemptible, how despicable!! He prefers liberty to glittering trash; when his heart beats joy, it is because he is free. . . ."

Yet, as Hunter carefully pointed out, Indian life also had its drawbacks. One was the almost continual warfare; others were the long marches, fastings, exposures just to procure subsistence. White people could thus congratulate themselves on their superior privileges and blessings. Here Hunter came startlingly close to using the modern term "cultural relativism" for his comparisons and contrasts: "But *relatively*, each conform to the peculiarities of their own respective *modes of life*, with a zealous preference [my emphasis]." The Indians could thus "reverse the position, and thank the Great Spirit for not having made them white, and subjected them to the drudgery of civilized life."

Hunter was convinced he had made his own choice and believed himself the exception in having left the charms of Indian life for refined society, books, and "social intercourse with civilized man, composed as he is of crudities and contradictions." But "the powers that be" in America could not have remained indifferent to his indictment of their Indian policy as cruel and unjust, to his condemnation of traders for corrupting and cheating the natives, or to his questioning whether frontiersmen could claim "the character of civilized beings." More disturbing still to citizens of the United States was the fact that Hunter's narrative afforded foreign critics a chance to dwell on their shortcomings. An English essayist echoed Hunter's characterizations of the traders and backsettlers in an important *Quarterly Review* article, for instance, and agreed that official policy toward the aborigines had been meretricious and murderous: "However it may be attempted to preserve appearances by fraudulent and compulsory purchases of Indian lands, and declarations of benevolent intentions towards their injured possessors, it has always been the boast of American policy, that 'the Indians shall be made to vanish before civilization, as the snow melts before the sunbeam.'" A writer in the *Monthly Review* put it still more succinctly: "The Whites civilize the Indians as settlers clear a forest—by felling all before them!"

Patriotic Americans understandably found all this intolerable. In their eyes Hunter stood self-convicted: he had written of the Indians as though they were moral and rational human beings; of their mode of life not as the black savagery it was, but as though it were merely another culture; and of red–white relations with criticisms that gave foreigners ammunition to attack the United States and the freedom it represented. Among those who rose to destroy Hunter were Jared Sparks, the editor of the *North American Review*, William Clark, the explorer and Indian official, Pierre Chouteau, the fur-trade baron, John Neal, the novelist, and Peter Stephen Duponceau, the pioneer linguist. Of them all, none was more ferociously determined than General Lewis Cass, Governor of the Michigan Territory.*

From the prestigious pages of the *North American Review* Cass denounced Hunter as one of the boldest impostors ever to appear in the literary world. In his long essay the general took up Hunter's claims point by point to show that he had misrepresented the history of his life, was guilty of errors and falsehoods about the tribes with which he claimed to have lived, and had blundered into stupid misstatements about the geography and botany of the Osage prairies and hilly woodlands. He buttressed this demonstration with letters from John Dunn, whose name Hunter claimed to have adopted, and from William Clark and others, all of which added to the evidence that the writer of *Memoirs of a Captivity* was unknown in the region and ignorant of the events and tribes he pretended to discuss from firsthand knowledge.

The article proved a sensation, with the *Niles Weekly Register* immediately pronouncing it conclusive proof that Hunter was "an arrant impostor." By 1848, the election year which saw Cass chosen presidential nominee of the Democratic party, a campaign biographer could claim for his famous article, with "its peculiarly eloquent style and engrossing interest of its subject," priority in exposing Hunter and his narrative, "which has since been acknowledged a palpable forgery." In the twentieth century a leading Western historian agreed, reflecting the general professional verdict, that "the evidence to that effect by Lewis Cass, William Clark, and Auguste Chouteau seems conclusive." Hunter was thus effectively silenced for the hundred and fifty years extending from his day to ours.

By any reckoning Cass made a formidable enemy. According to one of his biographers, he had preeminent claim to the title "Father of the West," for scarcely any other man had been for so many years so closely connected with "the rise and progress of the United States." Cass had grown up in New Hampshire, gone to Phillips Exeter Academy with Daniel Webster, moved West to take up the study and practice of law, shared a joint command with General Harrison in the War of 1812, and had become governor of Michigan in 1813. From then until his article denouncing Hunter, Cass had a dozen years and more of continuous dealings with the Indians. He negotiated almost a score of treaties with the various tribes and ultimately, before moving into Andrew Jackson's cabinet as secretary of war, extinguished Indian title to most of present-day Michigan, Wisconsin, and northern Minnesota. His article on Hunter was the first of three major essays in the *North American Review;* these firmly established his position as a scholar and gained him an honorary Doctor of Laws degree from Harvard in 1836. No one in the country, therefore, could hope to challenge his position as the foremost Indian expert. Colonel Thomas L. McKenney, an expert in his own right, once named Cass "the best informed man in the United States on Indian affairs." Or as Jared Sparks put it, "he is allowed to have a better knowledge of the Indians than any well educated man in the country."

Of course, as I tried to make clear in *White Savage,* Cass should have been allowed nothing of the sort. He in fact demonstrated a broad and deep ignorance of Indian life in his attack on Hunter and in his other writings. Specific proofs of this ignorance, on those few occasions when mention of them might help the reader, are better left to the endnotes below.* What bears pursuing here, however, is a simple question: Why did no one step forward to challenge the general's credentials and subject his charges to rigorous analysis?

In one of his articles Cass revealed he was drawing on William Robertson, the Scots author of *History of the Discovery and Settle-*

ment of America (1777), for views that delineated "the red man as we have found him." This meant that Cass had accepted, if he meant what he said, Robertson's grotesque assumptions, among which were that the Indians had no body hair, were "destitute of one sign of manhood and strength," and were forever fixed at the level of "mere animal." For Cass to accept Robertson's "faithful portrait of the Indians" meant that, in all his years of contact with native Americans, he had never *seen* a single one.

Yet this was precisely what made him preeminently qualified to become the nation's leading expert and what protected him from serious challenge. If Robertson said that tribesmen "waste their lives in listless indolence," Cass dutifully referred to the "listless indolence" of the natives and pleased white compatriots with his colonial vocabulary. As Frantz Fanon pointed out, for settlers the natives have always been "faces bereft of all humanity . . . that laziness stretched out in the sun."

Europeans in the New World had good reason, I have ventured, for not looking directly at the natives and the wilderness they were destroying. To have looked openly risked revealing that savages—from the devil-driven monsters of Cotton Mather's day to the forest beasts of Cass's—were like niggers: they existed only in the heads of whites. To have *seen* the natives risked discovering that these "ravening wolves" were merely that part of themselves Wasps found abhorrent, necessary to deny, and therefore necessary to project—these projections became what Cass actually called "wandering hordes of barbarians." Open-eyed scrutiny threatened to disclose that the headlong pursuit of God, Progress, the American Empire, and their own "higher nature" had hurled Wasps along a course of warring against what was natural in themselves and their environment.

Or consider this formulation of an answer to our question: Cass's savages were collective creations. He gained his reputation as an expert from the vigor with which he defended projections that were public property. His long career in appointive and elective office had placed him at dead center of mainstream American thought and politics. When he spoke on the Indians, therefore, he spoke for the vast majority of whites who shared his preconceptions and who already believed in his phantoms. But when Hunter wrote about the red people as *persons*—brothers, sisters, family, acquaintances—he threatened these phantoms and subversively suggested that two centuries of Indian extermination and dispossession might be all wrong. No right-thinking citizen would have thought of challenging the general's allegations against Hunter. Cass's countrymen did not have to be persuaded; they needed no more than the barest of excuses for believing the white savage a palpable fraud.

4

In the spring of 1824 John Dunn Hunter returned to the United States, pleased to be embarking on his great project and unaware of the storm of denunciations building up on the horizon. A summary account of what happened to him then is due the modern reader of his *Memoirs,* for the events of these last few months round out the narrative of his life and relate directly to the character of the attack against him.

In the fall Hunter paid Thomas Jefferson a final visit at Monticello. Before winter had really set in, he joined his friend Robert Owen in a memorable trip down the Ohio. Parting company with Owen in Indiana, where the latter stopped off to negotiate for the property which was to become New Harmony, Hunter continued on down to New Orleans. In early 1825 he returned to Arkansas to find his Quapaw friends in distress—they had recently signed a treaty ceding all their lands to the United States. In the months following he seems to have wandered through the Missouri and Arkansas country seeking some place of refuge for them and other tribes. But everywhere he went he found Indians being uprooted and driven farther and farther toward the Rocky Mountains. Still seeking some way to help all these "scattered and decaying" peoples, Hunter crossed over into the Republic of Mexico and, in the fall of 1825, turned up at the Cherokee *ranchería* some fifty miles north of Nacogdoches.

The Western Cherokees, along with other tribal fragments, had established a chain of villages on the rich red lands lying along the Trinity, Neches, Angelina, and Sabine rivers in East Texas. According to a report of the Mexican governor, the Indians worked "for their living and dress in cotton cloth of their own manufacture. They raise cattle and horses, and use fire arms. Many of them understand the English language." But the Indians had been unable to get title to the lands they had occupied and, worse still, they had recently learned that white colonizers had received grants to settle families nearby. When Hunter arrived their affairs had reached a crisis. Working closely with Richard Fields, one of their principal chiefs, Hunter assumed a position of prominence in their deliberations and was soon dispatched to the Mexican capital to act as their agent in one last attempt to gain legal recognition of their claims.

Hunter's mission to the City of Mexico was detailed in a message of Henry George Ward, the English chargé d'affaires. On March 19, 1826, he informed George Canning, the British Foreign Minister, of Hunter's arrival, of his account of how the Indians had been harassed by white settlers, and of his plan in return for a grant of lands,

Hunter proposed to bring 30,000 Indians into Mexico. They would take up farming and defend the frontier. Ward suggested to Canning that "a better opportunity would not easily be found of opposing a formidable obstacle to the designs of the United States on Texas." Hunter's plan fitted in nicely with George Canning's attempts to block American expansion into the former Spanish territories—the United States had just rejected his appeal for agreement on a self-denying ordinance and had instead enunciated the Monroe Doctrine, which was in effect a declaration of hemispheric imperialism—and fitted in as well with Ward's overriding concern to make Texas the crucial barrier for Mexico. The latter therefore welcomed Hunter's proposal to establish a buffer colony of Indians below the Red River. Fearing the ultimate incorporation of Texas by the United States, Ward had all the more reason, he reported to Canning, "to second his views."

With such a plan and with such support, Hunter quickly ran afoul of the first U.S. minister to Mexico. In one of his dispatches to Henry Clay, Secretary of State, Joel R. Poinsett reported Hunter's presence in the capital and revealed his own views:

> Hunter is certainly a shrewd active man—talking a great deal about the rights of the Indians, and as I believe not very friendly to the interests of the United States. . . . I do not think it would be politic on the part of the United States to suffer the emigration and establishment on the Mexican frontier of so large and powerful a body of Indian warriors, as it is Hunter's desire to move there.

Poinsett was unpersuaded Indians had any rights whites were bound to respect and, since he had been instructed to get Texas for his government, passionately opposed Hunter's projected settlement of tens of thousands of them on the frontier. In another dispatch to Clay he was able to report that the Mexican government had refused to give Hunter and the twenty-three tribes he represented "a large tract of land, where they might remain united in a body, but offered to settle them in different parts of the Country under Mexican Governors."

Though the failure of Hunter's mission meant that the Indians had lost their last, best chance to find a home or at least a place to make a stand against the tide of white settlers, there was a certain grim appropriateness in the fact that the decisive opposition had almost certainly come from the United States. It was consistent with the decree of Poinsett and his countrymen that the Indians vanish. They did not want the Indians where they were and so had launched a policy of removal beyond the Mississippi—Monroe was still talking in terms of their "voluntary" acceptance of this inevitability, but pressures were rising that would shortly produce Andrew Jackson's Removal Bill and a little later the Cherokee Trail of Tears. Yet the Indians could not remove to where they themselves might go, even if some of them temporarily found refuge in what was at the moment foreign territory. So Poinsett suspected Hunter of not being very friendly and had the effrontery to write that it would not "be politic on the part of the United States to suffer the emigration of so large and powerful a body of Indian warriors, as it is Hunter's desire to move there." Was it not a most peculiar Providence that had granted white Americans the right to decide whether or not to *suffer* the emigration of free peoples?

The dispatches of Ward and Poinsett provide an adequate synopsis of what happened when Hunter returned to the tribes he represented. As Poinsett reported to Clay:

> Accounts have been received from Texas of an insurrection. . . . A half-breed by the name of Fields, a man by the name of Edwards, to whom the Legislature of Texas granted a large tract of land, and John Hunter of notorious memory, are the ring-leaders. They have made Nacogdoches their Head-Quarters—have hoisted a red and white banner, indicative of the union of whites and Indians—and declared that district of the country as far as the Rio Bravo del Norte [Río Grande] independent.

Named merely a "half-breed" by Poinsett, Richard Fields was in fact also a man, an intelligent, dedicated man who joined Hunter, when he heard the latter's sad tidings, in forging an alliance with Haden Edwards, the *empresario,* and other whites in Nacogdoches. The unifying bond was the conviction of both reds and whites that they had been abused by the Mexican government. Together they drew up a Declaration of Independence, cut to the pattern of the original, and raised their red and white flag, symbolizing the Republic of Fredonia. Though their rebellion of late 1826 and early 1827 was short lived, it was a forerunner of that of 1836 and in its own way much more interesting. How many times in Western history, before or since, have settlers and natives come together in the realization that liberation for one depended on liberation for both?

Ward quite correctly reported to Canning that the role of Stephen F. Austin, head of the flourishing colony of whites to the West, had been central in putting down the attempted revolution. Austin, he observed,

> not liking the Neighborhood of the savage Tribes, whom the Whites of Nacogdoches wished to introduce into Texas, declared himself,

at once, against their Projects, and having united the Forces of his Colony . . . with the Mexican Troops under General Bustamente, decided the Contest without allowing Time for Hunter's Indians to cross the Frontier, and join Field, Edwards, and the other Chiefs of the soi-disant Republic of Fredonia.

To say that the "Founder of Texas" did not like savage tribes in his neighborhood, however, was a bit of an understatement.

Austin had grown up as Hunter's neighbor, as it were, in Missouri. After the death of his father, Moses, the delicately built former clerk took up the family claim in Texas. He secured from the Mexican authorities a concession to establish a colony on the Brazos and a premium for himself of 65,000 acres, some of it on the Pedernales, which extraordinary acquisitions his biographer attributed to his understanding "of Mexican racial qualities." Austin was in truth a pragmatist, but it would be a mistake to regard him as a mere opportunist. For him evil consisted quintessentially in the rejection of authority. He was thus opposed to the Fredonian revolution in principle and spoke out of some of his deepest convictions when he declared there were in Nacogdoches "some bad and rebellious men who must be expelled from the Country." To his mind "bad" and "rebellious" were synonyms. Like the Puritans and like his contemporaries, men such as Cass and Poinsett, Austin practiced a civil religion based on the sacred authority of "well-ordered" government: "For without Government, without law," he cried, "what security have we for our persons, our property, our characters, and all that we hold dear and sacred? None, for we at once embark on the stormy ocean of anarchy, subject to be stripped by every wave of faction that rolls along, and must finally sink into the gulf of ruin and infamy."

It followed that it was "our duty as *men*, to suppress vice, anarchy, and Indian Massacre." The three evils were not accidentally linked nor were the italics fortuitous: lacking government, the Indians were not *men*. For Austin, as for Cotton Mather, the Indians were and had been forever sunk in ruin and infamy or were ungoverned children of nature, which came to the same thing. The fact that the Fredonian uprising had been the work of a red-and-white alliance, then, was its most horrifying aspect: Austin's hatred of rebellion was so intensified by his racism as to make his words a torrent. "Great God," he exclaimed, "can it be possible that Americans, high minded free born honorable Americans will so far forget the country of their birth, so far forget themselves, as to league with barbarians and join a band of savages in a war of murder, massacre and desolation?"

Before joining in the campaign against the insurgents, Austin wrote Hunter a long letter designed to break him off from the alliance. Dated January 4, 1827, the letter lay bare with surprising directness the roots of the American response to people of color and to those whites so foolhardy as to take their side.

"My Dr. Sir, let us examine this subject calmly," Austin proposed, "let us suppose that the Indians over run the whole country and take possession of it for the present as far as the Rio Grande and drive out or massacre all the honest [sic] inhabitants. What will they gain?" The Indians would soon be fighting among themselves, he deliberately explained, for they could not establish *Government*. Hunter's plan to establish an Indian country was folly, therefore, for nothing but confusion and massacre would be the consequence. But say the Indians did get possession, how would they maintain it?

> The mexican Nation *has* force to subdue you, and even admitting they had not, she can procure it from the United States of the North, for both nations would unite in crushing a common enemy to both, and annihilating so dangerous and troublesome a neighbor as a large combination of Indians would be . . . the U.S. would soon sweep the country of Indians and drive them as they always have driven them to ruin and extermination.

After all this, Hunter hardly needed Austin's pointed reminder: "*You* know the Govt. of the United States and its policy as respects lands and Indians." By then he did and because he did, he could not have been too surprised by Austin's underlying message. Either the Indians submit to cultural subjugation or die. If not exterminated by Mexico, they would be by the United States, which "always have driven them to ruin and extermination."

Now if the modern word "genocide" means the deliberate destruction of "a part of an ethnic, national or religious group," as it has been defined, then Austin was simply enunciating, as known fact, that American Indian policy had always been genocidal in intent and performance. He threatened Hunter and the Cherokees with the same fate unless they were good; unless, that is, they gave up their mad efforts to be free.

Hunter and Fields, however, refused to give up. Accordingly Austin, Peter Ellis Bean, an American soldier of fortune, and others bought off the Indians with fake promises of lands and arranged to have the Cherokees kill the rebels. Fields was the first to be murdered. Then, on his way to join their allies in Nacogdoches, Hunter and two Cherokee braves stopped to water their horses at a creek near the Anadagua village. In this unguarded moment one of Hunter's companions shot him in the shoulder and toppled him off into the water. As his assassin raised his weapon for a final shot, Hunter reportedly implored him not to fire, "for it was hard, he said, to die by the hands of his friends." How the writer knew what Hunter said before this second shot is unknown. Hunter died his hard death, anyhow, in late January or early February 1827, near the present town of Henderson, Texas.

Austin had naturally earned the gratitude of Mexican officials. In fact, the acting governor furnished him with a document that certified he had earned "the highest opinion from the Government" for perfect discharge of his duties:

> Stephen F. Austin contributed most efficaciously placing himself at the head of his colonists in beating the rebels of Nacogdoches . . . having united his forces to the Mexican troops by which movement their dispersion was obtained, and the death of several of their ringleaders, by which the order and tranquility of the frontier were restored.

The document made it official: Hunter was shot by one of his "savage companions," but the Indian was simply acting as the agent of others. Though Austin did not pull the trigger, he could take major credit for putting Hunter's assassin out there on the creek bank.

So another savage bit the dust—albeit this time a white one—in the Three Hundred Years' War against the Indians. Individual responsibility aside, Hunter was silenced and killed by the same American nationalism and racism which made so many of his red friends "vanish." And he died doing exactly what his narrative was all about in the first place, trying desperately to help the Indians find some way out of their dilemma of extermination or cultural castration.

5

Memoirs of a Captivity among the Indians of North America remains as striking and singular as the life of its author. A first reading in 1967, as I have written elsewhere, "persuaded me that it was an important document, perhaps a minor classic in the American literature of self-discovery. Like the much more impressive works in this tradition—Thoreau's *Walden* (1854) and Whitman's *Leaves of Grass* (1855) come to mind—it seemed to have grown up outdoors someplace, perhaps at the edge of the woods like a sumac bush or a wild grapevine." Almost daily intercourse with the work in the half-dozen years since has made me a little apprehensive about the modesty of my original contentions. The claims of Hunter's narrative go beyond our literature of self-discovery.

At the time it proved a valuable repository of ethnological data. Impressive testimony that it did came from Sir John Franklin, the discoverer of the Northwest Passage, who had himself lived for almost a year with a tribe on the Coppermine River of northern Canada. At a Paris soirée in the 1820s Franklin defended Hunter and his work against the attacks of an American: "I am aware, Sir," he said, "of all that has been objected to Hunter's narrative, as I have both perused the work and conversed with the writer or author; and I do not hesitate to declare that he has given the best account of the manners and customs of the Indians of any author I have ever read. And," he added with emphasis, "allow me to be something of a judge!" In truth few were better qualified to judge than the celebrated explorer of the Arctic.

Two decades later George Catlin evaluated the narrative in almost the same words: Hunter's work, "as far as it treats on the manners and customs of the American Indians, and which could not have been written or dictated by any other than a person who had lived that familiar life with them, is decidedly the most descriptive and best work yet published on their every-day domestic habits and superstitions; and, of itself, goes a great way, in my opinion, to establish the fact that his early life was identified with that of the Indians." The great Indian painter and ethnologist, who had spent most of the 1830s with tribes west of the Mississippi, was one of the few even better qualified than Franklin to judge Hunter's work.

Over the intervening decades ethnologists have made frequent use of the *Memoirs* and have thereby underlined the validity of these two early evaluations. More recent students, including Clark Wissler, have found it an important source on the Osage Indians and on occasion invaluable for data obtainable nowhere else. Indeed, of all the captivity chronicles, Hunter's narrative is rivaled by only one or two others for authentic information, from the inside, on Indian manners and customs.*

All of which is not to say, of course, that everything in the narrative is authentic. Not for the first time, a systematic assessment of every part of a document is both desirable and impossible. The surviving evidence simply will not enable us to subject every statement or episode to ruthless testing. Our problem here was formulated very well by George Catlin, who had the advantage of several meetings with Hunter, had read his book, and had later visited Indian villages and talked to chiefs mentioned in it: "I felt assured, therefore, that he had spent the Indian life that he describes in his work," Catlin wrote; "and yet that he might have had the indiscretion to have made some of the misrepresentations attributed to him, I was not able positively to deny." Nor can I.

Consider a single illustration: while he was still with the Kansas, Hunter related, they had ascended the Platte several hundred miles to the entrance of the Dripping Fork, where they had fixed their camp and explored a nearby cavern. In this "abode of darkness" they discovered two human bodies, which they buried, "and then made good our retreat, half inclined to believe the tradition which prevails among some of the tribes, and which represents this cavern as the aperture through which the first Indian ascended from the bowels of the earth. . . ." The tradition made sense, for one of the versions of the Osage genesis myth had the first men ascending from the depths of the earth. But the existence of the cave has been questioned, and a close examination of the passage suggests it was not uninfluenced by Charles Brockden Brown's *Edgar Huntly* (1799). As if heeding Brown's famous preface, the Indians have a proper literary response to a Gothic setting that was the American counterpart of ruined castles and chimeras. This passage may have had its origin in an actual incident that was colored by Hunter's "infatuation with reading" after he left the Osages and took up "literary habits."

Or possibly it was a fabrication—not a relatively innocent "indiscretion"—and it may have been the work of other hands than Hunter's. No matter how exceptional, his *Memoirs* automatically became part of a popular literary genre that had its own imperatives. Publishers and hack writers the country over knew that, in order to reach a sensation-avid market, a captivity narrative had to include at least some scary incidents and exciting escapes and deliverances. Thus James Maxwell, Hunter's Philadelphia publisher, may have been instrumental in having a colorful incident made part of Hunter's text. Or Edward Clark, whose kind assistance Hunter acknowledged in his "Preface," might have contributed a literary touch or even invention of his own. Ominously enough, Clark was a Philadelphia inventor, the contriver of ingenious contraptions for navigating falls of rivers, as well as being a civil engineer and a member of the Academy of Natural Sciences. Given Hunter's ignorance of "the art of bookmaking," he could easily have been victimized by his publisher or by editor Clark: either could have been responsible for the Dripping Fork incident. And here further inquiry is blocked by a sign reading "No Evidence."*

But we need not pause here irresolutely. Many valuable works have passages that remain problematical, and many still more precious texts are not free from corruptions, whether from the author's indiscretions, outside additions, or both. No doubt there are some problems I have not detected and others I have misunderstood or failed to explicate adequately. With full recognition of this probability, I can still state flatly that I believe Hunter to have been an honest man.

His claims to authenticity were actually strengthened by the numerous instances of alleged misrepresentations that I investigated in depth—indeed, the accumulated evidence would have permitted me to build a stronger case that his detractors were guilty of imposture.

As you will observe, Hunter's work has two major divisions, a narrative section repeating the title "Memoirs of a Captivity" and an ethnological section bearing the title "Manners and Customs." When it was first published, George Procter, the *Quarterly Review* critic, held that Hunter's narrative, which "does not form above one third of his volume," is "by far the most interesting part of it." Perhaps this was an underestimation of the intrinsic interest of the remaining two thirds, but it remains true that the first section is more interesting and significant. It is therefore reproduced here in its entirety. Unfortunately the second section demanded more competent editorial assistance than Hunter received. Three additional chapters were simply inserted in the American edition for those copies published in London; his pamphlet "Reflections on . . . Society" was simply tacked on the end of the third English edition. As a consequence, closely related topics were separated by intervening chapters; matters discussed in one place reappeared substantially unchanged in another. I have therefore tried to tighten the organization of this section through some major excisions and transpositions.*

My goal has not been completeness and full annotation. It is rather a book, relatively unburdened by heavy scholarship, that can be read with some confidence, to be sure, but also with ease and pleasure. Success here would mean an edition that will help Hunter come alive and lead him to that place in our collective memory I think he richly deserves.

As the attentive reader will soon discover, Hunter was remarkable for more than his adventures. He was a splendid field observer of Indian life and occasionally displayed astonishing flashes of insight into white ways. What are we to make, for example, of his contrast of red and white "violence"? Asking the reader to understand the Indian desire to excel in warfare, "however their mode of conducting it may appear to civilized people, or *however it may differ from the legitimatized murders of more refined governments* [my emphasis]," Hunter sounded like the late Albert Camus reflecting on the guillotine. Hunter's anecdote about Round Buttons had elements of the dandy-frightening-the-squatter reversal that Mark Twain was to perfect. His lines lamenting the destruction of wild life, "the wantonness of civilized man," and this man's delight in body counts, of having "killed so many buffalo, deer, &c."—these lines speak directly to our own desperate ecology and to the recent presence of the United States in Indochina.

Or, finally, consider his analysis of what would happen once the Indians became farmers, as he was urging, and settled down in the "comforts of civilized life":

> And then, as population and wealth increased, science and refinement, and perhaps, disease and crime also, would commence their rapid march; never, from the constitution of the human mind, and the organization of things, to terminate, except in the wreck of universal nature.

It was as though he had a prevision of our crime-ridden thermonuclear present. But Hunter did no more than see the same logic in "Progress" that Edgar Allan Poe saw when he spoke of Americans "hurrying to some exciting knowledge—some never-to-be-imparted secret, whose attainment is destruction."

"Of all the traits which distinguish the Indian character," wrote Hunter, "that of nice discrimination is perhaps the most remarkable. Accustomed from his earliest life to no other guide to conduct him, and no other means to satisfy his wants than those with which Nature has supplied him, the Indian follows her footsteps in all his walks, and minutely watches her most secret haunts." Like Henry David Thoreau, who was keenly interested in his narrative, Hunter knew that his savage friends followed in the footsteps of nature and were at home in the wilderness, joyfully recognized its kinship with the animal in themselves, and saw it in all its shining beauty. Had white Americans not rejected him in fear and revulsion, Hunter might have helped them moderate, if not stop, their absurd war with the nature in themselves and their frenzied conquest of the nature without.

But better late than never. Lead on, gentle reader.

RICHARD DRINNON

London, England
March 1973

[A facsimile of the title page of
the third edition, printed in 1824.]

MEMOIRS

OF A

CAPTIVITY

AMONG

THE INDIANS

OF

NORTH AMERICA,

FROM CHILDHOOD TO THE AGE OF NINETEEN:

WITH

ANECDOTES DESCRIPTIVE OF

THEIR MANNERS AND CUSTOMS.

TO WHICH IS ADDED,

SOME ACCOUNT OF THE

SOIL, CLIMATE, AND VEGETABLE PRODUCTIONS

OF THE TERRITORY WESTWARD OF THE MISSISSIPPI.

By JOHN D. HUNTER.

THE THIRD EDITION, WITH ADDITIONS.

LONDON:

PRINTED FOR
LONGMAN, HURST, REES, ORME, BROWN, AND GREEN,
PATERNOSTER-ROW.

1824.

Messrs. Longman and Co.

Dear Sirs,
   The Editor of the *Eclectic Review*, in examining my *Memoirs*, has made a very natural inquiry, who is the gentleman alluded to in the Preface as my assistant? I am very happy to answer the question by referring to Col. Aspinwall, consul-general for the United States to Great Britain, and Mr. Toppan, 69 Fleet Street, London. I might refer to many of the most respectable persons in all parts of the United States, but perhaps a few will suffice: Robert Walsh, Esq., Editor of the *National Gazette*, Philadelphia; Col. William Duarre, Editor of the *Aurora*, Philadelphia; Dr. Waterhouse, Boston; Dr. Mitchell, Dr. Hosack, and Mr. Silliman, of New York; Professors Paterson and Potter of Baltimore.*
                                    Yours with esteem, &c.
                                        JOHN D. HUNTER

London
August 2, 1823

Preface

In presenting myself to the world as an author, I have complied more with the wishes of friends than my own inclinations. Indeed, I do so with reluctance, being fully sensible of my inability to do justice to the undertaking. This conviction arises from an imperfect acquaintance with the English language, and total ignorance of the art of book-making. Besides, I write from memory, of events, persons, and things, which are many years separated from the present, and some of them so remotely, as barely to come within my recollection. Under such circumstances, although kindly assisted by my friend Edward Clark, with interrogations respecting some of the subject matter, and the revisal and arrangement of the manuscript; still, as regards manner, I am not insensible that there is ample ground for the exercise of indulgence on the part of my readers. If I were a finished scholar, the case would have scarcely suffered any change, because the data would remain the same; and it is questionable, whether I could have improved its present form, at least within the prescribed limits. From the circumstance of writing altogether from memory, and at different periods of time, some repetition has been unavoidable. In the history of my early life, I could have mentioned many more incidents and anecdotes of a particular or general nature, which, though of some interest to myself, would not, I am persuaded, prove so to my readers. Indian life is full of adventures, privations, and dangers: and the history of many of their warriors would, in my opinion, prove much more interesting than mine: except from the circumstance of my being a sojourner amongst strangers, and comparatively a youth.

Here I ought to remark, as I omitted to do in my narrative, that I am ignorant of the length of time I lived with the Indians. I have reason to believe I was nineteen or twenty years of age when I left them, which was in the spring of 1816.

In telling the story of my captivity during the above-mentioned period, I found many things to say respecting the people among whom I lived, which tempted me to frequent and long digressions. To avoid the inconvenience that would have resulted from such a mode of proceeding, I have adopted the expedient of throwing into a detached form, under appropriate heads, my observations on the Manners and Customs of the Indian tribes dwelling westward of the Mississippi, and my notices on the climate, soil, and vegetable productions of the territory occupied by them. To the former I have ventured to add some anecdotes, which appeared likely to prove at once characteristic and amusing; while the latter have been augmented by such details as I was able to offer respecting the Materia Medica of the Indians. It is with great diffidence that I submit the volume to the critical examination of the British Public; and in bespeaking indulgence for its faults, I would remind the reader, that the information which it contains was acquired at a period when I had neither the hope nor the intention of communicating it in this manner, and that therefore it is given simply and entirely from memory.*

PART ONE

**MEMOIRS OF A CAPTIVITY
AMONG THE INDIANS
OF NORTH AMERICA, FROM
THE AUTHOR'S EARLIEST
RECOLLECTION TO HIS
ASSUMPTION OF THE HABITS
OF CIVILIZED LIFE**

Memoirs

Of the place of my nativity, and the circumstances of my parentage, I am altogether ignorant, and fear that I shall forever remain so, as I have assiduously explored every avenue through which I could expect information, both while I was with the Indians, and since my residence in the United States. I have had friends, whose exertions to serve me, in this particular, deserve my warmest gratitude; and whilst I have the gloomy reflection of knowing that their efforts, as well as my own, have been unavailing, I will cherish these manifestations of their kindness toward me with the devotion of a heart that knows how to appreciate favors. This part of my history, together with most of the incidents of early life, which generally, in works of this kind, form an interesting portion, will, in all probability, forever remain unknown. Nevertheless, some features in this period were so strongly marked as to leave indelible impressions on my mind; while others not so strikingly characterized, like the imperfect recollection of a dream, cross my memory, but fix on it no decided and satisfactory images.

I propose to treat on these, and the subsequent history of my life, before I enter into the details of the habits, morals, and polity of the Indians with whom I resided; because this arrangement will enable me to embody much matter in my narrative, which, if read, I am apprehensive, will prove tedious and uninteresting, and which thus disposed of, can be passed over at the option of the reader, for the subsequent and more interesting contents of the work, without interrupting the general connection. Besides, it will afford me the satisfaction of detaching myself, in a degree, from the view of the reader in the more important parts; a circumstance with which, in the capacity of an author, I may truly say I wished altogether to have complied, but which I could not consistently do against the opinions of many from whom I have received unequivocal tokens of friendship and regard, and whose advice I feel myself bound to respect.

I was taken prisoner at a very early period of my life by a party of Indians, who from the train of events that followed, belonged to, or were in alliance with, the Kickapoo nation. At the same time, two other white children, a boy and a small girl, were also made prisoners.

I have too imperfect a recollection of the circumstances connected with this capture, to attempt any account of them; although I have reflected on the subject so often, and with so great interest and intensity, under the knowledge I have since acquired of the Indian modes of warfare, as nearly to establish at times a conviction in my mind of a perfect remembrance. There are moments when I see the rush of the Indians, hear their war-whoops and terrific yells, and witness the massacre of my parents and connections, the pillage of their property, and the incendious destruction of their dwellings. But the first incident that made an actual and prominent impression on me happened while the party were somewhere encamped, no doubt shortly after my capture; it was as follows: the little girl whom I before mentioned, beginning to cry, was immediately despatched with the blow of a tomahawk from one of the warriors; the circumstance terrified me very much, more particularly as it was followed with very menacing motions of the same instrument, directed to me, and then pointed to the slaughtered infant, by the same warrior, which I then interpreted to signify, that if I cried, he would serve me in the same manner. From this period till the apprehension of personal danger had subsided, I recollect many of the occurrences which took place.

Soon after the above transaction, we proceeded on our journey till a party separated from the main body, and took the boy before noticed with them, which was the last I saw or heard of him.

The Indians generally separate their white prisoners. The practice no doubt originated more with a view to hasten a reconciliation to their change, and a nationalization of feelings, than with any intention of wanton cruelty.

The Indians who retained me continued their march, chiefly through woods, for several successive days; a circumstance well remembered by me, because the fear of being left behind called forth all my efforts to keep up with them, whenever from fatigue or any other cause they compelled me to walk, which was often the case.

After a long march and much fatigue, we reached their camps, which were situated on a considerable stream of water; but in what particular part or section of country, I am wholly unable to say. Just before our arrival, however, we were met by a great number of old men, women, and children, among whom was a white woman attired in the Indian costume: she was the wife of a principal chief;

was a great friend to the Indians; and joined with, and I believe surpassed, the squaws in the extravagancy of her exultations and rejoicings on account of the safe return of the warriors with prisoners, scalps, and other trophies obtained from their vanquished foes.

I think it must have been in the fall when I was taken prisoner, because the forests, and indeed the whole atmosphere, presented a smoky and peculiarly gloomy appearance; which most probably was owing to a custom which the Indians practice, of firing the leaves at this season of the year, to facilitate the collection of nuts for their consumption during the approaching winter.

After our arrival at their camps, and I had become reconciled to my new mode of living, and my adopted connections, nothing occurred for several years, to the best of my recollection, as worthy of notice, except our repeated removals; nor should I mention this, only that it serves to account for the obscurity with which everything connected with my early life is surrounded. I was adopted into the family of one of the principal warriors, named Fongoh, who claimed me as his property, from having taken me prisoner; his wife, a squaw of an intermediate stature, and dark complexion, proved to me a kind and affectionate mother.

It may appear somewhat extraordinary that I should recollect the above incidents so circumstantially, while others scarcely separated from them as to time, should have nearly or quite escaped my memory; but such is the fact, though I am persuaded from the faint traces still remaining on my mind, could either my parents or the location of my childhood be presented to me at this time, in the same state or condition that they were in previous to my being taken by the Indians, that I should recognize them individually. But the probable massacre of the former, and the changes in respect to the latter, which have rapidly succeeded each other in the country where most likely my being first dawned, forbid the hope of ever realizing these, to me, desirable and important events.

But notwithstanding this apparent incongruity in respect to memory, when the careless and playful manner in which children usually pass their time is taken into consideration, together with the violent changes that interrupted my youthful sports, the cause of surprise will, I am persuaded, cease to exist.

With respect to my parents, it is highly probable, as I before observed, that they perished at the commencement of my captivity. This I infer from the circumstances which generally precede, attend, and follow the destruction of some families who adventure to the western frontiers for a settlement, among which, from the manner of my capture, I suppose mine to have been; and as some of my readers may not be acquainted with them, a few remarks here on these subjects may prove interesting, and will not, I am persuaded, be deemed irrelative to the plan I have proposed to follow.

Inheriting certain districts of country from their ancestors, the limits to which are prescribed either by treaties with the several tribes, or are traditionary and mutually respected, the Indians are accustomed to roam with unrestrained freedom through their forests in search of game, or to cultivate so much of the soil as they may deem necessary to supply their wants and comforts. Every encroachment made upon their territory, whether with or without their consent, is, sooner or later, regarded as an infringement of their natural rights, and has frequently given rise to long, cruel, and exterminating wars, not only between different tribes, but between the Indians and the whites. They regard the latter with much the most scrupulous jealousy; because experience has taught them that every settlement on their part, within their boundaries, is a precursor to their [own] farther recess [or retreat], which, they most sensibly feel, will only terminate with their final expulsion, extermination, or incorporation with those they esteem their natural and most bitter enemies. With such feelings and views in regard to their neighbors, and their highest ambition being to excel in war, to improve themselves in which no opportunity is suffered to escape, however abhorrent their mode of conducting it may appear to civilized people, or however it may differ from the legitimatized murders of more refined governments, it ought not to be a subject of wonder that the Indian warriors should often seek to come in collision with the advanced settlers. They do seek it, and terrible is the vengeance they often inflict on these unfortunate outposts to civilized life, for the imputed infringements of their rights.

The outsettlers are generally men of indolent, and frequently dissolute habits: they, for the most part, hunt and fish to procure a livelihood; and this wandering mode of life makes them acquainted with the neighboring Indians, their manners, and languages, and finally, with the situations most propitious for their pursuits. Under such circumstances, perhaps with consent, though this courtesy is but little regarded, lured by the present prospects, and regardless of future dangers; first, one or two, and afterwards more families, venture into the territories of the Indians, till in fact the jealousy of the latter becomes excited, when, if possible, they scheme and execute their destruction. The Indians are also often provoked by other causes: such, for instance, as frauds and thefts practiced upon them, which provoke to retaliation and aggression; consequently, the innocent and guilty indiscriminately suffer. Such conduct, mutually practiced by them and the whites, along the whole extent of the conceived, though arbitrary boundary, is the cause of the inveterate hostility that exists between them, and leads to all the scenes of Indian cruelty that are practiced on the frontier settlers. The settlers are aware of the dangers to which they are exposed, and generally associate for their mutual defense: when sufficiently numerous they erect block-houses and pickets, to which all retreat on particular signals being given. In cases of emergency, where their number is not sufficiently great to encourage the hope of a successful resistance, should they apprehend an attack, they retreat to places of greater security, and wait till the angry passions of their Indian neighbors have subsided, or become appeased. This, however, does not often happen; because the Indians take their measures so secretly, and execute them with such expedition, as to cut them off before any definite suspicion of danger has been entertained. From the first, these encroachments are viewed with a suspicious eye by the Indians; and should any ill success subsequently attend their pursuits after game, the cause is at once ascribed to the white settlers. These complaints are for a while individual and feeble; but multiplying and becoming clamorous, a council is convened, the subject debated, the measure of redress fixed upon, and instantly carried into execution. Sometimes, however, secret combinations of the young warriors, with a view to acquire celebrity and distinction, anticipate this form; and the first intelligence the chiefs have of their plan, is their return from an expedition with scalps, prisoners, &c. But by far the most frequent and summary way of chastising those intruders is practiced by the hunting parties; who, while these hostile feelings exist, promiscuously destroy them, in whatever situation they may be found. For this conduct, the warriors generally receive the approbation and plaudits of the chiefs. When neither of the above modes amount to a radical cure of the evil, other measures having been determined on, and the arrangements made necessary to carry them into execution, the war-party starts for the settlement, on the destruction of which it is bent. On arriving in the neighborhood, should the settlements be strong, and capable of making much resistance, the Indians separate, and secrete themselves till a favorable opportunity presents for an attack; such, for instance, as the absence of the men; when, upon a signal being given, they rush simultaneously upon, and force an entrance into, their dwellings, block-houses, or pickets. Their conduct is then governed by the danger they have to apprehend from the sudden return or number of their enemies; should this be great, and the prospect of cutting them off by ambush appear doubtful, an indiscriminate slaughter of the inhabitants and destruction of property follow. But if the danger be less, they kill most of the men, reserving only such as would be likely to associate with them, or those against whom they entertain a pointed enmity for injuries received, which they intend to revenge before their assembled tribe, in the most exemplary manner. Should the settlement, however, be weak, the Indians commence the attack on their arrival; and if they prove successful, the men generally are treated as above, the women and children carried off as prisoners, and the houses pillaged, and then fired with their remaining contents. This is a brief outline of their mode of warfare with the whites, and is perhaps all that requires to be said on the subject.

As I grew larger so as to recollect the more recent incidents of my life, the Indian boys were accustomed tauntingly to upbraid me with being *white,* and with the whites all being *squaws;* a reproachful term used generally among the Indians, in contradistinction to that of *warrior.* This often involved me in boyish conflicts, from which I sometimes came off victorious. These contests were always conducted fairly, and the victor uniformly received the praises and encouragements of the men; while the vanquished, if he had conducted himself bravely, was no less an object of their notice; if otherwise, he was neglected, and much pains were taken to shame and mortify him; nor would this conduct be relaxed in the slightest degree, till he had retrieved his character. The Indians are not only spectators, but umpires in these contests; they display great interest in them, and always adjudge with the strictest impartiality. By such means the courage and character of the young Indians are tested; and when deficient, the remedy is at once applied, and so effectually, that instances of cowardice are seldom discovered among them after they have arrived at the age of puberty. From the above practice, it should not be inferred that they encourage discord and quarreling among themselves: the fact is otherwise; and in truth they experience much less than is met with in the lower orders of civilized life.

The white woman whom I noticed a little back was no way remarkable for any attention to me, which at this period of my life I think somewhat extraordinary; but perhaps, like myself, she had been taken prisoner by the Indians while young, and her sympathies had become enlisted for, or identified with those of the tribe. She had two children, was tall, healthy, and good-looking, as I judge from the impressions made on my mind at that early period of my life. She separated from us in company with her husband and a considerable party of Indians, who had become disaffected, while on a hunting excursion on some of the branches of the Mississippi, during the last year, except one or two that I remained with this tribe; since which, I have heard nothing concerning her. She was much beloved by the Indians, was in the prime of life, and I have no doubt is now living with some of the Kickapoos on the Mississippi, or some of its tributary streams.

Digressing a little, I may here observe that I met three or four white children, apparently of my own age, while traveling among the different tribes. They appeared, like myself, to have been at first forced to assume the Indian character and habits; but time and a conformity to custom had nationalized them, and they seemed as happy and contented as though they had descended directly from the Indians, and were in possession of their patrimony. I also met some, whose parents, either on the side of the father or mother, had been white: they sustained the character of brave warriors; but in general no caste, differing from that of the tribe, is held in repute or estimation. It is a remarkable fact, that white people generally, when brought up among the Indians, become unalterably attached to their customs, and seldom afterwards abandon them. I have known two instances of white persons, who had arrived at manhood, leaving their connections and civilized habits, assuming the Indian, and fulfilling all his duties. These, however, happened among the Cherokees. Thus far I am an exception, and it is highly probable I shall ever remain such; though, I must confess, the struggle in my bosom was for a considerable time doubtful, and even now my mind often reverts to the innocent scenes of my childhood, with a mixture of pleasurable and painful emotions that is altogether indescribable. But my intercourse with refined society, acquaintance with books, and a glimpse at the wonderful structure into which the mind is capable of being molded, have, I am convinced, unalterably attached me to a social intercourse with civilized man, composed as he is of crudities and contradictions.

While the Indians, with whom I lived, were engaged on the Kaskaskia River in making sugar, the season after they had separated from the white woman, as just noticed, a party of Patawattomies [Potawatomis] split the sugar troughs, hacked and very much injured the sugar trees, stole several horses, and committed other depredations on their property. The Kickapoos determined to make reprisals; and, accordingly, a party of their warriors pursued the aggressors down the river, put them to flight, and returned with most of their horses and some scalps, without having sustained any loss on their part. The Kickapoos, sensible that their hunting grounds were but indifferently supplied with game, while those adjoining them in some directions were quite the reverse, were in consequence much addicted to roving. Parties of them had already settled to the west of the Missouri, and those who remained usually extended their huts along the great lakes, or the Mississippi, much to the annoyance of their neighbors, and the interruption of their own peaceful relations. By such conduct, and by divisions among themselves, they had become comparatively weak; and it was the wish of the most influential warriors of the tribe to join their brethren beyond the Missouri; while those who had hunted to the north, and carried on a considerable trade at the post of Mackinaw, opposed the measure. The subject was debated a long time, with great warmth, and ended in a separation of the parties. Those in favor of migration immediately commenced their march, taking me with them.

They were obliged to pass through the hunting ground of the Patawattomies, which occasioned much skirmishing with some hunting parties of that nation; but they finally succeeded in crossing the Mississippi, without sustaining much loss. Thence they proceeded up the Marameck [Meramec] River, to a village of the Shawanees [Shawnees], the same, I believe, that is now called Rogerstown. The Kickapoos were cordially received, and the pipe went round in confirmation of mutual friendship. After remaining for some time here, the party proceeded for several days up the Marameck, leaving my mother behind; but for what reason, I was never able to learn. The separation filled me with the most painful sensations; but I had then become so old as to appreciate the importance of sustaining my Indian character, and therefore scorned to complain. We finally encamped on the banks of this river, considerably above the Shawanee town, in a delightful country, which was abundantly supplied with game. The hunters made frequent excursions to explore the country and take buffalo; in one of which they were attacked, and very roughly handled by a hunting party of strange Indians, who, it was supposed, claimed the hunting grounds, and considered the Kickapoos as violaters of their rights. This surprise and defeat, together with their own weakness, induced the Kickapoos to send runners to the Shawanees for assistance; but they returned, without being able to procure any: which induced the party to ascend the river to a greater distance, with a view to avoid their enemies. This step, however, proved highly detrimental to them; for by this time the hostile Indians had appeared in more considerable numbers below, and, as reported by some spies who had been sent out to make observations, cut off a retreat. In this state of things, the party, to avoid a surprise, crossed the river, and pursued their journey with great industry, without any interruption till they unexpectedly arrived opposite to a settlement of Kickapoos, which had been effected some time previously, by a party that had preceded them.

This settlement, when first made, consisted of about ninety warriors; their number now was much reduced, and, reinforced by our party, did not much exceed the original number. They were considered as intruders by the neighboring Indians, who carried on a desultory warfare with them; which, if they had remained where they were, must finally have terminated in their total destruction. To return would be attended with great danger; they therefore concluded to advance further into the country, which they considered would be flying from it; besides, in the latter direction, game, the most important object next to their safety, was very abundant. The execution of this resolution was hastened by several skirmishes, which the Kickapoos had about this time. They accordingly crossed the river, and coursed up its banks till they blended with the ridges and hills. During the early part of the march, the hunters had some engagements with hostile wandering parties, which, though by no means decisive, operated, in the aggregate, much against them. They, however, found, as they receded from the larger streams and good grazing grounds, that this annoyance almost entirely ceased; but then the game diminished with the danger: there was, nevertheless, a sufficiency to supply all their wants; and they again fixed their camps, with the hope of enjoying uninterrupted peace, till more of their nation should join them, and they were better prepared to repel injuries. In this they were, however, disappointed; for they were shortly after surprised by a large party of wandering Pawnees, which massacred and scalped nearly all their warriors, and took the remainder, including men, women, and children, prisoners. The march that followed was long, and over a broken country, which, to the best of my recollection, was not interrupted by any very large stream.

The Indians who now claimed me had many small engagements, some of which, I believe, were with the Osages,* as I heard that name frequently used. Some months must have transpired in this way, in which I do not remember to have suffered anything remarkable; nor were my affections enlisted in favor of my new masters by any particular kindness or attention shown me. We had now come to the hunting grounds of the Kansas† Indians, at least I learned so from the incidents that followed, and also from the Kansas themselves. The party I was with, as before observed, were wanderers; that is, having no fixed towns, and not scrupulous as to the infringement of the privileges of others. They pushed their hunting excursions into the neighborhood of the Kansas' hunting parties, had frequent skirmishes with them, and lost or took several scalps, according to whichever party prevailed; but nothing decisive occurred till the

*Wa-sagè
†*Konses,* } according to the Indian pronunciation. (JDH)

In his "Handbook of the American Indians," Frederick Webb Hodge lists Hunter's spellings of both tribal names (I, 655; II, 158). (RD)

Kansas' hunters received reinforcements from their villages on the Kansas River, when a bloody engagement ensued, which terminated in nearly an equal loss to both parties. Shortly after this, our party, while in their camps, were surprised by the Kansas, who had been reinforced, and almost entirely cut off: a few warriors escaped, and the remainder, including myself, were taken prisoners. The Kansas took us after a long march to their towns, situated on the Kansas River, several hundred miles above its confluence with the Missouri, which is three hundred and fifty miles above the entrance of the latter river into the Mississippi.

Shortly after my arrival, I was adopted into the family of Kee-nees-tah by his squaw, who had lost a son in one of their recent engagements with the Pawnees. I was exceedingly fortunate from this election; and not only the chiefs and squaws, but the whole tribe, treated me with regard and tenderness. This conduct in respect to myself was not singular, for all the women and children were treated in the same manner; while the warriors who were so unfortunate as not to fall in battle were nearly all tortured to death: a few of them, however, were respected for their distinguished bravery, and permitted to live amongst them. It is somewhat remarkable, that among the few who survived this tragic event, was an Indian named Nee-ke-rah, who, as I have since been informed by an officer of great respectability that served in Colonel Russel's regiment of rangers, subsequently returned to the hunting grounds of the Kickapoos, where he had formerly resided, joined the Indians hostile to the United States, and fell, either at the battle of the Wabash or Mississinua towns.*

In justice to my own feelings, I cannot avoid making some remarks in this place, on the difference of character that exists between the Kickapoo and Kansas Indians. The former are treacherous, deceitful, cunning, not tenacious of a good character, exceedingly remiss in their social habits and intercourse, and are held in humble estimation by the neighboring tribes: while the character of the latter, according to the estimation I formed of their conduct to me, is directly the reverse. In this difference of their general character, it is, however, possible for me to be mistaken; but gratitude is a virtue inculcated by all the Indian tribes with which I have been acquainted; and so great was the change of conduct towards me, after my transposition from the former to the latter, that I am persuaded my readers will excuse me, even should I have committed an error.

I was too short a time with the party from whom the Kansas took me to form any correct opinion of their character: their conduct to me was in no respect remarkable, and I am not positive to what tribe of Pawnees they belonged.

In the ensuing fall the traders came among us; and here for the first time, to the best of my recollection, I saw a white man. My surprise, as may be naturally supposed, was great: but in a short time my curiosity became satiated; and their conduct, demeanor, and employment, regarded under the prejudices I had imbibed from the Indians, left no very favorable opinion of them on my mind. It was in the fall season when I arrived at the Kansas' towns: the Indians were numerous and well provided with venison, buffalo meat, corn, nuts, &c.; and judging from the knowledge I have since acquired, had made greater advances toward civilized life, than any of the neighboring tribes. They had a large number of horses; and while with them I first learned to ride that animal. Here, after I had become acquainted with their language, I was accustomed, in company with the Indian boys, to listen with indescribable satisfaction to the sage counsels, inspiring narratives, and traditionary tales of Tshut-che-nau.* This venerable worn-out warrior would often admonish us for our faults, and exhort us never to tell a lie. "Never steal, except it be from an enemy, whom it is just that we should injure in every possible way. When you become men, be brave and cunning in war, and defend your hunting grounds against all encroachments. Never suffer your squaws or little ones to want. Protect the squaws and strangers from insult. On no account betray your friend. Resent insults—revenge yourselves on your enemies. Drink not the poisonous strong-water of the white people; it is sent by the Bad Spirit to destroy the Indians. Fear not death; none but cowards fear to die. Obey and venerate the old people, particularly your parents. Fear and propitiate the Bad Spirit, that he may do you no harm; love and adore the Good Spirit, who made us all, who supplies our hunting grounds, and keeps us alive."

He would then point to the scars that disfigured his body, and say, "Often have I been engaged in deadly combat with the enemies of our nation, and almost as often come off victorious. I have made long walks over snow and ice, and through swamps and prairies, without food, in search of my country's foes: I have taken this and that prisoner, and the scalps of such and such warriors."

Now looking round on his auditors with an indescribable expression of feeling in his countenance, and pointing to the green fields of corn, and to the stores collected from the hunting grounds, he would continue, "For the peaceful enjoyment of all these, you are indebted to myself and to my brave warriors. But now they are all gone, and I only remain. Like a decayed prairie tree, I stand alone: the companions of my youth, the partakers of my sports, my toils, and

---

*"Tshut-che-nau" means, in the Indian dialect, "Defender of the People." (JDH)

my dangers, recline their heads on the bosom of our Mother.* My sun is fast descending behind the western hills, and I feel that it will soon be night with me."

Finally, his heart overflowing with gratitude, with uplifted hands, and eyes directed heavenwards, he would close the interesting scene, by thanking the Great and Good Spirit, for having been so long spared as an example to point out to the young men the true path to glory and fame. I loved this old man, the Indians all loved him; and we always listened to his wise counsels with the greatest satisfaction and delight. I am convinced that much of this venerable chief's character would have adorned the proudest age of civilized life. Surely it was a bright example, in the western wilds, of uneducated virtue and practical piety.

Such, connected with the traditionary accounts of the Indians, of which I shall take notice in the progress of this work, were our more serious employments; while dancing, running races, wrestling, jumping, swimming, playing with the hoop, throwing the tomahawk, fighting sham battles, and holding councils, made up the most of our amusements. My employment, while with the Kansas, was similar to that of the Indian boys generally, and consisted in assisting the squaws to perform their various duties, and in taking fish and some kinds of game.

While with this nation, a party of hunters, consisting of about thirty, which had ascended the Kansas River, and crossed over to some of the branches of the Arkansas, was routed with some loss by a party of wandering Pawnees. On their return, a council was convened, and the subject of migrating to new hunting grounds, connected with which the recent excursion had been made, was solemnly debated. Tut-tes-se-gau, or the Rushing Wind, a brave and ambitious warrior, zealously supported the measure: he observed, that in the recent contest, he had lost a brother; that a removal would bring them into delightful hunting grounds, and place them in the immediate neighborhood of their natural enemies; that thus an opportunity of revenge would be offered, and new fields of glory be opened to exercise the courage and skill of the young warriors: while the chief, Kis-ke-mas, or the Waving Grass, as zealously opposed it. In discussing the subject, he observed, that the hunting grounds they already possessed were sufficiently extensive and well-furnished with game to supply all their wants; they were theirs by inheritance, and they were able and willing to defend them: and that to restrain and keep in fear their neighboring enemies, presented sufficiently brilliant and more just objects for exercising the bravery and ambition

---

*Meaning the Earth. (JDH)

of their warriors. "The hunting grounds we propose to acquire belong to powerful nations. They will unite and defend them, as we would ours, to the last. Such a measure would lead to a perpetual and exterminating war. How many women and little children it would leave without hunters to provide food for them, and warriors to defend them against their enemies! As for their bravery, none could doubt it; every stream that watered their vastly extensive country could afford proof of it; and if this is not sufficient, the scars they all bore would incontrovertibly establish it, as long as the fire of life burned." I heard this subject discussed: much division of opinion existed; but the wise counsels and appropriate eloquence of Kis-ke-mas prevailed. The Pawnees, Mahas [Omahas], and some other nations, were, to the best of my recollection, severally at war with each other about this time; and the two above mentioned were also hostile to the Kansas, and made, during the summer, several disconnected incursions upon their hunting grounds, killed several of their hunters, and stole many of their horses. The Kansas, determining to put a stop to these encroachments, and to make reprisals, pursued one of these marauding parties, belonging to the Pawnees, up the Kansas River to the shoals below Neesh-ke-nah, or the Willow Islands of the traders, where there is a safe ford, which is a thoroughfare for the Indians in their hunting and depredatory excursions. The Pawnees, perceiving that they were pursued, and taking advantage of the very dry season and high winds that prevailed, set fire to the leaves and prairie grass, and made safe their retreat across the river. The Kansas were in consequence compelled to abandon the pursuit, and escape with great difficulty from the smoke and flames, which spread with the most astonishing rapidity. About this time, the Mahas, who were and for a long time had been at war with the Kansas, and also with the Ottowas [Otoes*], made peace with the latter; and uniting their forces, determined to resist the ambitious views of the Kansas, as respected the farther extension of their hunting grounds.

After much skirmishing on both sides, in which no great advantage was gained, a decisive and bloody battle was fought, late in the fall, on the Gravelly Fork, a few miles above its confluence with the Kansas River, in which the Kansas came off victorious with the loss of the brave and gallant Kis-ke-mas, and fourteen or fifteen of his warriors. The loss on the other side was much more considerable; the Mahas and Ottowas having lost thirty-five killed, and twenty-five taken prisoners.

The return of the Kansas with their prisoners and scalps was greeted by the squaws, as is usual on such occasions, by the most extravagant rejoicings; while every imaginable indignity was practiced on the prisoners. The rage of the relict of Kis-ke-mas knew no bounds: she, with the rest of the squaws, particularly those who had lost any connections, and the children, whipped the prisoners with green briars, and hazel switches, and threw firebrands, clubs, and stones at them, as they ran between their ranks to the painted post, which is a goal of safety for all who arrive at it, till their fate is finally determined in a general council of the victorious warriors. A farther account of this ceremony will be subsequently noticed. The prisoners all arrived at the place of safety alive: though some of them were horribly mangled. In the course of a few days, a council was held, in which it was determined to spare the lives of all the prisoners except two, who were chiefs, and had rendered themselves conspicuous objects for revenge, from instigating the confederate war. These two chiefs were Mahas; they were never heard to complain during the protracted and cruel tortures inflicted on them by the squaws: one of them, on the contrary, did all in his power to provoke his persecutors; observing to the wife of Kis-ke-mas, "I killed your husband, I took his scalp, I drank his blood: I owe my country nothing; I have fought many battles for her, killed many of her enemies, and leave behind me warriors enough to revenge my death, to defend their hunting grounds, squaws, and little ones. I am a man: the fate of war is against me—I die like a warrior."

Not long after this, I experienced a painful loss. The squaw who had adopted me among her children, and who had treated me with great tenderness and affection, was accidentally drowned in attempting to collect driftwood during the prevalence of a flood. This circumstance was the cause of grief, apparently more poignant to be endured than is usually experienced in civilized life; because the customs of the Indians do not tolerate the same open expression of feelings, from the indulgence of which the acuteness of grief is relieved, and sooner subsides. The Indians regard tears, or any expression of grief, as a mark of weakness in males, and unworthy of the character of the warrior. In obedience to this custom, I bore my affliction in silence, in order to sustain my claims to their respect and esteem; but nevertheless, I sincerely and deeply felt the bereavement; and cannot, even at this late day, reflect on her maternal conduct to me, from the time I was taken prisoner by the Kansas, to her death, without the association of feelings to which, in other respects, I am a stranger. She was indeed a mother to me; and I feel my bosom dilate with gratitude at the recollection of her goodness, and care of me during this helpless period of my life. This, to those who have been bred in refinement and ease, under the fond and watchful guardianship of parents, may appear gross and incongruous. If, however, the imagination be allowed scope, and a lad ten or twelve years of age, without kindred or name, or any knowledge by which he could arrive at an acquaintance with any of the circumstances connected with his being, be supposed in the central wilds of North America, nearly a thousand miles from any white settlement, a prisoner or sojourner among a people on whom he had not the slightest claim, and with whose language, habits, and character he was wholly unacquainted; but who, nevertheless, treated him kindly; it will appear not only natural but rational, that he should return such kindness with gratitude and affection. Such nearly was my situation, and such in fact were my feelings at that time; and however my circumstances have since changed, or however they may change in the future, I have no hope of seeing happier days than I experienced at this early period of my life, while sojourning with the Kansas nation, on the Kansas River, some hundred miles above its confluence with the Missouri. Shortly after the death of my adopted mother, the sage and venerable Indian chief, Tshut-che-nau, whom I have before noticed, died. The whole nation grieved for his loss, a large concourse followed him to the grave, and the ceremony of burial was solemn and deeply impressive. Early in the following spring, a party of about thirty hunters and eleven boys, including myself, started on a hunting excursion: it was the first time the Indians had taken me with them, and the hunt excited great interest, especially as the boys, armed only with bows and arrows, were very successful in the chase. We ascended the Kansas River nearly to its source, till we arrived at the hills that separate it from the waters that flow into the Arkansas. From thence we directed our course to the right, and crossed the head waters of several streams that flow into the Missouri. We ascended one of these called the Kee-nesh-tah, or the River That Sinks, known to the traders by the name of the Platte, several hundred miles. This river takes its Indian name from flowing in some places through districts of sand, over which it spreads to a great extent, and sometimes nearly disappears. It is shoal; and not navigable, except for short distances, even for canoes. The districts of country remote from the watercourses, are generally prairie, and are abundantly supplied with buffalo, elk, deer, bears, and other smaller game.

We passed the summer in hunting and roving; and in the fall ascended the Platte several hundred miles, with a view more particularly to take furs. Near the place where we fixed our camps, which was on the Teel-te-nah, or Dripping Fork, a few miles above its entrance into the Platte, is an extensive cave, which we visited on several occasions, and always with great reverence and dread.

This cave is remarkable as having been the cemetery of some people who must have inhabited this neighborhood at a remote period of time, as the Indians who now occasionally traverse this district bury their dead in a manner altogether different.

The entrance to this cavern was rather above the ground; and though narrow, of easy access. The floor was generally rocky, and much broken; though in some places, particularly in the ante-parts, strips of soil appeared, covered with animal ordure. Parts of the roof were at very unequal distances from the floor: in some places it appeared supported by large, singularly variegated, and beautiful columns; and at others it supported formations resembling huge icicles, which I now suppose to be stalactites.

Lighted up by our birch-bark flambeaux, the cave exhibited an astonishing and wonderful appearance; while the loud and distant rumbling or roar of waters through their subterranean channels, filled our minds with apprehension and awe. We discovered two human bodies partly denuded, probably by the casual movements of the animals which frequent this abode of darkness; we inhumed and placed large stones over them, and then made good our retreat, half inclined to believe the tradition which prevails among some of the tribes, and which represents this cavern as the aperture through which the first Indian ascended from the bowels of the earth, and settled on its surface.

Our camps were fixed on a high piece of ground near the cave, in the vicinity of the Dripping Fork, a name which this stream takes from the great number of rills that drip into it from its rocky and abrupt banks. Near this place is a salt-lick, to which various herds of the grazing kind resort in great numbers. The buffalo, deer, and elk, have made extraordinarily deep and wide excavations in the banks surrounding it, where we used often to secrete ourselves; sometimes merely to observe the playful gambols of the collected herds, and terrible conflicts of the buffaloes, but more frequently to destroy such of them as were necessary to supply our wants. The beaver, otter, and muskrat, which find safe retreats in the cavernous banks of this stream, were very abundant; and our hunt was attended with great success.

About this time a young man, named Davis, who I have since learned was from Kentucky, came among us. He belonged to a party of adventuring hunters, which he supposed were all cut off, except himself, by a party of wandering Sioux. His appearance among us excited great sympathy; he claimed our protection, and received a cordial welcome. This occurrence, not without cause, created great apprehension for our own safety; for the Sioux, who had attacked Davis' party, were numerous, and not very far off. We had hitherto experienced no incidents calculated to mar the pleasures always connected, in a high degree, with the chase on safe grounds: we had taken much game; the cold, changeable weather had commenced;

and our party, after maturely deliberating the subject, determined forthwith to commence their return to the Kansas towns. A division of opinion, however, existed as to the route which ought to be taken: some were for descending by the Platte and Missouri, as by this route the watercourses would direct them, and food would be more easily obtained, as game was much more abundant. As, however, the rich and abundant furs, with which the waters of this district were supplied, had become objects of importance to the several tribes which inhabited thereabouts, and contentions had arisen between them respecting the right to these hunting grounds; it was finally concluded to course back on the high lands that divided the waters of the Arkansas from those of the Missouri, in preference to inviting the hostility of the belligerents, by passing through the territory in dispute. We accordingly commenced this long and tedious march, and proceeded for several days, without any thing remarkable occurring. We then fell in with a party of Osages, belonging to the Grand Osage nation, who treated us very friendly, and from whom we learned the difficulties and dangers we should have to encounter, provided we continued on our route to the Kansas towns. They, pointing in a homeward direction, observed "The sky is overcast with clouds; all is hostility and war. The tribe of Osages under White Hair, has joined the confederacy against the Kansas; and war parties from the Mahas, Ottowas, and Pawnees, now occupy their hunting grounds, and cut off your return."

The Osage party with whom we were, could afford us no protection: to remain on these grounds, or to retreat farther back, would have ensured no safety; for the whole country hereabouts was frequently traversed by hostile parties of Indians; and to give ourselves up to the Mahas or Ottowas, our inveterate enemies, would have been inviting our destruction. It was probable, although the Osages under White Hair were at war with our nation, that no engagements had taken place between them to inflame a deadly hatred. Besides, they were considered by all the neighboring tribes to be magnanimous and sincere, and were accordingly much esteemed and respected. A council was therefore held, at which the principal Osages attended; and it was determined by their advice, all the circumstances having been maturely weighed, to surrender ourselves to the protection of the hostile Osages, as a measure though exceeding painful, yet offering the best prospects for our safety. We parted from these friendly Osages, with strong expressions of gratitude and regret, after having received their assurances that our reception by White Hair's tribe would be friendly, and might be depended on. They also sent a wampum and greetings, as tokens of their favor, and our peaceful intentions.

We now crossed several ranges of hills, and then coursed down a considerable stream, which, from the incrustations we found on its margin, I now suppose was the Grand Saline of the Kansas River. On its bank, in the neighborhood of extensive swamps, while pursuing our route, we were surprised by a strolling party of independent Pawnees. They were more numerous, and better armed than we were; but, notwithstanding, our party came off victors. I do not know what number the Pawnees lost, as we took no scalps; it is probable, however, it must have been considerable, from the circumstances of their retreat, which was accompanied with the most hideous yells, and the bearing off of their dead; a practice which they most tenaciously adhere to, even at the risk of their lives. We lost no scalps, but four of our party were killed, including two boys, who had acquired much reputation before they left the Kansas towns, for having, in conjunction with a squaw, killed two of the Ottowas in the act of stealing horses on the banks of the Kansas River. I ought before to have remarked, that these boys had been presented with rifles, in consequence of their good conduct on the above occasion, which probably was the cause of their deaths in the recent engagement. The Indians applauded Davis, who had continued of their party, and was one of the combatants, for his bravery and good conduct in this affair. This was the first engagement I had ever been in: I was armed with a bow and arrows, which I applied to the best of my ability; but probably with little or no effect. From this place, apprehensive of another attack, we made all the expedition in our power, taking our dead with us, which we buried in the course of the following night, in silent grief. After this ceremony had been performed, we descended this Saline a considerable distance; thence, crossing a hilly country, a large river, probably the Kansas, and several smaller ones, we arrived on a stream, called by the Indians, Leshfaus-keeh, and by the traders, Vermillion River, on account of the red earth through which it flows, and from which the natives procure red paint.*

We next entered upon the hunting grounds of the Osages hostile to the Kansas nation. The buffalo herds were here more numerous than I had ever before witnessed; but, apprehending that we should be considered as depredators, and treated as enemies, we did not discharge a single shot, or in any other way disturb them.

As we proceeded, our apprehensions increased, from the appearance of moccasin tracks in the sand, signs of recent encampments, &c., which plainly indicated that we had nearly arrived at the crisis which was to determine our relations, as to peace or war. These indications continuing to increase, we concluded, and rightly, that we were in the immediate neighborhood of their settlements: in consequence of which we encamped on elevated grounds near the river, and dispatched two peace-runners, with friendly tokens to the Osage chief. Our messengers were at first, as is common among the Indians, regarded with suspicion, and strict scrutiny; but on giving a satisfactory account of themselves and their party, they were retained, and treated in a friendly manner. In the meantime, the chief convened a council, and sent six of his warriors to welcome our arrival. They were received by our party, divested of their arms, with great satisfaction and joy. Kee-nees-tah, the chief of our party, and my father by adoption, saluting the principal Osage according to the customs of the Indians, observed, "Our people are now at war. I left them friends at the time I started on a hunting excursion, many moons ago, without any hostile intentions to yours, or any other tribe. I cannot return to my people in safety, and come to claim of you the rights of hospitality." The Osage, in the same respectful manner, assured him and our party in the name of his nation, of his friendship and regard, and invited us to sit at the same fire, and smoke the same pipe with them. We accordingly accompanied them to their town, where we were welcomed by all the inhabitants, amounting probably to fifteen hundred, in the most cordial and friendly manner.

I had not been long with the Osages, before I was received into the family of Shen-thweeh, a warrior distinguished among his people for his wisdom and bravery, at the instance of Hunk-hah, his wife, who had recently lost a son in an engagement with some of the neighboring tribes. This good woman, whose family now consisted of herself, her husband, a daughter almost grown, and myself, took every opportunity, and used every means which kindness and benevolence could suggest, to engage my affections and esteem. She used to weep over me, tell me how good her son had been, how much she loved him, and how much she mourned his loss. "You must be good," she would say, "and you shall be my son, and I will be your mother." The daughter, in many respects, imitated the mother; and the greatest care was taken to supply my wants with the choicest things they had in their power to bestow. They made and ornamented moccasins and leggings for me, and furnished me with a beaver cap and buffalo robe, habiliments not usually worn by the Indian boys. In fine, so constant and persevering were their attentions, and so kind and affectionate their care of me, that not to have loved and esteemed them, would have argued a degree of ingratitude and apathy of feeling to which, if I know myself, I then was, and shall forever remain, a stranger. Several months had now transpired since the death of my Indian Kansas mother. My Indian father, it is true, had accompanied me throughout our recent excursion to the Dripping Fork: but then, as is customary among the Indian warriors, with respect to their offspring, or those whom they may adopt, he showed little or no regard or tenderness for me. Thus, the indulgence of my filial feelings, which I think were proportionally excited as the necessity of parental support increased, was in a measure interrupted. The treatment I received from Hunk-hah and her daughter chimed in harmonious concordance with the vibrations of my bosom: I gave loose to their indulgence, and sincerely loved and respected them, as much, it appears to me, as if they had really been allied to me by the strongest ties of consanguinity. The Osages generally were fond of and kind to me, particularly the children; in whose sports, which much resembled those of the Kansas, I invariably joined, and often excelled. The party of Kansas whom I accompanied to the Osage nation were distributed in different families, and shared in their hospitality, amusements, and toils of the chase. It may be proper, in respect to them, to observe in this place, that the hostility between the Osages and their nation continuing, they were not permitted to return; but suffered in no other respect any restraint whatever. I arrived among the Osages early in the winter season, and no occurrence took place, in respect to myself or this nation, worthy of being noticed, during the following year. I passed my time much in the same manner as while among the Kansas, only with the exception that I occasionally joined the Indians in their hunting excursions.

The next fall, however, a party of hunters, consisting of Osages and Kansas, took me with them on an excursion, several hundred miles up the main Arkansas River. This expedition, in some respects, proved very fortunate; for we not only collected a large quantity of furs, venison, and buffalo meat, but had the additional satisfaction of gaining a victory over a party of wandering Pawnees, who had the temerity to attack us. In this engagement, we only had two wounded; the enemy was entirely routed, with the loss of fifteen scalps. I took part in this engagement; but being only armed with a bow, was not more successful than I had been in my first essay on the Grand Saline.

We returned to the Osage town late the next spring, where a part of our furs were bartered with the traders, who frequently visited the Osages, for rifles; with one of which, each of the boys who had been on the recent hunt was supplied. Thus armed and otherwise properly accoutred, I felt all the self-consequence of a veteran warrior; and panted more to distinguish myself in war, than in any peaceful pursuits, though probably not more than fourteen or fifteen years of age. I soon learned the use of my rifle in the chase, and used it with great success; in consequence of which, the Indians gave me the name of the *Hunter*. The following summer, with nearly all the winter, was spent in short hunting excursions, with a view, for the most part, to procure provisions; hunting of furs being considered by the old men, whose opinions operate with nearly as much force as their acknowledged laws, as highly detrimental to the morals of the Indians. It led to too great a superabundance, which created factitious wants, and afforded the means of their intemperate indulgence, particularly as respected ardent spirits, which had been introduced in considerable quantities among the Osages, after our late successful hunting excursion. Here, I first saw drunken Indians, and witnessed, with indescribable astonishment, its unsocial effects on the women as well as on some of the warriors. No state of society is, in my opinion, more exempt from strife and contention between husband and wife, than that of the Indians generally. The warrior thinks it beneath his character to meddle in any way with the province of his squaw; but, when this *evil spirit* is introduced among them by the traders, this character undergoes a great modification, particularly during the paroxysm of its influence. In fact, a drunken Indian and squaw act more like demons than rational human beings; and nearly a whole town in the same situation, as I have since frequently witnessed, would, according to the representations given of them by some poets, bear a strong resemblance to the *Infernal Regions*. Indeed, no language can describe its mischievous effects. The traders take advantage of such occasions to defraud the Indians; who, when they become sober, very often seek redress in the destruction of their property, or in that of the white people themselves. Hence, quarrels and commotions are fomented between them and their trading visitors, and no hope can be rationally entertained by the benefactors of the human family to improve their condition, till this bane to social life be wholly excluded from them.

Resuming my narrative, I think it was in the winter following the Indians were filled with great terror, on account of the repeated occurrences of violent tremors and oscillations of the earth: the trees and wigwams shook exceedingly; the ice which skirted the margin of the Arkansas River was broken in pieces; and the most of the Indians thought that the Great Spirit, angry with the human race, was about to destroy the world. I have no doubt part of New Madrid was sunk by one of these earthquakes; and if so, they must have happened in 1811, which period accords with the subsequent events of my life. Davis, who joined the Kansas party while at the Dripping Fork, left the Osages this winter: I heard from him some time after, but do not now recollect the particulars; and what has since become of him I know not.

After I had been some time with the Osages, an occurrence took place, which, as it had, beyond a doubt, considerable influence on my ultimately leaving them, deserves to be noticed.

While I was out with my Indian sister Wees-keh collecting fuel, she made some very particular inquiries about my people, which, of course, I was unable to answer. These inquiries frequently recurred to me, and led to a train of reflections in my youthful mind of a most extraordinary kind.

The accounts of the white people, which the Indians had been very particular in giving me, were no ways flattering to my color; they were represented as an inferior order of beings, wicked, treacherous, cowardly, and only fit to transact the common drudgeries of life. I was at the same time assured, that my transposition from them to the Indians was for me a most fortunate occurrence; for now I might become an expert hunter, brave warrior, wise counsellor, and possibly a distinguished chief of their nation. All this I considered as true, till the arrival of the traders among us. They were particularly kind and attentive to me, and made me several trifling presents; in consequence of which I in general formed strong attachments for them. They gave me to understand, that what the Indians had told me was incorrect; they informed me, that the white people were numerous, powerful, brave, generous, and good; that they lived in large houses, some of which floated on the great waters; that their towns were very extensive, and filled with people as numerous as the sand; and that they fought with great guns, and could kill many at a single fire. They used various methods to induce me to visit them; but although these reports were in part believed, my curiosity much excited, and my mind filled with wonder and astonishment, at the existence of such extraordinary things, yet I could not bring my feelings to consent to such a measure.

After some reflection, the prejudices imbibed in early life returned in their full strength; and I still thought the white people were in their characters what they had been represented, and even worse, from the conduct which some of them had practiced while among us. Besides, they were on all occasions represented by the Indians in the most hideous and objectionable colors, no doubt with a view to strengthen my first impressions, enervate my curiosity, and suppress any desire that possibly might exist to visit the white settlements.

On several occasions, when I made inquiries respecting this strange people, and expressed a wish to visit them, and see the singular things of which I had heard, and which continued a long time to occupy my thoughts, the Indians told me I was too young for so long a journey; that if I undertook it, I should be seized, forced to work in the fields even after I had grown to the size of a warrior or hunter, and never be suffered to return. They also told me that when I had grown up, taken many scalps, and become a renowned warrior, I might visit the white people with impunity; that then they would not dare to touch me, but would behold me with consternation and dread. In this way my inquiries were answered, and my curiosity repressed; and though reflections on these subjects frequently recurred to my mind, yet it is highly probable that nothing short of the powerful incitement that finally led to the measure could have induced me to abandon my Indian brothers.

In the following spring, a party of thirty hunters and six or seven squaws started on a visit to some of their connections, who remained at the Osage towns on the Grand Osage River,* taking me with them. Our course was up the Arkansas for a considerable distance; thence across the highlands, till we struck the headwaters of the Grand Osage River, which we descended, to the village belonging to Clermont, or the Builder of Towns, a celebrated Osage chief.* We remained among the Grand Osages, till early in the next fall. During our stay, I saw a number of white people, who, from different motives, resorted to this nation: among them, was a clergyman, who preached several times to the Indians through an interpreter. He was the first Christian preacher that I had ever heard or seen. The Indians treated him with great respect, and listened to his discourses with profound attention; but could not, as I heard them observe, comprehend the doctrines he wished to inculcate. It may be appropriately mentioned here, that the Indians are accustomed, in their own debates, never to speak but one at a time; while all others, constituting the audience, invariably listen with patience and attention till their turn to speak arrives. This respect is still more particularly observed toward strangers; and the slightest deviation from it would be regarded by them as rude, indecorous, and highly offensive. It is this trait in the Indian character which many of the missionaries mistake for a *serious* impression made on their minds; and which has led to many exaggerated accounts of their conversion to Christianity.

Some of the white people whom I met, as before noticed, among the Osages, were traders, and others were reputed to be runners from their Great Father beyond the Great Waters, to invite the Indians to take up the tomahawk against the settlers. They made many long talks, and distributed many valuable presents; but without being able to shake the resolution which the Osages had formed, to preserve peace with their Great Father, the President. Their determinations were, however, to undergo a more severe trial: Te-cum-seh, the celebrated Shawanee warrior and chief, in company with Francis the prophet, now made their appearance among them.

*To understand this subject fully, it should be borne in mind that a part of the Osages, not long since, with the chiefs Big Track and White Hair for their leaders, had separated from the Grand Osage nation, settled on the Arkansas River, and sustained their independence. (JDH) See my note below, pp. 234–35. (RD)

He addressed them in long, eloquent, and pathetic strains; and an assembly more numerous than had ever been witnessed on any former occasion listened to him with an intensely agitated, though profoundly respectful interest and attention. In fact, so great was the effect produced by Te-cum-seh's eloquence, that the chiefs adjourned the council, shortly after he had closed his harangue; nor did they finally come to a decision on the great question in debate for several days afterwards.

I wish it was in my power to do justice to the eloquence of this distinguished man: but it is utterly impossible. The richest colors, shaded with a master's pencil, would fall infinitely short of the glowing finish of the original. The occasion and subject were peculiarly adapted to call into action all the powers of genuine patriotism; and such language, such gestures, and such feelings and fullness of soul contending for utterance, were exhibited by this untutored native of the forest in the central wilds of America, as no audience, I am persuaded, either in ancient or modern times ever before witnessed.

My readers may think some qualification due to this opinion; but none is necessary. The unlettered Te-cum-seh gave extemporaneous utterance only to what he felt; it was a simple, but vehement narration of the wrongs imposed by the white people on the Indians, and an exhortation for the latter to resist them. The whole addressed to an audience composed of individuals who had been educated to prefer almost any sacrifice to that of personal liberty, and even death to the degradation of their nation; and who, on this occasion, felt the portraiture of Te-cum-seh but too strikingly identified with their own condition, wrongs, and sufferings.

This discourse made an impression on my mind, which, I think, will last as long as I live. I cannot repeat it *verbatim*, though if I could, it would be a mere skeleton, without the rounding finish of its integuments: it would only be the shadow of the substance; because the gestures, and the interest and feelings excited by the occasion, and which constitute the essentials of its character, would be altogether wanting. Nevertheless, I shall, as far as my recollection serves, make the attempt, and trust to the indulgence of my readers for an apology for the presumptuous digression.

When the Osages and distinguished strangers had assembled, Te-cum-seh arose; and after a pause of some minutes, in which he surveyed his audience in a very dignified, though respectfully complaisant and sympathizing manner, he commenced as follows:

"*Brothers*—We all belong to one family; we are all children of the Great Spirit; we walk in the same path; slake our thirst at the same spring; and now affairs of the greatest concern lead us to smoke the pipe around the same council fire!

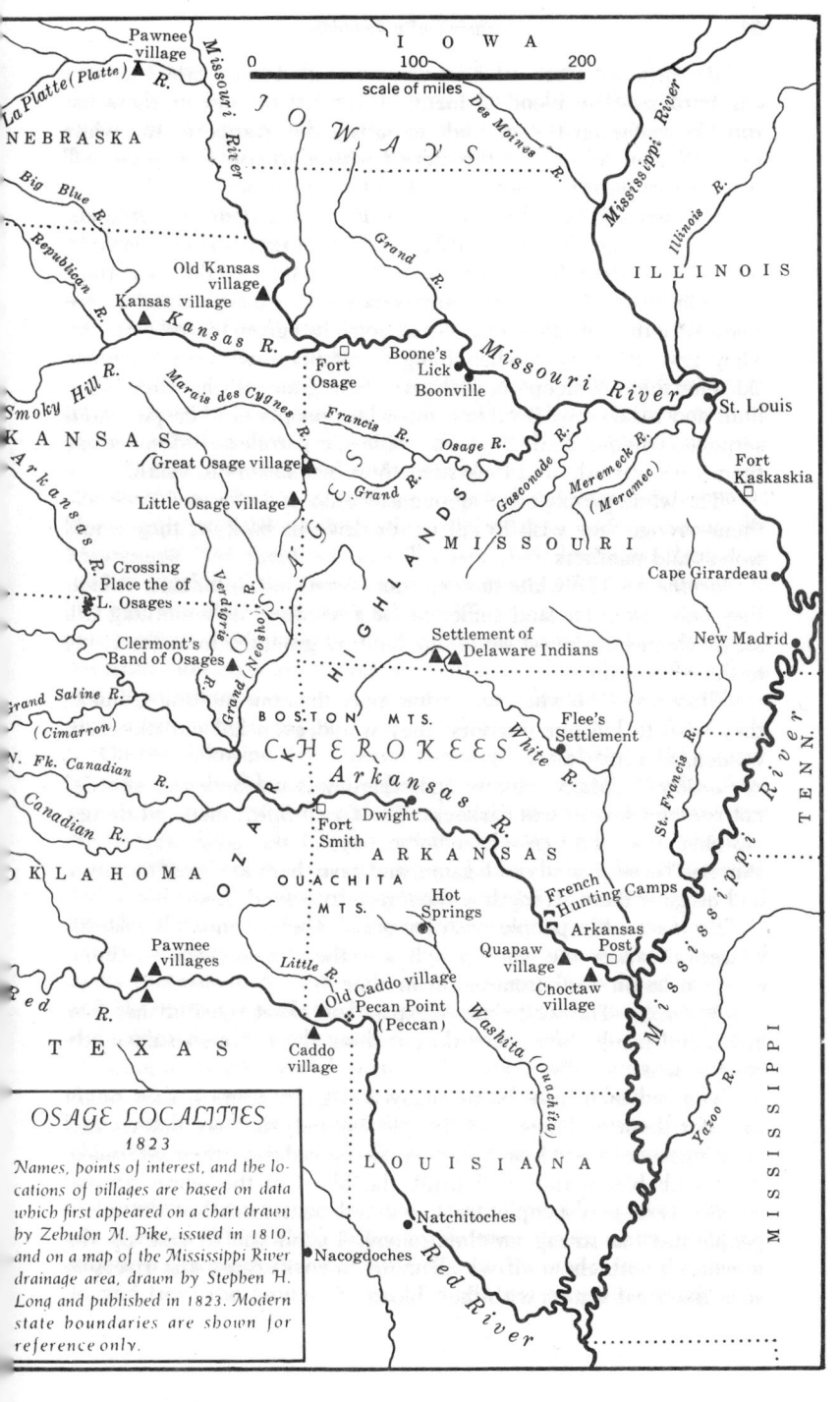

remarks on the excellent fruits with which we often regaled ourselves. These, on our way out, consisted of very large red and white strawberries, red and purple raspberries and gooseberries; and on our return, of various kinds of grapes, great Osage plums, and a variety of nuts; all which were in astonishing abundance. Before our return, the Osage hunters on the Arkansas had gone on an excursion up that river; in consequence of which I was only engaged in desultory hunting for the following winter. In the spring the hunting party returned, with an abundance of furs and other game. They had, during the winter, an engagement of no great importance with a party of wandering Indians, and brought back with them a gentleman whose name I think was M'Clure: with the object of whose tour through that country I am wholly ignorant. He left us, after a short stay, with warm expressions of gratitude for the kind treatment and protection he had received; and I know not what became of him afterwards, though it would be to me peculiarly gratifying to learn, as he asked me many questions, appeared to take great interest in my situation and welfare, and expressed much surprise at my inability to give any account of myself prior to my residence among the Indians. From the circumstance of his speaking the Osage language so as to make himself readily understood, I infer that he had been much among the Osages, and perhaps other nations of Indians.

A new event worthy of remark grew out of some depredations of the wandering Pawnees on the property of the Osages. Some squaws, who had gone after the horses for the purpose of bringing in game, surprised a party of this description, in the very act of stealing them. The Osages had, on several former occasions, lost their horses; but from the manner in which they were taken, knew not on whom to retaliate the injury. The discovery being made, a party of about sixty of their warriors, including myself, started in pursuit. We followed their tracks up Grand [Neosho] River for a considerable distance, when the signs indicating that they were not far in advance, a council was held to decide whether we should continue the pursuit forthwith, or wait till they had encamped for the night. We determined to proceed on; but with the greatest caution. In the meantime two spies were sent ahead, with a view to make discoveries, while the main party marched slowly and quietly after them, in single file.

About two miles from the place where we halted, there was a sand beach, bounded by the river on one side, and on the other by high abrupt cliffs, which in time of floods could not be passed. On arriving at this place, which was now passable, the spies discovered that a part of the Pawnees had left the direct route, and taken a circuitous one round these cliffs through the prairie grass, which good watering place, and encamped for the night. Four days after this, they arrived at their towns, and were received with general demonstrations of joy. To these succeeded the wailings and mournings of those who had lost connections and friends; and then followed the burial of the dead, which was performed in the most solemn and impressive manner.

My wound was severe and painful, and confined me several weeks; but from the skill of our physicians and the kind attentions of my Indian mother and sister, I soon was enabled to rejoin the hunting parties. After the return of the hunters from their excursion up the Arkansas River, a party of thirty-seven hunters, consisting chiefly of the Kansas, and including myself, started on an exploring and hunting expedition, up the Arkansas. It is proper here to remark, that although the Osages had declared war against the Kansas, yet no hostile operations were carried on by the parties against each other. A sufficient number of the former had, however, joined parties of the Mahas and Ottowas in their depredations on the latter, to keep alive their mutual feelings of hostility. In consequence of these animosities, the Osages kept a steady eye on the Kansas party that had thrown itself on their protection, and usually so contrived their hunting parties as to have a majority of their own nation in them. This, I am satisfied, was their policy, though it was executed with delicacy, and apparently without imposing any restraint. The Kansas suspected their motives; and, when by themselves, had frequent conversations on the subject: plans for their escape had been proposed; but it was utterly impossible for their whole number to co-operate simultaneously, without exciting a suspicion that would either defeat them altogether, or prove fatal to a portion of their party. They were well supplied, and otherwise treated kindly; and therefore thought the maintenance of a friendly relation, and their own safety, at least for the present, objects of paramount consequence.

Under such feelings, and with a view to relieve the inquietude of their minds, growing out of the peculiarity of their situations, some of the leading and most restless of the Kansas planned the expedition before named. I have no doubt they intended to include their whole party, so that should an opportunity offer, they might return to their towns on the Kansas River, though such a design was never declared. I was merely asked to volunteer, whenever the excursion should be proposed. But however adroit the plan was, or whatever it had for its object, the whole of the Kansas could not be induced to embark on it.

Some of them were sick, some had married among the Osages, and some, probably, did not approve of the measure.

The trees had just begun to show their foliage when we commenced our journey up the Arkansas: we pursued our course very steadily, at the probable rate of thirty or thirty-five miles a day, stopping only when we required refreshment or rest. On arriving at the usual crossing-place of the Indians between the Arkansas and Kansas rivers, one of the principal Kansas of our party proposed privately to me and some others, to separate from the Osages, and return to the Kansas towns. I strenuously opposed the measure; because my Kansas father remained at the Osage towns, who, together with the other Kansas, not included in our party, might, I was apprehensive, be sacrificed to requite such treachery; and because my ambition, which had been much excited by the prospective results of our contemplated expedition, would in consequence suffer a total disappointment. Besides, I had been a long time from the Kansas, and was not particularly attached to any of the tribe; while with the Osages I had left a mother and sister, who were dear to me, and who loved me in return.

The scheme was finally abandoned; and we continued our course considerably further up the Arkansas; we then left this river, and crossed a hilly country, and several of the heading branches of the Kansas River, and subsequently arrived at our old camping grounds on the Dripping Fork, a few miles from its entrance into the Platte. We remained here several days, again explored the cavern before noticed, and took a considerable quantity of game on the adjacent prairie grounds. A council was also held, and the subject of our future route debated. A small number were for descending the river and returning home; while a very large majority, including myself, were for pursuing an opposite direction. We accordingly crossed to the Platte, and followed the main stream, in a generally direct course, nearly to its source among the Rocky Mountains. This stream, for a great way up, continues shoal and rapid, flowing generally over a sandy or gravelly bed; though it is occasionally interrupted by rocks and falls: it frequently branches and then unites, thus forming many large and beautiful islands; some of which contained wigwams, and cultivated spots of ground. The prairies continue a great distance up; but they do not, except in a very few instances, border on the river, and when they do, the distance is inconsiderable, and the grounds are barren and rocky.

These prairies are generally undulating and rich, in their hollows; but, receding from these, they gradually become sterile, and terminate either in sandy or clay ridges. The margins of this river, and of the streams generally flowing into it, for an extent of from one to three miles in breadth, are covered with thick and large growths of cottonwood, ash, sycamore, elm, various kinds of walnut, and many other trees and shrubs common to the western states.

But so variable are the features of this section of country, and so totally disconnected with its future reclamation and improvement were my views when I visited it, that any attempt on my part to a particular description would be the extreme of folly, and merit no consideration. In fact, many years, if not centuries, must yet elapse, before a correct account of this extensive district can be obtained. Travelers may pass over and write volumes on it; but Indian titles have to be extinguished, forests planted, and roads formed, before any satisfactory and circumstantial information, as connected with the purposes of civilized life, can be arrived at. Suffice it to say, that no person unacquainted with this vast extent of country, and the fertility of a large portion of its soil, can form any idea of the luxuriance of its vegetable productions, or of the immense herds of buffalo, deer, elk, &c., that riot, if I may use the expression, on the varied suffusion of perpetual plenty.* Besides the wild rice, which grows on the wet lands, and various kinds of grass and herbage, either strawberries, gooseberries, blackberries, raspberries, or grapes, all in their proper seasons, and of a size and richness of flavor surpassing any that I have seen in a state of cultivation, carpet the whole surface of the fertile prairies.

On our way up, we fell in with a party of friendly Maha Indians, who were ascending the river, to a former battle ground, with a view to collect the bones, and pay the last solemn rites to the manes of their unfortunate countrymen, who, sometime before, had been surprised and all cut off by their enemies, except one, who was their pilot on this occasion. This individual escape had something of the miraculous in it, and some account of it here may not prove uninteresting to my readers. The Mahas, to the number of forty or fifty, were on a hunting excursion, and had encamped on the banks of a considerable stream that flows into the Platte. In this situation, they were surrounded on all sides, except that of the river, by a numerous party of Indians; who made their advance so cautiously, as not to be perceived till they had singled out and fired upon their objects. The war-whoop and rush then followed; and all, except four or five who fled to the river, were massacred on the spot. Those who took to the river were pursued, and all, except Nee-kish-lau-teeh, the subject of this anecdote, were shot as they were swimming. Nee-kish-lau-teeh, though twice slightly wounded, escaped to the opposite shore, and took a circuitous route through some woods that bordered on it, struck the river again some distance below, but in sight of his camps, and there secretly observed the motions of his enemies. He supposed that all his companions had been slain, and that no efforts of his foes would be wanting to number him with them, in order more effectually to screen themselves from detection, and avert the just vengeance which their atrocious conduct merited.

In this supposition he was not mistaken; for, on arriving at the bank, as just noticed, he observed the Indians making preparations to cross after him. In consequence of which he again took to the woods, following the course of the river, till he came to a bend, where he reswam it, and then changed his course directly back towards the place where his party had been surprised. On arriving within a suitable distance to notice whatever might transpire, he secreted himself in some drift-grass, with which the willows adjacent to the stream were thickly interwoven, and there patiently waited for two days and two nights the events that followed. The Indians, to the number of ten or twelve, crossed the river in pursuit; showed themselves at several places on the banks, both above and below their crossing-place; and, towards night, recrossed, and joined their main party. Early next morning, a still greater number crossed the river, and took its course downwards; while another party took the same direction, on the side where Nee-kish-lau-teeh had secreted himself. This party was so arranged as to sweep the whole of the thick undergrowth along the shore: it proceeded slowly, and searched apparently in every place but the one which contained the object of their pursuit. The Maha had nearly buried himself in the sand, and was otherwise completely hidden: he saw his blood-thirsty foes almost in the act of treading him under their feet, and heard them encouraging each other, and threatening him with cruel tortures, and a lingering death; but he fortunately escaped their search. At night, the parties returned and encamped; and the next morning, having abandoned the search, crossed the river, and journeyed into the country along its banks. The Maha remained in his hiding-place all that day; and at night, in hopes of procuring some food, cautiously approached, first the recent encampments of the hostile Indians, and then those of his unfortunate companions.

He found buffalo meat, satisfied his appetite, slaked his thirst at a neighboring spring, cleansed and dressed his wounds, and made such provision as he could for a long journey.

He was feeble from long fasting and the wounds he had received, and was without any offensive or defensive weapons whatever; but, nevertheless, in the dead of the night, with sensations too painful to be described, he left this ill-fated spot covered with the mangled carcasses of his brother warriors.

On his journey home, he traveled in the night time, secreted himself by day, and subsisted altogether on roots; after much suffering, however, he carried the distressing intelligence to his countrymen.

A party of Loups [Pawnees*] committed this horrid massacre; a long and bloody war followed, in which the Mahas fully satisfied their desire for revenge. They had beaten them wholly from those grounds, and could now hunt on them, without the fear of being disturbed. Such at least is the account that Nee-kish-lau-teeh gave of the transaction, and the consequences that followed. This Maha was probably fifty years of age, when I saw him: he spoke the Kansas language so as with some difficulty to be understood. He had been once across the Rocky Mountains, and much among the neighboring tribes and nations; by whom, as well as by his own people, he was held in high estimation. They even supposed him to be more under the immediate protection of the Great Spirit, than the generality of the Indians: hence his influence was great; and besides the duties of a chief, he often performed those of a prophet and physician.

The description this old man gave of his excursion to the great hills of the west excited the curiosity and ambition of our whole party, and was the primary cause that led us to the execution of a similar expedition.

We continued with the Mahas several days, on the most friendly terms; were advised of the country over which we should pass, of the tribes we might meet, and, in particular, cautioned to be on our guard against the Sta-he-tah,* a small but barbarous tribe of Indians, which inhabit the grounds bordering on the headwaters of the Platte. We parted from these friends with sincere regret. On our way farther up we met several parties of hunters, belonging to different tribes, most of whom, particularly as we approached the mountains, were armed only with bows, arrows, and spears. Whenever we discovered recent trails, we secreted our arms as much as possible, carried the muzzles of our rifles downward, marched on with an apparent carelessness, though in reality with much caution; and when in view of any party, boldly approached it with the customary ensigns of peace.

We were, at first, uniformly met with great suspicion and distrust; but, when the motives of our excursion and the place of our hunting grounds were made known, we were as uniformly received with friendship, and treated with hospitality. We were able to hold talks with some of the parties we met: although our languages were very dissimilar, a few words in each were, in two or three instances, found to be precisely the same; others had some similitude, but by far the greatest number were altogether unintelligible. We met some with whom we were obliged to communicate wholly by signs. These resided high up the river, or among the mountains; were generally well made, robust, and peaceably disposed. They were neither very cleanly nor well provided; and were probably, as they never appeared in large parties, the remnants of more powerful nations, who had sought safety from their enemies in retired or wandering lives. They frequently accompanied us on our route, and partook of our game; in the destruction of which, we were, of course, much the most successful. In return they gave us such things as their ill supplied stores afforded, among which was the Pash-e-quah,* a farinaceous, nutritive, pleasant-tasted, bulbous root, which is found in the valleys in great abundance, is much used by these Indians, and is not a bad substitute for bread, particularly when roasted. They also gave us nuts and a species of wild rice; the latter of which might be collected in considerable quantities in the low grounds of this district, notwithstanding the depredations of the numerous herds which occasionally subsist on it. These Indians, particularly the squaws, treated me with singular attention, probably on account of my being the only white person they had ever seen. I forbear, however, going into details, because they might by some be considered as clashing with propriety.

Before we arrived at the upper confines of the prairies, by the advice of some friendly Indians who had been with us for several days, we directed our course up a considerable branch of the Platte to the right, in a northernly direction from the main river, in order to avoid the Sta-he-tah tribe, of whom some mention has previously been made.

After pursuing this stream several days, we passed a hilly country, covered with oak, chestnut, beech, hickory, and other upland trees, indicative, as I have since learned, of a good soil; and then struck upon a small stream, that flowed in a direction nearly opposite to the one we had recently left. Here we stopped a day; and, after debating the subject, unanimously agreed to proceed onwards, as far as the summits of the Great Western Hills, and still further, should circumstances prove favorable. A division of opinion, however, existed as to the direct route; but it was finally determined to course along the base of the dividing hills, which we did, till we arrived on the banks of a stream rather larger than the Platte was where we left it. It may here be observed, our party generally thought that the accomplishment of this journey, would, on our return, entitle us to as much applause from our people as though we had gained a signal victory over our enemies; and the desire for fame, or a high reputation, urged us on, and made us bear with patience the fatigues of the journey. At a short distance above the place where we struck this river, our course was interrupted by a remarkable cliff, which we could not ascend, and between which and the water, there was no possibility of passing: we, therefore, having examined a considerable fall in the river, and ascertained the foregoing facts, varied our course, till this range of hills afforded a convenient pass.

Having crossed them, we directed our way along the banks of this stream, till it terminated in a lake or large pond of remarkable transparency. We observed many small but no large streams flowing into this heading reservoir, probably, of some one of the branches of the Missouri. The country around, as far as the eye could extend, was hilly, and in a westward direction swelled into mountains of great height. We here met small parties of Indians [Shoshoni?], comparatively poor, but, nevertheless, hospitable and friendly. In character they resembled those before described; though, receding from the grazing prairies, they became more timid.

Some of them accompanied us constantly, and served us virtually as guides to the Mountains of Snow; towards which they frequently journeyed, during the summer seasons, on account of the greater safety this route afforded in the chase.

After passing the lake above noticed, I accompanied two of our party in pursuit of game up a small stream which disembogued through a deep ravine, rendered peculiarly gloomy by a tall and thick growth of evergreens. We soon discovered two unusually large brown bears, which, so far from being intimidated at our approach, made directly for us, in a rapid and threatening manner. When first seen they were only at a short distance from us, and we scarcely had time to level our pieces and fire, before one of my companions was in the grasp of one of these ferocious animals, now rendered furious by a wound we had inflicted. Fortunately for us the other had been shot through the heart, and fell immediately dead, so that all our efforts could be directed to relieve our companion from his perilous situation. Our rifles had all been discharged, and the urgency was too great to attempt to reload them; we therefore resorted to our long knives and tomahawks, and although we thrust the former their whole length repeatedly into the bear, and cut it in an extraordinary manner with the latter, yet some time elapsed before we could extricate him from the potent fangs and claws of his rapacious adversary. It is well known among the mountain tribes, that these bears are not only ferocious and daring, but remarkably tenacious of life; and we came very near proving these facts, by the loss of one of our party. The poor fellow was shockingly bitten and torn, and in great danger of losing his life in this desperate conflict. This affair delayed our progress considerably, and made our hunters more wary. Nevertheless we proceeded onward, coursing occasionally the streams, and then crossing one range of hills after another, till our patience was nearly exhausted.

We had received from some of the Indians, a general description of the route; but we had no trails or marks to guide us, except the transverse direction of the hills, which being covered either with thick growths of evergreens, fallen trees, rocks, or snow, and not infrequently with all of them together, and swelling occasionally into mountains sometimes precipitous, rendered our journey tedious and difficult. We found very little game to supply our wants, and were obliged to waste our ammunition on pheasants and small game, which, in some of the valleys, were very abundant. We also shot some mountain goats, and a few black-tailed deer. The cold was at times severe, and we experienced several falls of snow, hail, and rain. At length we arrived on the last range of mountains, from the top of which an apparently delightful country presented itself below: on reaching it, however, it was quite the reverse, and very little game was to be found.

Soon after, we struck a small stream, on the banks of which three or four huts were situated; but no Indians were perceived. We followed this stream some distance, and finding game still scarce, owing as we supposed to the sterility of the soil, we crossed to our left several ranges of hills, where were some deer, and in the course of two days came to an Indian settlement, on the margin of a considerable stream. These Indians were armed with bows and spears, appeared very friendly, and were less suspicious than any we had before met. This conduct and apparent security grew, no doubt, out of their own poverty, and that of their hunting grounds. They were small in stature, well made, but exceedingly filthy; and subsisted mostly on fish, roots, and berries, of which they were generally parsimonious. They had a few horses, and many dogs; the former were of no great account among them; while the latter were held in high estimation. They spoke a singular, and to us an unintelligible language, and called themselves Lee-ha-taus.

This tribe was not numerous, and inhabited the neighboring country. Some of these Indians accompanied us down the country, to other villages belonging to the same nation. We stopped but a short time, smoked the pipe of friendship, and still accompanied by some of them, continued our route down the river. As we advanced, we found the Indians more numerous, equally friendly, and more liberally disposed, than those we had passed in the upper country. Game was everywhere scarce, and we were indebted to the hospitality of strangers for a portion of what was necessary to our subsistence. Sometimes we assisted in taking fish, but the stores of this article were generally so abundant, and so little valued, as to render our efforts in this way rather a source of amusement than consideration to our friendly hosts. We accepted these proffered obligations in preference to running the risk of giving offence, by destroying their game, which was esteemed by them in proportion to its scarcity. The nations through which we passed, did not possess the warlike character of the Indians of the Missouri and Mississippi regions. They were all at peace, and had frequent intercourse with each other, without exciting the least suspicion or jealousy. These circumstances facilitated our progress very much, for we were always accompanied by some of them, from one tribe to another. Besides, we frequently had the use of some of their canoes or rafts, to assist us on our way. In this manner, we continued our route, sometimes over barren prairies, hills, &c. and at others, through woods, till we arrived at the great Pacific Ocean. Here, the surprise and astonishment of our whole party was indescribably great. The unbounded view of waters, the incessant and tremendous dashing of the waves along the shore, accompanied with a noise resembling the roar of loud and distant thunder, filled our minds with the most sublime and awful sensations, and fixed on them as immutable truths, the tradition we had received from our old men, that the great waters divide the residence of the Great Spirit, from the temporary abodes of his red children. We here contemplated in silent dread, the immense difficulties over which we should be obliged to triumph after death, before we could arrive at those delightful hunting grounds, which are unalterably destined for such only as do good, and love the Great Spirit. We looked in vain for the stranded and shattered canoes of those who had done wickedly. We could see none, and we were led to hope that they were few in number. We offered up our devotions, or I might rather say, our minds were serious, and our devotions continued, all the time we were in this country, for we had ever been taught to believe, that the Great Spirit resided on the western side of the Rocky Mountains, and this idea continued throughout the journey, notwithstanding the more specific water boundary assigned to him by our traditionary dogmas.*

We soon satisfied our curiosity; but what, however, contributed most to hasten our departure, were the almost incessant rains that fell while we were there. The food with which we were supplied, over the few elk and deer we killed, was disagreeably loathsome; yet to have rejected the hospitality of our kind hosts, would have given great offense, as we learned, in one instance, by experience. We arrived at the ocean, on the south side of Chock-a-li-lum (Columbia River), and coasted southwardly, to a small inlet, around which several detached huts were situated. The Indians inhabiting them were not very numerous; they subsisted chiefly by fishing: and the manner in which they managed their canoes, was a source of much surprise and satisfaction. These Indians, as well as those along the tide waters of the Columbia, are small and deformed in their persons, and exceedingly filthy in their habits and appearance. They paid particular attention to their women, who frequently took part in their debates, and generally in their fishing excursions. I remark this, because it was so different from the privileges enjoyed among the Osages, Kansas, and other nations of Indians on the other side of the Rocky Mountains. The men generally have but one wife, though, if I mistake not, polygamy is permitted. The married women totally disregard the obligations of continence, and boldly indulge in its violation; but such conduct led to no breach of hospitality or friendship between this tribe and our party, whilst we remained with it.

They take fish in great abundance, with wooden spears, pointed with bone, or some other hard substance. They took many, while we were with them; they were five or six feet in length, and very oily: they are not eaten till they become soft from keeping, when they are mashed with water, in wooden troughs, and cooked with hot stones. We roasted some while fresh, which proved tolerably palatable, but they did not approve of our mode of cooking. Each family have their winter supplies on hand, consisting of membranous sacks of oil, dried fish, and some roots. Elk, deer, and wild fowl, are taken by them in small numbers, but with great difficulty, and are esteemed great luxuries. They cultivate no ground, depending on the earth's spontaneous production for the roots they obtain, which are few, and not very nutritive. In fact, none of them agreed with us; some produced the water-brash, and others, *nausea*, and cathartic effects.

These Indians called themselves Calt-sops [Clatsops*]: the country around them is mountainous, and covered with a large growth of evergreen trees. From these they make their canoes, with great labor, and then launch them into the ocean; from which, after every expedition, they are carefully withdrawn for their preservation.

These canoes are highly valued, in consequence of the difficulty experienced in constructing them. They are articles of traffic only in matrimonial negotiations; and a young Indian was busily employed, while we were there, in making one, which was to be exchanged for the daughter of his intended father-in-law, with whom all the courtship is carried on.

We remained but a few days with these Indians, for the reasons above stated, and because a general anxiety prevailed among our party to be on their journey homeward.

After having taken our leave of them and of the Great Waters, which had excited and still maintained an indescrabable interest in our minds, we returned by the route we descended, till we arrived at the entrance of the Mult-no-mah (River of much game),* into the Columbia. From whence, by the advice of the Mult-no-mah Indians, we pursued the course of that [Willamette] river, nearly to its sources, on account of the hunting grounds in its vicinity being reputedly supplied with an abundance of game. The navigation of this river is interrupted by many rapids and several falls; one of which was very considerable, and appeared at some distance, curtained with a semi-halo of the most brilliant colors. It flows, particularly towards its sources, through a hilly, or more properly speaking, mountainous country. The soil of the valleys appeared fertile; and was, for the most part, covered with a large growth of trees. The Indians settled along its course, received us in a very friendly manner.

They differ very little in their habits and modes of life, from those on the Columbia River. The hunting grounds were ill supplied with game, and the water afforded but a limited supply of fish, in consequence of which they paid some attention to tilling the soil. They raised considerable quantities of a peculiar kind of corn; the ears of which were short, small, and set on stalks near the ground; the grains were also small, flat, and of a very deep blue color. They also raised beans and squashes, and to make up the remainder of their stores, collected nuts, roots, and wild tobacco. The leaves of this last article were narrow, long, and thin; and when dried, mild, and very superior for smoking.

A small tribe of Indians, calling themselves Leesh-te-losh,* reside on the headwaters of the Mult-no-mah; they were larger, better made, more warlike, and of a whiter color than any others we saw to the west of the Rocky Mountains. They received us at first, with some distrust, but afterwards were very friendly; they supplied us with such articles as they had to spare, and put us on the route eastwardly, across several ranges of hills. Passing these, we found, as we had been told we should, considerable game on the borders of a very large lake.

The Indians here, however, were not so friendly as we could have wished; but we conciliated their chief with presents, consisting of a tomahawk and two knives. They were not very numerous, but were athletic, and good warriors, being armed with stone tomahawks, clubs, spears, and unusually large and strong bows. The lake was well supplied with fish, which they took in considerable quantities with spears made of hard wood or pointed with bone. Their canoes were small, and clumsily made from the trunks of trees, but they were managed with great dexterity. They called themselves Ne-was-kees; we learned a few words of their language; but from the circumstances before noticed, remained only a short time with them. Journeying eastwardly, along the side of this lake, we fell in with many other parties of Indians, and killed what game we wanted, without any incident happening worthy of remark. We next crossed several ranges of hills, and found ourselves among a tribe of poor, inoffensive, and friendly Indians, with whom, if game had been plenty, or their stores abundant, we should have remained all the winter, as the season had now become cold, and snow had fallen on the level country, so as to render the traveling difficult.

We, however, pursued our route over a country whose surface was considerably varied, but which could not be called mountainous. On our way, we fell in with many Indians, of nearly the same character, habits, and dispositions of those last described, and were always kindly treated, though we received little or no supplies from their hands. We had now arrived at the neighborhood of the Great Mountains, and concluded, if in the summer we suffered extremely from the cold, in crossing them, that the attempt at the inclement season of winter, might, and probably would, terminate in the destruction of our whole party. It was therefore determined to form camps, and remain where we were, till the approach of milder weather. We accordingly set at work, and with poles, the barks of trees and brush, constructed lodges under the declivity of some lofty rocks, in a pleasant southern exposure.

Near by were several springs of water; one of which was of a temperature nearly sufficient to have cooked food, though we made no particular use of it. From the appearances, however, just below the efflux of the water, it must have been much resorted to as a bath; and, no doubt, by some of the Indians we had recently passed: because many of them appeared to suffer from cutaneous diseases, which probably owed their origin to a restricted and long-continued diet on crude and partially medicinal roots, and leguminous substances.

Our powder and ball had now become scarce; with a view, therefore, to husband them to the best advantage, we provided ourselves with bows and arrows, and parties of our hunters used them sometimes with considerable success, in procuring game for our subsistence. They always, however, took some rifles with them, in order, if chance should offer, to kill larger game at a distance, and to defend themselves against the white and brown bears and panthers which frequent these regions. The game we took consisted of elk, black-tailed deer, a species of mountain goat, some wild turkeys and pheasants, and we were generally well supplied. The panther and wolf, attracted, probably, by the scent of our food, frequently prowled round our camps; and so much were they to be apprehended, particularly the former, that no one ever ventured to go out alone, even on the most trifling occasion.

We killed several of them, and one under such peculiar circumstances as to deserve notice. This one, as is the usual habit of the animal, in taking its prey, had secreted itself in a crouching position, behind a rock, close to the spring we frequented, and was not discovered by two of our party, who were going for water, till they had arrived within its leaping distance. They, however, were not thrown off their guard by the violent agitations produced by the discovery; but exercised a presence of mind, which, I think, few men in their situation would have done, and which, in all probability, saved at least one of their lives. Tare-heem, who was in the advance, the moment he discovered the danger he was in, gave directions to his companion, and stepped cautiously backward, keeping his eyes riveted, if I may use the expression, all the while on those of his adversary. In this manner they soon retreated beyond its bounding distance,* and finally reached the camp in safety, though not without great apprehension. Tare-heem shot it a few moments afterwards, in nearly the same position in which he left it, and it proved to be the largest panther that any of our party had before seen. He brought the skin with him to the Osage nation, and took great pains to preserve it.

Apart from hunting, we dressed the skins of the animals we took in our hunts, and made them into moccasins, leggings, and robes. To amuse ourselves, and beguile the time, we played at several games of hazard, which will be noticed in another part of this work. Small parties of the neighboring Indians frequently visited us, with whom we always shared the products of our hunts gratuitously. We received from them, occasionally, small presents of beans, roots, nuts, and tobacco; with the latter of which, in the customary form, we often renewed and strengthened the relations of friendship.

At the breaking up of the winter, having supplied ourselves with such things as were necessary, and the situation afforded, all our party visited the spring from which we had procured our supplies of water, and there offered up our orisons to the Great Spirit, for having preserved us in health and safety, and for having supplied all our wants. This is the constant practice of the Osages, Kansas, and many other nations of Indians located west of the Mississippi, on breaking up their encampments, and is, by no means, an unimportant ceremony. On the contrary, the occasion calls forth all the devotional feelings of the soul; and you then witness the silent but deeply impressive communion the unsophisticated native of the forest holds with his Creator.

From our winter's encampment we soon arrived at, and crossed, the various ranges of mountains which divide the waters, flowing eastwardly and westwardly from each other. They did not appear so high, numerous, or difficult to pass, at the place we recrossed,

---

*Should this animal fail to seize its prey on the first leap or bound, it seldom continues the pursuit, but retires to its crouching posture and place, and there waits for a more fortunate opportunity. It is also said by the Indians, never to spring on its prey while they are mutually eyeing each other. (JDH)

as they were where we crossed them; our progress was, nevertheless, slow, on account of the snow, which was in some places deep, and gave way under our feet. We experienced some intensely cold weather, particularly on the tops of the mountains. We also found it exceedingly difficult to procure game, so that this part of our route might with propriety be termed one of suffering, though not the slightest complaint was heard to escape from the lips of one of our party. As we descended from the mountains, eastwardly, the difference in climate and vegetation was too obvious to escape our notice. When we left our winter camps, the warmth of the sun was considerable, the snow had nearly disappeared, and was dissolving rapidly; the nights were, however, rather cold, and not a sign of resuscitating vegetation presented itself to our view. A few days' journey, however, brought us upon grounds from which the snow had wholly disappeared; where vegetation had put on its gayest habiliments, and showed forth its joyful thanksgivings in concert with the melodious warblings of the feathered tribes. We had supposed, from the course pursued on our recrossing the mountains, and inclining northwardly, that we should strike upon our old tracks; but in this we were disappointed.

We made several excursions, first in one direction, and then in another, without procuring to ourselves any satisfaction as to the place where we were, or the course which ought to be pursued, to conduct us to our homes. Much time transpired in these perplexed circumstances; our whole party was completely lost, which, in fact, was the first time in my life, that I had ever known of an individual occurrence of the kind, though they sometimes happen; and this was the more extraordinary, as we were thirty-seven in number. We knew that we had returned by a route more to the south than the one by which we went out, and finally determined to course our way north and eastwardly, inclining considerably from the parallel direction of the mountains. We were induced to adopt this measure on account of the streams, where we then were, flowing in a southward direction.

We obliquely crossed a series of valleys, formed by gently swelling hills, and then successively arrived at, and crossed, two ranges of high mountains, whose tops were covered with snow. Shortly afterwards, we arrived on the banks of a small stream, which flowed in nearly a northern direction, and afforded toleraby good hunting grounds. This circumstance led us to change our route, which was now conformed to that of the stream. In a few days after this, we came to a much more considerable one which flowed eastwardly, and discovered buffalo, and recent Indian trails; but met with no interruption, till this stream, swelled by the confluence of some others, and the rain which had recently fallen, had become a large river. Here we discovered a small party of Indians, who, though we proffered every token of peace and friendship, fled with great precipitation.

We concluded rightly that they were only a hunting detachment from a more numerous party, and accordingly determined to guard against a surprise, in case they should prove hostile, by crossing to the opposite side of the river. This done, we proceeded slowly on, carrying our arms in the attitude of peace. In two or three hours we unexpectedly arrived near several temporary wigwams, which, notwithstanding all our efforts to prevent it, were deserted by some old men, women, and children, their only tenants, who fled, in the utmost consternation, to the neighboring woods. To have proceeded onwards at this time, without essaying to conciliate the good feelings of these Indians, would have been an act of defiance; and if the warriors of the village had been sufficiently numerous, would have invited our own destruction, as soon as they became acquainted with the circumstance, and could accomplish it. We therefore sent Tareheem unarmed in pursuit, in order to explain our friendly intentions, and, if possible, to smoke the pipe of peace with them. He returned in a short time in company with some of the old men, among whom was one who could speak the Mahas' language, which was also spoken by some of our party. We explained the nature of our situation, told them to what nation we belonged, inquired where we were, and tendered them wampums and the pipe of peace. They were, at first, exceedingly cautious, but relaxing as they became more acquainted, they smoked with us, in token of friendship. The women and children returned soon afterwards, and we were offered food; and, much to our satisfaction, told that we were now on the main Arkansas River. We had scarcely regaled ourselves before some hunters came in; they appeared far from being satisfied with their new guests, and the reception they had received. We, however, secured their friendship, very timely for us, with the presents of a rifle to the principal chief, and several tomahawks and knives to others of less distinction. We had barely terminated this negotiation, when a party of fifty or sixty warriors arrived in pursuit of us; among them, as we afterwards learned, were the Indians who fled from us in the early part of the day. They at first appeared ferocious, but as they belonged to the same tribe of Indians whose friendship we had purchased, and under whose roofs we now were, they forbore the commission of any hostile acts. A new negotiation was now set on foot, and we gratuitously parted with two more rifles and a few tomahawks; and subsequently bartered two more of our rifles for beaver skins. It is highly probable, had there been no lodges at this place, or if the hunters had been at their encampments when our party arrived, that we should have been wholly cut off. These Indians were principally armed with bows, tomahawks, and spears; appeared ferocious and warlike, and belonged to the Tetau [Teton*] nation. They were particularly hostile to the Pawnees, who had recently stolen some of their horses, and against whom a party of their warriors had then gone. We placed but little confidence in them; and, therefore, as soon as we had prepared four canoes from the skins of buffaloes, &c. we took our leave, not, however, without strong apprehensions of being pursued and destroyed; for we had now parted with several of our rifles, and our ammunition was too far exhausted to authorize any resistance, except under the most desperate necessity. What contributed most to our fears, was the circumstance of there always having existed a strong animosity between these Indians and all the various tribes located north and east of them.

We, however, finally escaped beyond their reach, without any occurrence happening worthy of notice. We afterwards fell in with three or four small parties, all Pawnees, with whom, after our mutual distrusts were removed, we exchanged several of our rifles, at their request, for beaver skins, which we transported in our canoes, now increased in number sufficient to contain our whole party. The navigation continued good for several days after we left the Tetaus: lower down it was interrupted by rapids and shoals, to such an extent as, in my opinion, to render the passage even of light canoes exceedingly difficult in dry times, though at this time there was sufficient water for the passage of large river boats.

The river flows from its source for nearly half the distance above the Vermillion [Verdigris*], through a hilly and broken country; the remainder of its course is through prairies, separated in some instances from the water by sand hills of considerable magnitude, but, for the most part, by forests of various kinds. The herds of buffalo, elk, and deer, were numerous; and we were always able to obtain supplies of food, after we struck the main stream, without much difficulty, though all our ammunition except one or two rounds, had failed several days before our return.

The Rocky Mountains, where we recrossed them, were not precipitous, nor of very difficult passage. Their sides were covered with considerably large growths of trees, principally cedars and pines, which diminished in size, till they altogether disappeared near the summits. The soil in the valleys between them, though somewhat broken by ridges and ravines, appeared from its vegetable productions to be good, and it was well watered. The streams which we crossed between the mountains, as already remarked, flowed southwardly, and, no doubt, were the heading branches of the Rio del Norde [Río Grande] or of some other river, flowing into the empire of Mexico or New Spain.

The Osages had looked upon us as lost, and greeted our arrival among them in the most joyful and tumultuous manner. My Indian mother and sister wept aloud, and the squaws, young and old, danced around us to the cadence of their festival songs, and decorated our persons in the same manner as though we had returned triumphant over the enemies of our country. The old men and warriors listened with wonder and astonishment at the narration of our adventures, and lavished on us the meeds of praise, and high encomiums, heretofore only bestowed on the most distinguished of their nation. In fine, Tare-heem, who before ranked as a distinguished and leading warrior, was now listened to among the sage counsellors: the rest of the party were ranked among the bravest of the warriors, and many of the unmarried men received from the young squaws, some a greater and some a less number of *ears of corn*, as so many individual invitations to enter into matrimonial alliances.

This journey occupied nearly sixteen moons.* The following seasons were passed in short hunting excursions, festivals, and amusements, till the spring arrived, when a considerable party, including myself, visited the Grand Osage nation, where we remained a few days. I became acquainted with, and received particular marks of favor from Clermont, the principal chief, and some of his most distinguished warriors. There was at this time, among the Osages, a trader named Manuel Lisa, a Spaniard or half Indian, who was now bound on a trading expedition up the Missouri, in company with a Mr. M'Lane,* another trader, and several Spanish, French, and American boatmen.

This Manuel Lisa was an artful, cunning man: he had several private interviews with me, and used every argument in his power to persuade me to accompany him in his intended voyage. I finally concluded to go with him, on condition that some of the Kansas and Osages, from White Hair's tribe, would join the party, which they consented to, and about twenty of us, in addition to the hunting party, descended the Osage River, and proceeded up the Missouri, in boats constructed for the purpose. In general the boatmen were competent to propel the boats; but where rapids or embarras* occurred in the river, we assisted at the cordelle, or towing line, from the shore. Sometimes it was necessary to wade up to the waist or arms in water, which was the cause of much discontent among

---

*Places where the navigation is rendered difficult, by the accumulation of driftwood, trees, &c. (JDH)

the boats' crew, but more particularly so among the Indians. The above was the first labor to which I had ever been confined. It was occasionally severe, but encouragement and praise, the tyrants to which all mankind are slaves, timely lavished by Manuel Lisa, made me forget my sufferings, and excited me to increased efforts and turmoils.

On our way up, we stopped at a Kickapoo settlement, at which were several who had connections in the party of their nation to whom I belonged, and who were nearly all cut off on the headwaters of the Marameck. They had already been informed of the circumstances connected with that unfortunate event.

Much interesting conversation took place between us: I made many particular inquiries respecting myself and my family, from a curiosity that had been excited by similar and often repeated inquiries which the Indians, particularly the squaws, and several traders, had made of me; but without being able to obtain the least satisfaction. In fact, if they had known, I believe they would not have made the disclosure; for it is natural to conclude that such information would have created a disquietude not to be allayed, short of the fullest research, which, if successful, would probably have terminated in estranging me from their modes of life, and social relations.

On arriving at the confluence of the Kansas River with the Missouri, all the Kansas that were of our party abandoned the expedition, and returned home, much to the vexation of the traders. I was invited to join them, and reflected on the course I ought to pursue with deep concern. I had been a considerable time from that nation, and, as my Kansas mother was dead, and my Kansas father had again married among, and incorporated himself with the Osages, I felt no particular attachment to this tribe; while among the Osages I had a fond mother and sister, and was much respected and esteemed by the whole nation. These circumstances, joined to the artful persuasions and promises of Manuel Lisa, determined me to remain, for the present, in his employment, and finally to return to the Osage towns. From this place we ascended the Kansas River to the towns where I had formerly resided. I was received here with every mark of the warmest friendship and affection; we soon, however, returned to the Missouri, and pursued the course of that river toward its source. This digression up the Kansas was undertaken by Lisa to form new connections with the Indians, to trade and take game, in all which he succeeded to his expectations. During this trip, I witnessed, for the first time in my life, with painful sensations, the wide and wanton destruction of game, merely to procure skins; and so much disgusted was I, on seeing the buffalo carcasses strewed over the ground in a half-putrefied state, that my reluctance to fulfill my engagements was so much increased, as to occasion me to reflect seriously on absconding from the party.* No opportunity, however, offered, and I gradually became more reconciled to this barbarous practice: such, to the shame of human nature, is the effect of custom. Just before we arrived at the entrance of the Platte into the Missouri, we experienced the most violent and long-continued rains, accompanied with heavy thunder, and the most vivid and incessant flashes of lightning, that I ever before or since witnessed. Our engagements were now such as to render a constant exposure necessary; in consequence of which, our sufferings were great, and many of the party became sick. The river swelled into a devastating flood, covered the islands and alluvial grounds, and bore off whole herds of buffalo and forests of trees on its surface: the sight was so distressing and awful as to surpass my powers of description. In a few days the rain abated, and we pursued our route. We occasionally fell in with parties of Indians, belonging to the Mahas, Ottowas, and Pawnees, who were friendly, and with whom Lisa entered into engagements for such furs, &c. as they might take, previous to his descending the river. The Sioux, whose grounds we next entered, were not considered friendly; we therefore made all the expedition in our power, keeping on the shores opposite to where we should be likely to fall in with them, and avoiding every act that might be construed into an apology, on their part, for attacking us. Passing the Sioux without any interruption, we reached the villages of the Ric-ca-ras* [Arikaras], where we remained several days. These Indians are well provided; and they treated us in a very friendly manner. Lisa entered into trading engagements with them, and made them several small presents, as he had done to those Indians who had concluded similar contracts with him. We next arrived among the Mandans, who received us in the same manner as the Ric-ca-ras had, and laid themselves under similar obligations to our traders. Hitherto, Lisa had treated me with a well-dissembled kindness and indulgence. Having, however, ascended the river so far as to render my return by the Sioux exceedingly hazardous, and being, as he now thought, sure of my services, he threw off the disguise, in order, no doubt, if possible, to make me sensible of my dependence on him, and to secure my entire obedience to his will: but he found himself mistaken. The obligations he, myself, and our whole party, knew were due from and not to him.

Several harsh words passed between us, when, on my assuming a position that threatened a summary and perhaps more severe chastisement than his offense merited, he submitted to ask my pardon;

*Pronounced by the Indians A-ric-ca-ra. (JDH)

and for some time afterwards treated me not with a real, but an affected tenderness and regard.

My conduct on this occasion was much approved, and secured me the friendship of all our party, except the original transgressor. From this place we continued up the Missouri till we arrived in the neighborhood of the Great Falls. On our way, we had frequent interviews with the several tribes of Indians inhabiting its borders, and the traders entered into similar engagements with most of them, as they had before done with those lower down. Otherwise, nothing worthy of notice happened, till several days after our arrival near the falls above named, when on account of a general dissatisfaction at the conduct of Lisa, all the Osages, who were ten in number, and myself, after having explained our motives to the traders, and their party, abandoned them, and took our course down the river, in the most direct manner. Lisa did all in his power to prevent our departure, on account of the important services he well knew we were capable of rendering him, in procuring furs, &c., and on which he had calculated with certainty and great expectations; but finding our determinations not to be changed, he parted from us apparently reconciled.

Since my return to the territories of the United States, he has, nevertheless, on several occasions, as I have been informed, complained of our conduct, which defeated in some measure the objects of the expedition, he having made use of some of the Osages to conduct his negotiations with many of the tribes he fell in with on his course up the Missouri.* On the third or fourth day after we left the traders, one of our party was bitten on the fleshy part of the leg by a rattlesnake. The wound was deep; but was immediately cut out with a sharp knife, and the incision cauterized with a heated stone. This occurrence delayed us but a short time when it happened, though subsequently it occasioned us much delay, on account of the sufferings it produced.

Some days afterwards, we met a party of English traders, with whom we bartered such furs as we had taken, for powder, ball, &c. They had just arrived on the Missouri by a portage connecting with some of the headwaters of either the St. Laurence or the Mississippi River. By signs, we made them understand our apprehensions of the hostile Sioux, which were settled lower down, on the Missouri. They, in a similar manner, advised us to avoid them altogether, by changing our direction south-eastwardly, after we should arrive at the Mandan villages, till we struck on the waters of the Mississippi, and then, to descend that river. After separating from this party, our progress was slow, and much interrupted by the lameness and indisposition of one of our party, occasioned, as before noticed, by the bite of a rattlesnake. The exposure and irritation produced by traveling had induced a high local inflammation and fever, which threatened the life of the sufferer, and rendered an encampment necessary. In consequence of this circumstance, we were detained several weeks; and finally resumed our journey, bearing our patient on a litter.

In a few days, however, we were amply compensated for all our delays and troubles, in his entire recovery. This Indian's name was Wen-ga-shee: he was a powerful and brave warrior, proved of essential service to us on our journey home, and, when I left them, continued to be much respected by the Osages. On arriving at the Mandan settlements, we attempted to follow the advice given us by the English traders; and after traveling for several days, in which we scarcely once observed the sun, on account of the fogs or smoke which prevailed, we came to a stream that flowed, as indicated by the rising of the sun, in nearly an eastward direction. Our party, to a man, supposed this stream to be one of the heading branches of the Mississippi, and were so elated with the happy result of their comparatively blindfold excursion, through woods and swamps, and over prairies and hills, that they continued their journey with redoubled efforts, notwithstanding the continuance of fogs, clouds, and occasional rains.

In a few days afterwards, however, we discovered, very much to our surprise and mortification, the sun rising obliquely behind us on the right; and, at a short distance ahead, a much larger stream than the one we were on, which flowed in nearly a westward course.

We all now concluded, and rightly, that we had taken a wrong direction, and had not inclined sufficiently to the right, after having left the Mandans. It was also evident, that the streams on which we now were flowed from the highlands dividing them from the headwaters of the Mississippi.

In consequence of this, it was concluded to follow the largest stream, in a direction considerably south of east, which we did for several days.

Some of our party were now for crossing obliquely to the right, over to the stream which we had first struck, after leaving the Missouri, and from thence directing our course for the Mississippi, as first intended; but Tun-gah,* to whom all looked as their chief, preferred the present route, and the others acquiesced.

Previous to this, several snows had fallen, and it had now become so cold that the rivers were, in most instances, sufficiently frozen to admit of our walking on the ice; but deer, and some other kinds of game, were plenty, and we performed our daily marches without experiencing much other anxiety than what proceeded from the doubts that existed as to the correctness of our route. We next arrived at a considerable lake, and met a party of Chippewa Indians, who treated us kindly, and informed us where we were, and of the route we ought to pursue. Following their advice, we altered our course to that of nearly south, and the next day experienced a most severe snowstorm, which, terminating in hail and severely cold weather, obliged us to encamp. A crust was now formed, which broke through at every step we took, and let us above our knees into the snow; and what was still more disagreeable, our moccasins and leggings soon gave out, and our feet and legs became nearly frozen, and very much lacerated. To repair them, and obviate this suffering, we first cut up the few spare skins we had, and, when those were exhausted, commenced on our buffalo robes: but with all the exertions we could make, our progress was slow, seldom amounting to twenty miles a day. The weather moderating, however, and the traveling becoming less difficult, we soon arrived upon waters flowing southwardly, where we again found a few lodges of the Chippewas, and were well treated. We obtained from them a few bearskins; repaired our robes, &c. and continued our journey over several small lakes and ponds, till we arrived at a more considerable stream, which ultimately proved to be the Mississippi. Here we experienced another snowstorm, which was more severe than the former, and rendered the traveling still more difficult and painful. We nevertheless continued slowly on, and should, I believe, have accomplished our return home, had not two of our party unfortunately become so badly frozen in their feet, as to make an encampment essential to their preservation.

We therefore soon cleared a spot in a small growth of woods, fixed poles, thatched them with brush, and finally covered the whole with a thick stratum of snow; which, with the fire we kept, and the few skins we had, formed, as to temperature, a comfortable lodge.

We often attempted to hunt, but the snow was too deep to wade through it, and too light to support us; we therefore were compelled to remain in our lodge, at the imminent risk of starvation. It is probable, if these difficulties had not existed, that our situation would not have been much improved, as game of every kind was exceedingly scarce.

We occasionally shot a wolf, as they prowled round our lodge, and in one instance an animal of the cat kind, neither so large nor of the same color as the panther of the Arkansas.

With these, including their skins and offals, and the bark of some shrubbery, we made out to sustain the flame of life, till those who were frozen had recovered, and the weather had apparently moderated; when, though so much reduced as barely to be able to walk, we renewed our journey, in hopes of finding some Indian lodge, or falling in with game.

We, however, suffered disappointment in both; and what added still more to our distress, on the second day's march, we were overwhelmed in one of those boisterous and tempestuous snowstorms, which sometimes happen in those northern regions, towards the breaking up of the winter, and of the severity of which no idea can be formed without experience. The flakes fell in such rapid succession, as nearly to fill the atmosphere; and were driven by the vehemence of the winds with such force as almost to obstruct our vision. The weather was intensely cold, and no retreat was to be found to shelter us from these threatening catastrophes. We spread a few skins on the snow, crowded in a heap upon them, covered ourselves with what remained, and, under the strongest conviction that our existence would here terminate, devoutly resigned ourselves to the disposition of the Great Spirit. The place where we had thus committed ourselves proved afterwards to be situated on the borders of a thin, stinted growth of pines, on one side of which was a field of snow extending beyond the reach of vision, through which the terminating branches of some shrubbery occasionally made their appearance.

How long we remained in this state is altogether out of my power to say; but we had fallen asleep, and were awakened by the howling of a wolf, which sometimes was very near us, and at others, receded till it was lost in remoteness. The repetition of this circumstance induced the belief that our retreat had been discovered by one of these animals, which, not being sufficiently courageous to attack us alone, had raised the cries we heard to rally others to his assistance. With a view, should such prove the fact, of resisting them and procuring some food to resuscitate our nearly exhausted frames, we attempted to rise, but found ourselves confined by an almost irresistible barrier of snow; and thinking it more advisable to dig ourselves a passage out, than to continue efforts, which, if they succeeded, would spoil our lodge, we soon made an aperture through which we might pass with facility, though none of us, at this time, ventured out. To the tempest, which so lately threatened our existence, had succeeded a most brilliant moonlight night; the winds had hushed, and all, except the distant howls of the wolf as before noticed, was profound silence. In this state of things, Wen-ga-shee, one of our party, placed himself in the outlet of our lodge with his rifle, and much to our joy and relief, shot the wolf soon after, as it approached him. From long abstinence our desire for food had become voracious; and part of this animal was literally devoured by us, without undergoing any preparation, while it was yet warm in its blood. This repast, although made in an intensely cold night, on the surface of a deep snow, and with very little more to cover us than the ethereal arch, was by far the most delicious that any of our party had ever before enjoyed. We had scarcely completed it, when our ears were again assailed with the approaching howls of another wolf; we therefore retreated to our snowy cell, lay in wait as before, and on its arrival shot this also. In the course of the night we killed four more, which were probably attracted in succession to the place by the howlings of those that preceded. Several more approached us in the forenoon of the following day, but they were so shy that we could not get within shooting distance of them. The snow, in the late storm, fell in great quantities; and, in consequence of the violence of the winds, had formed into deep drifts, particularly where we were. Our cell, for such the place we now occupied might with propriety be called, was directly under one of them, which was several feet deep. The warmth of our bodies had occasioned the snow to settle somewhat beneath us, but not sufficiently so to afford room for a comfortable sitting posture. We therefore set to work, and in a short time, with the assistance of our skins, excavated the snow to a depth and extent sufficiently great to contain us in any desirable posture.

With the stock of food we had on hand, we might have remained several days, comparatively comfortable, provided it had been possible to have kept a fire; but such a measure was incompatible with the existence of our mansion, and to have removed from it would be to expose ourselves to other, and perhaps greater dangers and inconveniences. We therefore formed a curtain door to our habitation with a bearskin, secured our provisions as well as we could, lighted our pipes, and smoked the day away in gloomy silence. The night following, we watched by turns for the wolves, and killed three more early in the evening, which were the last we saw while in this singular encampment, though we often distinctly heard their howls at a distance. We had suffered much from cold on the preceding day, and determining, if possible, to obviate a similar occurrence, we cut down several of the neighboring pines, with the trunks of which we pitched a roof over our lodge, thatched it with branches and leaves, and finally made it tight with the snow which we broke away from the arch and walls of our snow cell below. Soon after we made a fire in it, but found ourselves, in the course of the following day, extremely uncomfortable from the dampness of our situation. We remedied this inconvenience in a short time, by forming a sort of floor of the same materials, omitting the snow, as used for the roof, and subsequently kept ourselves, in respect to temperature, tolerably comfortable. In respect to food, our situation was far otherwise: we were constantly on a very limited allowance, and, towards the close of this extraordinary sojourning, without anything to eat except moss, and the inner bark of trees, for several days together; so that our situation became extremely alarming, from the prospect of starvation.

Some attempts were made to take game, but not a trace of any living creature, except wolves, could be discovered: we tried various arts to decoy some of them, but without success. Although the weather had moderated very much, and the snow was rapidly dissolving, yet, as we were comparatively without covering, three of our robes, or rather skins, having been much burnt, and others cut up for moccasins, it would have been exceedingly hazardous, and perhaps fatal to some of us, to have abandoned our encampment, circumstanced as we were. At this period, scarcely a single ray of hope glimmered between us and the grave: we were nearly in a helpless situation, and despondency had seized on us; but in the midst of our distress, the Great Spirit forsook us not.

On the morning of a very pleasant day, I had strolled, or rather crawled, a short distance from our cell with my rifle, in hopes that game of some kind or other would make its appearance. In this expectation, extraordinary as it may seem, I was not disappointed; for I had scarcely proceeded one hundred yards, before my attention was attracted by an extraordinary large elk, which was approaching me in rather an oblique direction, in a careless and easy gait. Fortunately, there happened to be a slight elevation, or drift of snow, just ahead, behind which I screened myself, and when it had arrived, as I thought, sufficiently near, shot at, and wounded it; but notwithstanding it made off at full speed. Some of the strongest and best provided of our party, hearing the report of my rifle, came up to ascertain the cause, joined in pursuit, and soon discovered, to our surprise, a large panther fixed upon its throat, and devouring it with great rapacity. We shot two balls through the body of this intruder, which, on first discovering us, as though aware that he should be forced to dispute the prize, had put himself in an attitude of defense; showing his fangs, and growling defiance. As soon as the panther had received our balls, he made several bounds of surprising length, directly towards us, and then, perhaps fortunately for us, fell dead. We now repaired with a part of the elk to our camp, and after having indulged our appetites immoderately, we brought in the balance in the course of the day. This seasonable supply at first occasioned a distressing sickness to all our party; but, finally, it reanimated our drooping spirits, and enabled us, shortly after, to visit the haunts of the elk, where we killed two more, which, like the former, were from a third to a half larger than any we had before seen. We found great difficulty in carrying these animals to our cell.

We next dressed their skins, repaired our moccasins and robes, dried some of the meat, and after returning thanks to the Great

Spirit for having preserved us through so many perils, commenced our march down the Mississippi. We soon came to some lodges of Chippewa Indians, where we received such attentions as our necessities required. From thence, continuing our course along the river, through the Chippewa hunting grounds, we were generally welcomed, and kindly treated; but, on arriving among the Sioux, we found ourselves in a very perplexed situation.

The friendly salutations we made were returned with threatening and hostile gestures and expressions. They closed their doors uniformly against us, and set their dogs on, no doubt with a view to provoke us to the commission of some act, which might be construed by them as a sufficient offense to justify an attack on us.

Sensible of the danger of our situation, though they were few in number, we suffered these indignities to pass unnoticed, though we felt them deeply, cursed the perpetrators in our hearts, and would, if our force had been sufficient, have revenged them on the spot.

We found our situation so unpleasant, that, after passing their first settlement, we determined to change our route; accordingly, we passed over to the west side of the river, and took our course nearly southwest, leaving the Sioux on our left. Crossing a broken, and somewhat hilly country, and several considerable streams, we at length arrived at a settlement of Sauk [or Sac] Indians, on Grand River, a considerable stream, which flows nearly south into the Missouri. We were received by them without the least distrust, and treated kindly: we attended the ceremonials of a wedding, joined in the festive dance, and, taking with us some presents to their kindred, who were settled about two hundred miles lower down, on the same river, left them with mutual tokens of friendship and regard. On arriving at the Sauk villages, Nee-he-gah, or The Rocky Hills, a chief of considerable note, received us in the most hospitable manner, supplied all our wants, and, as is customary among them in regard to those they esteem real friends, offered us the attendance of their women, who are more cleanly in their habits, and more handsome in their persons, than those of any tribe with which I am acquainted. Our party, however, to a man, declined the acceptance of their services.

From the Sauk villages, we passed over the country, crossed the Missouri near the mouth of the Kansas River, struck the Osage, and coursing along its banks, arrived at the villages of the Osages, who received and treated us as relations and friends. It was towards the termination of the busy sugar-making season when we reached this place: we remained among them till it was over, and partook of the festivities usual on such occasions.

From the Grand Osage villages, we crossed the country by the usual route to the Osage settlements of White Hair's tribe on the Arkansas, where we were received in the same manner as we had formerly been, on our return from the Pacific Ocean.

On my arrival, I found several white traders and hunters with the Osages, among whom were Colonel Watkins, and a Mr. Combs, who treated me with particular attention and kindness. They gave me some small presents, acquired my confidence, and, in the most pressing and persuasive manner, invited me to accompany them back to the white settlements. I was strongly attached to the habits and manner of life I had acquired, and regarded my relationship and connection with the Indians of too sacred a character to be thus violated, without any real, or even ostensible cause. I therefore peremptorily rejected all their offers. In our hunting excursions, I visited the camps of these traders, and these overtures were often renewed by them, but as often, and as unwaveringly opposed by me.

About this time, however, ardently as I was attached to the Indian mode of life, and to my adopted country, relations, and friends, an incident of the most trying and painful character occurred, which violently ruptured all those ties, brought me at once into their measures, and produced a highly important revolution in my life; a revolution, which, I am persuaded, few circumstances, and perhaps no other, could have effected.

Shortly after my return, a party of about thirty, including myself, consisting mostly of young men, started on a hunting excursion up a small river, known to the traders by the name of the Brushy Fork, which enters into the Arkansas about thirty or forty miles below the mouth of the Vermillion River. The success we met with was but indifferent, and the cause, as it generally is on such occasions, was ascribed to the white hunters, who had, in reality, just returned from scouring the smaller streams and hills for game. It perhaps deserves to be noticed, that the hunters, after the beaver season is over, generally terminate their hunting campaigns in pursuit of the smaller kinds of game, which resort to the small streams and hills for their appropriate food, which is generally there more abundant. While the principal part of our hunters, in accordance with this custom, were scattered on the upper branches of this stream, six of our number visited Colonel Watkins' main encampment on the Arkansas, below the confluence of the Brushy Fork. They were treated with kindness, but unfortunately permitted to barter for too much whiskey; a circumstance which came near proving fatal to the traders, and all their party. On leaving the encampment, these Indians stole six horses from Watkins, which were grazing on the prairies, and returning up the Brushy Fork, killed and scalped Mr. La Fouche, a French trader, and plundered his camp of all the furs, goods, &c. which it contained.*

With their hands thus stained in blood, and rendered furious by the excessive use of whiskey, they returned to our camps, distributed the poisonous and infuriating liquid among the rest of the hunters, and, raving in the most frantic manner against the whites, threw down their spoils and trampled them under foot; at the same time exhibiting the scalp of the unfortunate La Fouche, and threatening a similar vengeance on all the whites.

The skin† with its potent contents went frequently round, and in a short time nothing was to be seen or heard but the war-dance, the war-song, and the most bitter imprecations against all those who had trespassed on their rights, and robbed them of their game.

They next mentioned the great quantity of furs that Watkins had collected, which, if suffered to be taken away, would only serve as an inducement for other and more numerous parties to frequent their hunting grounds. "In a short time," said they, "our lands, now our pride and glory, will become as desolate as the Rocky Mountains, whither perhaps we shall be obliged to fly, for support and protection." These addresses produced the intended effect on the now pliant and overheated minds of their audience; and it was immediately determined to cut off and spoil the whole of Watkins' party. These proceedings produced in my bosom the most acute and indescribably painful sensations. I was obliged, nevertheless, to suppress them, in order to avoid suspicion; for, should they have entertained the least, either against me or any one of the party, the consequence, at this time, would have been instant death to the person suspected, and that, too, without any ceremony. Therefore, with an apparent cordiality, I lent my consent, and joined among the most vociferous in approving the measure, and upbraiding the conduct of the traders. This deceptive conduct was also another source for painful reflection; because on no former occasion had I been so situated, but that the opinion I expressed, or the part I took, was in perfect concordance with my feelings, and the maxims I had been taught. From the first proposition that was made to cut off this party, I never hesitated, in my

---

*This Mr. La Fouche was an excellent hunter: he was in the habit of frequenting several of the tribes alone, because it afforded a better opportunity for traffic with them. On the present occasion he had ventured among strangers, and accompanied Colonel Watkins for the sake of protection; he unfortunately failed of this, and fell a sacrifice to the Indians, who, in a drunken frolic, barbarously murdered him, as above recited. (JDH)

†The Indians generally make use of small skins, instead of bottles, &c. to contain their liquors. (JDH)

own mind, as to the course of conduct I ought to pursue. After I had matured my plan to my own satisfaction, I dissembled, very much to my surprise, with as plausible assurance as I have since sometimes seen practiced in civilized life. In fact, I not only acted my part so well as to avoid suspicion, but maintained so high a place in their confidence, as to be entrusted, at my own solicitation, to guard our encampment. This office is of great importance among the Indians; but it seldom exists, except when a measure of consequence has been fixed on, for the successful termination of which, secrecy and dispatch become necessary. The whiskey being exhausted, and the Indians retired to rest, under its stupefactive influence, I silently and cautiously removed all the flints from the guns, emptied the primings from the pans, took my own rifle, and other equipments, and mounting the best horse that had been stolen on the preceding day, made my escape, and gave the alarm to Watkins and his party.

I made considerable noise in taking my horse, and disengaging the others from their fastenings, so as to prevent their use, in case the Indians should discover my absence, and determine on pursuing me. Our dog heard me, and gave the alarm; at least I suppose such was the case, as it barked very loud, at first pursued me, and then alternately broke off and renewed the pursuit with increased ardor, as though it had been recently urged on and encouraged. The distance from our camp to Watkins' was between twenty-five and thirty miles; more than half of which was through thick briars and brushwood, where there was neither path nor trail to direct me. It was before the dawn of day, and quite dark when I left them, in consequence of which, and the expedition I made, I lost everything I had except my rifle.

On arriving at the crossing place of the Brushy Fork, I left the main, or Wells's trace, which, to avoid a rocky hill, led circuitously round and over a tremulous swamp. I apprehended, in case I followed it, that my horse might be swallowed up, and that I should be overtaken by my pursuers and destroyed. I therefore took my course over an almost impassable acclivity, which detained me nearly as much time as Wells's trace would, had it been passable for a horse.

When I had passed this hill, and struck the path I had just left, it had become light, and, not discovering anyone in pursuit, much against my own inclination, but in obedience to a necessary policy, I shot the dog, reloaded my rifle, and then continued my flight as fast as my horse could possibly carry me.

The dog had hitherto been a constant source of annoyance and apprehension to me, on account of the continual barking it kept up; which, if the Indians were following, as I had reason to believe was the case, served to pilot them in their pursuit.

Relieved from my perplexing companion, I varied my course at the first stream of water I came to, by following its channel a short distance downward; and then striking off to my left, I soon crossed the prairies, and arrived at Watkins' camp before anyone had left it in pursuit of game, as heretofore had been the daily practice.

From the darkness of the night, the interruption and roughness of the way, and the haste I had made I had lost my apparel, was badly lacerated, bleeding, and much exhausted.

The powerful agitations under which my mind labored, my gestures and features, and the manner and unusual hour of my arrival, spoke in a language not to be mistaken, that something extraordinary had, or was about to happen, and filled the whole party with surprise and the deepest anxiety. In very few words I informed them of the murder of La Fouche, and the danger they themselves were in. The hunters in general were exceedingly alarmed, and proposed an immediate retreat; but Colonel Watkins, who was a brave and courageous man, would not listen to it. He instantly ordered the preparations to be made to repel any attack that might be made on them, and I was requested to join in the defense, should one become necessary; but I refused, stating that it was sufficient for me to have betrayed my countrymen, without augmenting the crime, by fighting against, and possibly killing some of them. Colonel Watkins replied that they were not my countrymen; that I was a white man; and what I had done, and what he requested me to do, were no more than my duty to the white people required me to perform.

My prejudices against the whites generally were at this time as great as they had ever before been: my attachment for the Indians and Indian mode of life was ardent and enthusiastic; I therefore could not, or rather would not, understand this new relationship. I now hated the very looks of Colonel Watkins, who, before, had appeared so amiable and good; despised myself for the treachery of which I had been culpable, and almost regretted the part I had performed. This change in my conduct and feelings could not escape the notice of Watkins; who, sensible of the obligations he was under to me, and having, previously to my arrival, nearly completed his arrangements for descending the Arkansas, ordered instant preparations to be made for a decampment. I descended the river with this party, nearly to its junction with the Mississippi.

On the way, we had interviews with other traders, to whom Col. Watkins made known the extraordinary obligations he felt himself under to me; in consequence of which, frequent and pressing invitations and offers were made to induce me to leave the party I was with, and join them. The one I was now with, though no pains were spared to reconcile me to the change I had suffered, was scarcely to be endured; these overtures were therefore as foreign to my inclination as would have been a proposal for me to return to the Osages, whose confidence I had abused past all hopes of forgiveness. Indeed, so much dissatisfied had I become with my situation and relations with the whites, that, in spite of the most pressing solicitations, advantageous offers, and friendly advice from Col. Watkins, I determined on abandoning his party, in search of consolation and quiet to my half-distracted mind, among some tribe of Indians, who, ignorant of my treachery towards the Osages, would receive me to their fellowship. I thought that my life, passed among some of the most degraded tribes, would be infinitely more tolerable than it possibly could be, associated with the white people, even though I should realize all the gilded prospects which they incessantly held up to my view. Accordingly, after having received from Col. Watkins some presents, such as a powder-flask, powder, lead, balls, bullet-molds, flints, &c., which at that time were of great value and consequence to me, I left this party, I believe, to their sincere regret.

I journeyed nearly north, over a country which at first was level and partly composed of prairie land, though afterwards it was somewhat hilly; and in the course of a few days struck upon the waters flowing, as I have since learned, into White River, at which I afterwards arrived, and gradually ascended in a northern direction till it became only a small stream.

The prairie lands I passed over were covered with a very luxuriant grazing vegetation, and afforded subsistence for exceedingly numerous herds of buffalo, elk, and deer.

Rattlesnakes, both black and parti-colored, were larger and more numerous than I had ever before seen; and they would infest the country, to a much greater extent, were it not for the hostility that exists between them and the deer.

This animal on discovering a snake, as I have repeatedly witnessed, retreats some distance from it, then running with great rapidity alights with its collected feet upon it; and repeats this maneuver till it has destroyed its enemy.

The hunting season for furs had now gone by, and the time and labor necessary to procure food for myself was very inconsiderable. I knew of no human being near me; my only companions were the grazing herds, the rapacious animals that preyed on them, the beaver and other animals that afforded pelts, and birds, fish, and reptiles. Notwithstanding this solitude, many sources of amusement presented themselves to me, especially after I had become somewhat familiarized to it. The country around was delightful, and I roved over it almost incessantly, in ardent expectation of falling in with some party of Indians, with whom I might be permitted to associate myself. Apart from the hunting that was essential to my subsistence, I practiced various arts to take fish, birds, and small game, frequently bathed in the river, and took great pleasure in regarding the dispositions and habits of such animals as were presented to my observations.

The conflicts of the male buffaloes and deer, the attack of the latter on the rattlesnake, the industry and ingenuity of the beaver in constructing its dam, &c., and the attacks of the panther on its prey, afforded much interest, and engrossed much time. Indeed, I have lain for half a day at a time in the shade to witness the management and policy observed by the ants in storing up their food, the maneuvers of the spider in taking its prey, the artifice of the mason-fly (*Sphex*) in constructing and storing its clayey cells, and the voraciousness and industry of the dragon-fly (*Libellula*) to satisfy its appetite. In one instance I vexed a rattlesnake till it bit itself, and subsequently saw it die from the poison of its own fangs. I also saw one strangled in the wreathed folds of its inveterate enemy the black snake. But in the midst of this extraordinary employment, my mind was far from being satisfied. I looked back with the most painful reflections on what I had been, and on the irreparable sacrifices I had made, merely to become an outcast, to be hated and despised by those I sincerely loved and esteemed. But however much I was disposed to be dissatisfied and quarrel with myself, the consolation of the most entire conviction that I had acted rightly always followed, and silenced my self-upbraidings. The anxieties and regrets about my nation, country, and kindred, for a long time held paramount dominion over all my feelings; but I looked unwaveringly to the Great Spirit, in whom experience had taught me to confide, and the tumultuous agitations of my mind gradually subsided into a calm: I became satisfied with the loneliness of my situation, could lie down to sleep among the rocks, ravines, and ferns, in careless quietude, and hear the wolf and panther prowling around me; and almost feel the venomous reptiles seeking shelter and repose under my robe with sensations bordering on indifference.

In one of my excursions, while seated in the shade of a large tree, situated on a gentle declivity, with a view to procure some mitigation from the oppressive heat of the midday sun, I was surprised by a tremendous rushing noise. I sprang up, and discovered a herd, I believe, of a thousand buffaloes running at full speed directly towards me; with a view, as I supposed, to beat off the flies, which at this season are inconceivably troublesome to those animals.

I placed myself behind the tree, so as not to be seen, not apprehending any danger; because they ran with too great rapidity, and too closely together, to afford any one of them an opportunity of injuring me, while protected in this manner.

The buffaloes passed so near me on both sides, that I could have touched several of them merely by extending my arm. In the rear of the herd was one on which a huge panther had fixed, and was voraciously engaged in cutting off the muscles of its neck. I did not discover this circumstance till it had nearly passed beyond rifle-shot distance, when I discharged my piece, and wounded the panther. It instantly left its hold on the buffalo, and bounded with great rapidity towards me. On witnessing the result of my shot, the apprehensions I suffered can scarcely be imagined. I had, however, sufficient presence of mind to retreat and secrete myself behind the trunk of the tree, opposite to its approaching direction. Here, solicitous for what possibly might be the result of my unfortunate shot, I prepared both my knife and tomahawk, for what I supposed a deadly conflict with this terrible animal. In a few moments, however, I had the satisfaction to hear it in the branches of the tree over my head. My rifle had just been discharged, and I entertained fears that I could not reload it, without revealing and yet exposing myself to the fury of its destructive rage. I looked into the tree with the utmost caution, but could not perceive it, though its groans and vengeance-breathing growls told me that it was not far off, and also what I had to expect in case it should discover me. In this situation, with my eyes almost constantly directed upwards to observe its motion, I silently loaded my rifle, and then creeping softly round the trunk of the tree, saw my formidable enemy resting on a considerable branch, about thirty feet from the ground, with his side fairly exposed. I was unobserved, took deliberate aim, and shot it through the heart. It made a single bound from the tree to the earth, and died in a moment afterwards. I reloaded my rifle before I ventured to approach it, and even then, not without some apprehension. I took its skin, and was, with the assistance of fire and smoke, enabled to preserve and dress it. I name this circumstance, because it afterwards afforded a source for some amusement: for I used frequently to array myself in it, as near as possible to the costume and form of the original, and surprise the herds of buffaloes, elk, and deer, which, on my approach, uniformly fled with great precipitation and dread.

On several occasions, when I awaked in the morning, I found a rattlesnake coiled up close alongside of me: some precaution was necessarily used to avoid them. In one instance I lay quiet till the snake saw fit to retire; in another, I rolled gradually and imperceptibly two or three times over, till out of its reach. And in another, where the snake was still more remote, but in which we simultaneously discovered each other, I was obliged, while it was generously warning me of the danger I had to fear from the venomous potency of its fangs, to kill it with my tomahawk. These reptiles, as before observed, especially in stony grounds, are very numerous: the black ones are short and thick, but the parti-colored ones are very large and long.

I saw many that would, I am certain, have measured seven or eight feet in length. They are not, however, considered by the Indians so poisonous as the former; but, from the distance they are able to strike, and the great depth of the wounds they inflict, they are much the most to be dreaded. They never attack till after they have alarmed the object of their fears, and on account of this conceived magnanimity of character, the Indians very seldom destroy them. Indeed, so much do they esteem them for this trait, that I have known several instances in which the occupants of a wigwam have temporarily resigned its use, without fear or molestation, to one of these visitors who had given due notice of his arrival. The regard the Indians have for this snake has been illiberally construed into an idolatrous veneration; which is far from being the case. Bravery, generosity, and magnanimity, form most important traits in the character of the warrior; and the practice of these qualities is much more strictly inculcated in early life, and observed in maturer years by them, than are the commands of the Decalogue by the respective sects which profess to believe in and obey them. It is from impressions arising from these sources that the Indian, surrounded by his most bitter enemies, and the implements of cruel and vindictive torture, derives his consolation, and is enabled, when put to the most severe trials and excruciating pains, to bear them without complaint; nay more, to scorn the feeble efforts of his enemies, to make him swerve from this character, and to despise death unequivocally, approaching in its most terrific form. The same impressions teach him to respect those who also possess them, even though such should be his most implacable and deadly foes. Hence is derived the respect they show the rattlesnake; whose character, as before observed, they have construed into a resemblance to these qualities; and I can assure my readers, as far as my knowledge extends, whatever other people and nations may do, that the Indians adore and worship only the Great Spirit.

In the solitary and roving manner before noticed, I passed several moons on a number of small streams, which flowed into White River. This led me to an acquaintance with the best haunts for game, which this district of country afforded, and latterly I had employed a considerable portion of my time in making preparations with a view, when the proper season arrived, to employ myself in collecting furs. I had constructed several falls and blinds* in the vicinity of the beaver houses, and was one morning occupied in this manner, when, to my surprise and regret, I discovered some white people approaching

---

*The former is a sort of trap which the Indians construct to take beaver, &c.; the latter is only a screen, from behind which game is shot. (JDH)

me. From their dress and equipments I knew them to be hunters, and therefore apprehended nothing from them; though they were nevertheless unwelcome visitors, and I felt much distress at having my haunts encroached on and my solitude interrupted, especially by white people. I received them rather cautiously and cavalierly; but on being addressed by one of them, named Levous, in a complaisant and friendly manner, and that too in the Osage language, my conduct and feelings underwent a total and instant revolution, and I actually danced for joy.

This party consisted of five Frenchmen, who were on an exploring excursion to search out the most favorable places for taking furs, as soon as the hunting season should arrive. From the knowledge I had obtained of the adjacent country, I saved them the trouble of any further research: they therefore returned down the river to a place called Flees' Settlement.* After some persuasion I accompanied them, and on my arrival found a number of white people located at this point and in its vicinity, for the various purposes of cultivating the soil, grazing, trading, and hunting.

My appearance excited considerable interest, more particularly as a large portion of the inhabitants were affected with intermittent fevers, had no physician to relieve their sufferings, and at the same time entertained a high opinion of the Indian mode of practice.

In consequence of these circumstances, numerous applications were made to me to prescribe remedies for this, and also for some other diseases. With a few barks, roots, and herbs, such as the Indians resort to on similar occasions, I treated their cases with the happiest success, though much to my own surprise, for it was my first essay in the practice of the healing art.

The ignorance in the treatment of diseases displayed by the whites, who, in my intercourse with them, had uniformly inculcated their own superior skill and excellence over those of the Indians in every moral and physical department, was matter of great astonishment to me, and contributed in no small degree to many unfavorable contrasts, which I afterwards made.

While in this place, I acquired a knowledge of many words in the English language, and, at the repeated and not to be denied instance of the American women, for the first time in my life arrayed myself in the costume of the whites; but it was a long time before I became reconciled to these peculiarly novel fetters.

The people at this settlement generally were removed but a small degree above the Indians in their modes of life, which, considering the uncultivated state of the country, could not reasonably be otherwise expected. This circumstance had, however, a great effect in reconciling me to the change I was about to experience. It served as a gradation, seasoned by *other incidents,* to make every succeeding step to civilization not only tolerable, but highly desirable: whereas, if I had been ushered at once from one extreme to the other, it is highly probable that a mutual dissatisfaction, and perhaps disgust, would have been the result; which, most likely, would have deprived me of the superlative pleasures I now derive from associating in refined and highly cultivated societies, and thrown me back, no doubt, with self-congratulation to my former unreclaimed state of being.

The hunting season arrived, and, having furnished myself with several traps and other essentials, I started with Levous and some others, on our contemplated hunting excursion. The hunters with whom I now associated became attached to me, and followed my advice on all occasions; and the consequence was, the collection of an extraordinary quantity of valuable furs.

During this winter, a party of Delawares, eight or ten in number, who had been on a deputation to some American post on the Mississippi, crossed our hunting grounds, and accidentally fell in with our party. They had, previous to reaching our camp, under the influence of whiskey, killed some women and children belonging to some graziers in the vicinity of Flees' Settlement, who were absent on a hunting party. The alarm occasioned by this hostile conduct reached us before the arrival of these Indians, and nothing was heard among our party but a determination to revenge these murders. On more mature reflection, however, it was thought most advisable to let the offenders pass unmolested; particularly as the number of whites on this river, including hunters, traders, and all, was too inconsiderable to encourage the hope of success in a war that would be likely to follow any hostile conduct on their part. Besides, the Delawares were more numerous farther up the country, and were also on very friendly terms with some of the tribes in their neighborhood.

These Indians were sensible that the offense they had committed was known to our party, and dreaded the consequences: but, as I had lived with the Osages, with whom they were now friends, and conversed with them in the Osage language, I acquired their confidence, learned the particulars, and finally effected a reconciliation that secured them from any hostility on our part, and enabled us to pursue our hunts without the fear of molestation. Shortly after, we were visited by another party of Delawares, with whom we traded to a considerable amount. I exchanged my traps for their full value in furs. We separated from them on good terms, and then returned down the river to Flees' Settlement, where we made a short stay, and subsequently continued our route to the Mississippi, with an intention of descending that river in search of a market: but, meeting with some traders at Maxwell's Fort, just above the mouth of White

River, I concluded to dispose of my furs, and remain for the present at this place.

Some people of respectability, particularly Messrs. Wyatt, Finley, and Henderson, informed me of the value of my furs in the current money of the country, advised me to dispose of them, to vest the proceeds in lands, and to turn my attention to agricultural or some other useful pursuit.

I had several offers for them, one in particular from a man calling himself Davis, who had in a peculiar manner attached himself to me, by professions of the deepest interest for my welfare, and for whom, believing him sincere, I entertained a very high respect.

On account of the supposed reciprocity of good feelings, I sold my pelts to this individual in preference to any other, for six hundred and fifty dollars. On making payment, he counseled me in the most friendly manner, to be cautious how I disposed of my money. He stated, that the white people, generally, would be on the alert to take advantage of my ignorance of the value of things and modes of negotiation, to defraud me of it; and further, that many of them, if they knew how large an amount I had, would not hesitate to rob, and, to prevent detection, even to kill me. He urged me to avoid these dangers by accompanying him; to this proposition, however, I objected, and he took his departure down the river, laying me under the strongest injunctions to secrete my money in some safe place, and whenever I wanted some, to take only a single note at a time. I regarded all that this fiend in human shape had said as truth; and, not having any immediate wants to satisfy, which made an expenditure necessary, a sufficient time elapsed for him to escape, before I found out the fraud he had practiced on me. The discovery, however, was soon made, and happened in the following manner: Mr. Wyatt, whom I just before mentioned, had frequent interviews with me, and expressed great solicitude to see me settled in some employment that would restrain my roving disposition, concentrate my efforts and desires to a single object, and establish habits of industry and usefulness. He recommended agriculture to me, as the most certain, independent, and elevating in its results, and disinterestedly offered to assist me in the purchase of a tract of land. This gentleman had a large family, was easy in his circumstances, and very highly respected by all who knew him; and his counsel had its intended effect on me, not so much, however, on account of any of the foregoing circumstances, as because he was aged: for I had been taught, and still believed it my duty, to attend to the advice of age and experience, even though emanating from a white person. I accordingly accepted of his offers, and deposited in his hands all my treasure, stating at the same time the amount. The old gentleman counted it over in the presence of his family, and, with indignation and surprise strongly depicted in his countenance, inquired if this was all I had. I answered, as was the fact, that it was all I had obtained for my furs, except five or six dollars. "The villain, the Yankee* villain," he replied, "has cheated you: instead of six hundred and fifty dollars, you have only twenty-two!!!"

This I found to be the case; and my agricultural schemes were wholly defeated, for the present. Before this fraud was discovered, I had expended five or six dollars for some necessary articles of clothing, &c.; so that the whole amount I had received did not exceed twenty-seven or eight dollars. I was at first advised by Mr. Wyatt and some others to pursue Davis in the first boat that should descend the Mississippi; but as considerable time had elapsed in which Davis might, and probably had made his escape, as I was comparatively without money, and an entire stranger to the language of the country, they subsequently changed their opinions, and I adhered to their advice.

I was exceedingly anxious to follow him, not, however, so much with a view to recover my money or furs, as to chastise him for his egregious duplicity and contemptible breach of friendship. I openly threatened, and, had he crossed my path, I certainly should have chastised the villain in a very summary manner; and the apprehension of such an event was probably the real cause why Wyatt and his friends finally advised me to abandon the pursuit. This transaction, from the manner of its accomplishment, disgusted me more than ever with the white people. The Indians had constantly inculcated on my mind, while I was with them, that fraud, cupidity, and perfidiousness, were indiscriminate traits in their character. Thinking now these precepts were dogmas not to be questioned, I determined to abandon for ever all farther connections with them.

Wyatt, who was then and has ever since proved my sincere friend, resolutely opposed such a measure. "You cannot suppose," said he, "that either myself, Mr. Finley, or Mr. Henderson, or such and such individuals," repeating the names of several respectable persons, "would, on any account, have served you so. There are but few among us that would; and as you advance into the settlements the proportional number of such wicked people becomes very much diminished. The Indians themselves have some among them who are bad, of which you yourself are a witness; and you cannot hope, and ought not to expect, to meet with any state of society wholly exempt from them."

However consistent his mode of reasoning was, it made little or

*The term Yankee is universally applied to all rogues in the western states, without any regard to their place of nativity. (JDH)

no impression on me; and taking my leave of him, and the few acquaintances I had formed, I started with a determined resolution to make no considerable stop, till I arrived at the Kansas towns, where I had formerly resided. On arriving at Flees' Settlement, I was much embarrassed from information I received there, that some of the Delawares had committed hostilities on the whites, and massacred a Mr. Hendricks and some others at a temporary settlement farther up on White River. These Delawares had formerly resided in the state of Indiana, and had moved across the Mississippi in consequence of some negotiations, effected, I believe, by General Harrison. Subsequently they became displeased with this arrangement, and showed their resentment in the commission of the before-named massacres. The people at Flees' Settlement had become acquainted with my disposition towards the whites, and my intended return to the Indians, and used all the means in their power to conciliate my good feelings, and prevent the execution of my plan. In this, I am persuaded, they never would have succeeded, had it not been for the previous conduct of the Delawares; for when they had exhausted all their arguments and offers, to no purpose, I was told, that my intended movement was of an unfriendly and hostile character; that I had now become an enemy to the white people, and was going to join their Indian foes. This charge wrought my feelings up to a degree of excitement bordering on frenzy. Such an idea had never entered my mind: I entertained no enmity against the whites generally, and the Delawares were entirely strangers to me: I could not, however, deny that appearances were so much against me, as to justify a language so derogatory to my honor, and for which, under less specious circumstances, I would have exacted an exemplary atonement. Nevertheless, in the present exigency, I restrained my feelings and resentments, as far as was in my power; determined neither to give offense to the whites by making a movement in the direction of their enemies, nor to risk the displeasure of the Delawares, by passing through their territories, as I must have done, on my journey to the Kansas nation, without enlisting in their quarrels.

This determination satisfied the settlers; but it was indirectly forced, and consequently (apart from other considerations) was not calculated to render a residence among them agreeable to my feelings, nor even to reconcile them to me. Though constrained to abandon the route I had contemplated, the measure itself was still uppermost in my mind, and I concluded still to accomplish it, in some more circuitous direction. I was diverted from my purpose, however, by two young men, named Tibbs and Warren, who resided in the neighborhood of New Madrid, but were now on their way to the St. Francis River, in search of good hunting grounds. The mere mention of their intended excursion was sufficient to induce me to join them, and we forthwith proceeded on our journey. We passed some time on some of the branches of this river, in pursuit of our object, and then descended it to a small French settlement, where we remained till the hunting season arrived. While here, I became acquainted with an elderly French woman, named Mashon, who took great pains to instruct me to read, and to convert me to the Roman Catholic faith. I made some progress in the former; but with respect to the latter, notwithstanding her zeal in the pious office was unremitting, I made no proficiency. My mind was too strongly prejudiced by early education to yield either to her persuasions or arguments. I worshiped the Great Spirit, and entertained too exalted an opinion of his attributes to consent to exchange the adoration of him for that of a small ivory crucifix, the symbol of her faith, with which she had gratuitously presented me, as I supposed, for that purpose.

Finding all her labors to convert me of no avail, in the most fervent manner she pronounced me a heretic unworthy of the blessings of the Gospel, and gave me over to the buffetings of the father of sin; notwithstanding which, and the efforts she made to inflame my mind against the Americans, on account of the heresies of their religion, I still feel a regard for her memory, because she first taught me the elements of the English language, and because I believe her conduct proceeded from pure, though mistaken motives, having my spiritual welfare singly in view.

According to a previous agreement which I had made with Tibbs and Warren, I started in their company up the west fork of the St. Francis River, on a hunting and trading excursion, where we passed the whole of that hunting season. In the spring, we descended the river to its junction with the Mississippi, and proceeded down to Natchez, where we disposed of our furs. My part of the proceeds came to rising eleven hundred dollars; the most of which I deposited for safekeeping in the hands of Doctor Sanderson, a very respectable physician of that place. Soon afterwards, I engaged, in company with the above named Tibbs and Warren, in the capacity of boatman, with some Kentuckians who were short of help, and continued down the Mississippi to New Orleans. Here new scenes for both my admiration and disgust presented themselves to view. The arrangement, comparative elegance, and number of buildings; the magnitude, finish, and great collection of ships or vessels; the vast multitude of people, and the extent and bustle of business, excited the former; while the tumultuous revelry, intemperance, and debauchery of the boatmen and sailors, the abandoned demeanor of some unfortunate females, and the assemblage of a filthy multitude of blacks and whites, motley in all the intermediate shades, scarcely submitting to any moral restraints, and degraded in servitude and its concomitant vices, too low to be associated in the scale of rational human beings, were but too well calculated to produce the latter. The first occasioned reflections corresponding with the peculiarity and extraordinary grandeur of their character, while the hideousness and deformity of the latter, caused me again to sigh for the woody retreats and uncontaminated manners of the tawny children of the wilderness.

In my humble capacity of boatman, I did not expect to form any respectable acquaintances in this city; nor did I at this time, though subsequently I am happy to say that I can rank some of its most distinguished citizens, among those of a similar character in various parts of the United States, who have given me the most decided proofs of their friendship and regard, and to whom I thus gratefully tender the homage of a public acknowledgment.

Leaving New Orleans, I returned in company with my employers, through the Cherokee and Choctaw nations, to Kentucky, and from thence to the neighborhood of Cape Girardeau, in the Missouri territory, where I remained about six weeks engaged in acquiring a rudimental knowledge of the English language, in a respectable school, conducted by Mr. G. Simpson, a native, I believe, of the state of New York. While in this place, I was distinguished by as many different names as there were pupils in the school, much to the amusement and playful ingenuity of my companions. Indeed, the license taken with me in this respect was so great as to give umbrage to some of my friends; who advised me to obviate the grounds for such a practice, by assuming some appropriate one to be known by thereafter. While with the Indians, they had given me the name of Hunter, because of my expertness and success in the chase; I therefore determined on retaining that as my patronymic. And as Mr. John Dunn, a gentleman of high respectability, of Cape Girardeau County, state of Missouri, had treated me in every respect more like a brother or son, than any other individual had since my association with the white people, I adopted his for that of my distinctive, and have since been known by the name of John Dunn Hunter.*

In the following fall, I ascended the Mississippi and Missouri rivers as far as Boone's Lick, in company with several others, on a trading expedition. At this place I became acquainted with the celebrated Col. [Daniel] Boone, the gentleman who *first* adventured to settle among the Indians, in that part of Virginia now known as the state of Kentucky.

Both of our lives having been somewhat singular, and in a great measure identified with the aborigines of the country, nothwithstanding the disparity of our ages, we soon became strongly attached to each other: I passed much of my time with him; and he treated me with so much kindness and friendship, that his memory will ever remain dear to me.

While at this place I again met with Manuel Lisa, of whom I had occasion to make some remarks, in a prior part of my narrative. He still continued hostile to me, on account of our previous disagreements at the Mandan villages, and higher up on the Missouri River, and resorted to clandestine measures to prejudice the Indians against me, and defeat the object of my voyage. Nevertheless, I managed so as to effect all the negotiations I desired, without increasing the misunderstanding between us; at least, so far as my own feelings were concerned.

From this very successful expedition I returned to St. Louis, where I exchanged my furs for produce from Kentucky, and descended the Mississippi River with it to New Orleans. On my way down, I was near losing my life and property at a place which I think was called Bayou Sira, in a violent storm. Several boats were wrecked, and some lives and much property lost. I disposed of my produce on advantageous terms at New Orleans, and returned up the river to Natchez in a steamboat. This mode of traveling, and the ease with which the boat appeared to be navigated against the current of the Mississippi, without the aid of the wind, or any perceptible human force, filled me with amazement, and almost induced the belief, that it was effected through the agency of invisible spirits; of whose favorable dispositions towards mankind I had no reason to doubt.

I passed the following summer and fall, in obtaining a further knowledge of the English language, under the tuition of Mr. Robert Currie, a very respectable teacher, who conducted a flourishing seminary in the vicinity of Pearl River, in the Mississippi territory. I remained at this school, under that gentleman, and Mr. John Lewis his successor, at subsequent intervals between the trading seasons; so as to make the whole period of my studies amount to about two years and a half, exclusive of about six weeks, which I passed, in the autumn of 1821, at Mr. Samuel Wilson's academy, near Walnut Hills, in Mercer County, Kentucky. At first, my instructors experienced some difficulty with me, on account of my supposed intractable disposition. Mr. Currie acknowledged, after we became intimately acquainted, that his prejudices were so great against me, at the time I delivered an introductory letter to him from Mr. Philip Sublette, that he was on the point of refusing me admission to his school, notwithstanding the highly respectable character and standing of the gentleman who had recommended me to his care and instruction. There was, perhaps, some cause for these prejudices: for while I was at school at Cape Girardeau, my fellow students, as before noticed, were disposed to and did take greater freedom with me than I thought was proper or justifiable, and I never suffered them to go unnoticed, notwithstanding the injunctions of my teacher to the contrary. This conduct, it is true, irritated Mr. Simpson at first; but subsequently, I believe, I secured his esteem; though not by the same means that I did the respect of my school companions.

For some time after I entered school, I experienced great difficulty in learning the pronunciation and meaning of words; this, however, being once partially surmounted, my progress was easy, till I could read, so as to understand all the common schoolbooks that were placed in my hands. During the recess of my school employments, I seldom went anywhere without a book. I had access to some respectable libraries, and became literally infatuated with reading. My judgment was so much confused by the multiplicity of new ideas that crowded upon my undisciplined mind, that I hardly knew how to discriminate between truth and fable. This difficulty, however, wore off with the novelty, and I gradually recovered, with the explanatory assistance of my associates, the proper condition of mind to pursue my studies, which were again renewed and continued, as above noticed, with great interest and solicitude. They were confined to reading, writing, English grammar, and arithmetic. On leaving this school, my instructors respectfully complimented me for the proficiency I had made; but they were remarkable for courtesy, and I ascribed their conduct to that cause.

I passed my winters as I had heretofore, since I left the Osages, in taking, or trading for furs, which I subsequently disposed of, on profitable terms, at New Orleans.

During my last visit at this place, I accidentally met my friend, Colonel Watkins; the interview was highly interesting, and sincerely affecting to us both. He made various propositions to induce me to form a connection with him in the fur and cotton trade, to which I thought it inadvisable to accede, on account of my ignorance of commercial transactions, and my anxiety for the attainment of more extensive knowledge. He gave me much useful advice respecting my future intercourse with the world; treated me, in every respect, with the interest and attention that a fond father would an affectionate son; inquired into the state of my affairs; and enjoined it on me, as a matter of *right*, to call on him, should I ever stand in need of his assistance.

Since this interview, I have heard that Colonel Watkins was profitably engaged in the fur and cotton trade; though I have only received one communication directly from him, since we separated at New Orleans. This was in April 1821, while near Shawneetown, in the state of Illinois. And, as it alludes to the circumstance of my preserving him and his party from destruction by the Osage Indians, as previously detailed, I trust no apology will be deemed necessary for giving it a place in my narrative. It is as follows.

Cape Girardeau, Missouri,
March 15, 1821.

My dear Friend,

I have just received information from Mr. Combs and Colonel L. Bean, that you are lying very low with the fever, at Shawneetown; yet am much gratified to hear from the same respectable source, that you are on the recovery.

I am in haste, and am sorry I have but a few moments to devote to this tribute of gratitude and respect, for one to whose goodness and enterprise I am indebted, under Providence, for my life; and that too, at the sacrifice of everything valuable to you. I hope you will not venture to start before you recover your strength. Mr. Combs informs me, that you have started, without taking any recommendations with you from your friends, excepting Dr. Syme.*

If this will be of any service to you, it is with the greatest pleasure I tender it. Your confidence may carry you too far; your resources may fail; and recommendations be rendered necessary. If my recommendation will do you no good, it will not be any disadvantage; so, as to taking it along or not, you will exercise your own pleasure; but however you may receive it, be assured, that if any favor I can do you, would be of tenfold the advantage which it possibly can be at present, I would be far from supposing I have relieved myself from the obligations which your intrepidity and goodness have laid me under.

I have been to Philadelphia and Baltimore: you may derive information by going to either. I would advise you to spend some time at both places, as you can, without any difficulty, procure letters of introduction to the first characters in either place, from your friends in Cincinnati, Louisville, or Lexington; which I would advise you by all means to accept, as the politeness of those people will be certain to offer them to you—and, if you were aware of the necessity of friends, in a strange country, as I have been, you would not neglect any facility in extending, even among strangers, your singular history.

I am willing to certify upon oath, at any time, if required, my delivery from inevitable destruction, by your timely and hazardous undertaking.

I know your clerical friends were very solicitous for you to go through Boston, and obtain a theological education. I cannot say what course to advise you, as to that: I do not know the moral tendency

---

*In this respect Mr. Combs labored under a mistake—*Author.* (JDH)

of your mind, and cannot advise. Let me hear from you often: I shall be generally at Natchez or Baton Rouge.

Permit me, dear Sir, to subscribe myself, your most affectonate and sincere friend and well-wisher.

(Signed) GEORGE P. WATKINS.*

Previous to receiving the above letter, I had visited several of the largest towns, and formed an acquaintance with some of the most respectable people in the Western States. There were many among them, who were particularly friendly; and who advised me to journey eastwardly as far as Baltimore, Philadelphia, and New York, with a view to publish the history of my life, and such information as I possessed, respecting the Indian nations settled west of the Mississippi River.

In addition to the inducements held out by the advice and solicitude of my friends, I had, for some time preceding, fostered an ardent desire to become acquainted with some one of the learned professions. My views in this respect had been very much influenced by the advice of the truly venerable Mr. Wyatt, whose name I have previously had occasion to mention.

He had explained to me the difference between the comparatively natural rights enjoyed by the Indians, and those essential to the harmonious preservation of civilized society.

He demonstrated the observance of industry, perseverance and prudence, as necessary to secure even a moderate share of the comforts and happiness of life, and taught me the importance of sustaining my relation with the world independent of its bounties, rewards or fears.

In fine, it was he, who first satisfactorily unfolded to my benighted mind the *Identity* of the Great Spirit with the Creator of all things, and the *Salvator* of the human family. He also taught me rationally to unbend my selfish, evil propensities, and to gird on the armor of self-denial, charity, and truth, and to *square* my life by them, as acceptable offerings to the Great I AM.

As I entertained very great respect for that gentleman, his opinions were treasured up by me as oracular; and I have since often reflected on them with a mixture of pleasurable sensations and painful solicitude that defies my powers of description.

But besides my desire to acquire a professional knowledge, my ardent imagination depicted to me all the beauties that had been unveiled in the intellectual world. From the ready proficiency I had made, I thought of nothing less than the subjugation of the empires of science and literature, and when this had been accomplished, to have penetrated into unexplored regions in search of new truths.

With my mind thus filled with lofty expectations; ignorant of the world, of my own powers, and the vanity of the attempts I contemplated; unknown to a single human being, with whom I could claim kindred, except from common origin; and even indebted to circumstance for a name; in the fall of 1821, I crossed the Alleghany [Allegheny] Mountains, and, as it were, commenced a new existence. By this, however, I intend no local reflection, for wherever I visited. hospitality and friendship have been inmates, and often hailed me in the silent though expressive language of the heart, "thou art my brother." In truth, the kindness and respectful attention I have received since I left the Indians, from all classes of people with which I became acquainted, have been of a nature calculated to inspire and fill my soul with gratitude and respect, and that I may merit their continuance will be the high ambition and constant endeavor of my future life.

PART TWO

**MANNERS AND CUSTOMS
OF SEVERAL INDIAN TRIBES
LOCATED WEST OF THE
MISSISSIPPI**

Considerations on the Physical and Moral Condition of the Indians

1

Under this head I propose to treat of their migrations, and separations into tribes, language, signs, modes of writing and delineation, structure, complexion, mental capacity, &c. I shall commence on their migrations and separation into tribes or nations.

The Indians are very thinly dispersed over the country . . . bounded on the east by the state of Missouri and Mississippi River; north by the British dominions; west by the Rocky Mountains; and south by the Arkansas River and territories of the Mexican empire. [They are particularly scarce*] in the temperate and more fertile parts; where, all circumstances taken into view, one would, with apparently great reason, look for the contrary.

But the abundance and variety of game, the spontaneous production of a great number of plants, mild climate, and facilities for satisfying all the wants of Indian life, have rendered the possession of these regions a perpetual subject for contention, and are the proximate causes of this unnatural reversion. The Indians generally are disposed to rove; and in their excursions, they frequently encroach on the privileges of their neighbors, which is seldom suffered to pass unnoticed, and usually terminates in war; a result frequently courted with no other view than to school the young warriors, and afford the older ones opportunities to acquire distinction. These wars are sometimes of short duration; at others they only cease with the extermination or removal of one of the parties. Discomfited bands or tribes are sometimes met with, which have scarcely males sufficient for the chase, without regarding the subject of their defense. In such instances they commonly retreat for protection and safety to the most unfrequented or mountainous regions, or form alliances with their more powerful and friendly neighbors. But in general they incorporate themselves with some other tribe, and become either virtually extinct, or acknowledged dependents. The Peorias, Missouri, and Little Osage tribes, are instances to the point.

If closely pressed by their foes, instead of becoming tributaries, and contrary to what generally results among reclaimed nations, they abandon their country and homes, apparently without experiencing those acutely painful sensations incident on similar occasions to civilized life. But before they resort to such measures, they accomplish all that their means will permit, more to support their claim to the character of an independent and brave people than to their territory. In this way the strong and more powerful press upon the weak; while the weak dispose of themselves as above described.

The migratory disposition of the Indians consequently becomes in part forced. Remotely, according to the tradition of many of the tribes, it has been from the north or northeast, southwardly; and no doubt it has been induced by the very same causes which contribute to depopulate the more fertile regions of this country, with which the Indians, from their mode of life, could not fail progressively to become acquainted. To these causes may perhaps be added the more favorable disposition of a northern climate to an increase of population, and exemption from the jealousy and envy of their more southern neighbors, because of the severity of their climate and the poverty of their hunting grounds. These circumstances combined would allow of an accumulation of people greater than those regions could support, so that, from necessity, a portion would be compelled to a change of residence. Or Asia, as some have supposed, may have, by some means at present unknown to us, sent out, either by accident or design, a succession of colonies, which, pressing one upon the other, have contributed to keep up this change of location among the several tribes.

There now exists an implacable enmity between the Sioux and Kansas, which originated, at no very remote period, in the former having forced the latter to abandon their hunting grounds on the Missouri. The Osages have a similar tradition in regard to their removal, though it does not extend to the nation that coerced them to the measure.

Most of the Indian nations, although now occupying territories, which they have possessed for periods extending very far beyond their chronological data, have like traditions, which are no doubt founded on facts; but the problems, as to the remote or succeeding causes which led to those results, I shall resign to abler pens for solution.

These migrations recently have been much influenced by the advance of the white settlers; and they will continue to be so, I apprehend, till terminated by the total destruction of all the Indians on the eastern side of the Rocky Mountains.

In regard to those settled on the western side, I entertain more favorable hopes; because they are less warlike, appear to entertain far less elevated notions respecting the sovereignty of their tribes, and their own individual natural rights, and have not so unconquerable a contempt for all servile labor; and because the game, fish, and roots on which they subsist, having become comparatively scarce, they will the more readily be persuaded to adopt agricultural pursuits, to obtain a less precarious subsistence. Such changes, if history may be relied on, are the concomitants of civilization, and they must prove conducive to an increase of population; so that if brought about among those people, they will be redeemed from the annihilation to which those on the eastern side of the mountains appear to be rapidly advancing. When a nation of Indians becomes too numerous conveniently to procure subsistence from its own hunting grounds, it is no uncommon occurrence for it to send out a colony, or, in other words, to separate into tribes. Preparatory to such a measure, runners or spies are sent in various directions to ascertain the most suitable location. A national council next hears the several reports, determines on the plan, and elects chiefs to carry it into operation. The pipe is then sent round, and all who smoke it are considered as volunteers. Sometimes the number is too small to warrant the enterprise; at others it is so large as to occasion the migration of the whole nation. Where, however, it is properly proportioned, the ceremony of separating is at once accomplished, and is truly affecting.

The tribe so separated maintains all its relations, independent of the parent nation; though the most friendly intercourse is commonly maintained, and they are almost uniformly allies. Separations sometimes take place from party-dissensions, growing generally out of the jealousies of the principal chiefs, and not infrequently out of petty quarrels. In such instances, in order to prevent the unnecessary and wanton effusion of blood, and consequent enfeebling of the nation, the weaker party moves off, usually without the observance of much ceremony. These divisions seldom last long; reconciliation follows reflection, and a reunion is effected. Instances, however, have been known, in which the two parties became the most irreconcilable, rancorous, and deadly foes, and raised the tomahawk against each other, with a malignity surpassing, if possible, that exercised between hostile nations totally distinct in consanguinity.

To the above causes for the Indian nations separating into tribes, may be added that of belligerency; in which, as in wars among civilized nations, the strong generally triumph over the weak; but the consequences are very dissimilar. Among the civilized, the vanquished are very seldom disturbed in their possessions, or undergo even a change of masters, though such a measure might often prove highly advantageous; while among the Indians, to prevent entire destruction, they are obliged to flee from their possessions, and are frequently dispersed into different tribes or bands, which, being prevented from reuniting, by the interposition of their enemies, connect themselves with other nations, or seek safe retreats, and maintain their independence in the manner as before observed.

Of some one of these characters have been the divisions which not very remotely took place, respectively, among the Sioux, Pawnees, and Osages; and it is highly probable that the Kansas and Osages descended from, or constituted originally a single nation, as there is a striking resemblance in their languages.

LANGUAGE. It has been supposed by some, that all the Indian nations speak different dialects of the same language; but the case is far otherwise.* There are scarcely two nations, between whom no intercourse exists, whose languages are so similar as to be mutually understood by the respective individuals of each; indeed, I believe there are none; although the circumstances of origin, descent, immediate neighborhood, intermarriages, voluntary associations, friendly intercourse, and the incorporation of the vanquished of one tribe with another, have materially modified, and, in many instances, effected a strong resemblance in some of them. Among nations more remote, some words of the same pronunciation, and of the same and of different imports, are used; but instances of this nature do not occur sufficiently often to materially alter their character, and they maintain their claims to distinctiveness with as much force, perhaps, as do the English, French, German, and Russian languages. It is true, that an individual of one nation may, by the assistance of signs, make himself sufficiently understood to hold a conversation on all ordinary subjects, with strangers of almost every other, but then it should be remembered that their languages are pantomimic, and that their poverty is, to a considerable degree, made up for by those impressive and common auxiliaries.

The Indians settled in towns and villages speak languages more stable, comprehensive, and full, than those do who have no fixed residence, or lead more solitary lives. And, as they have neither records nor standards, but depend wholly on recollection and habit, it is not extraordinary, under the many other casual and arbitrary circumstances influencing them, that their languages should, as they actually do, suffer frequent and considerable changes.

SIGNS. In regard to the signs used by the Indians to connect their words, and render their languages intelligible, very little of a satisfactory nature can be said; because they are so variously adapted to their different subjects of conversation, as in general to baffle description. In order to comprehend them fully, it is necessary to understand their idioms and habits. In talking of an enemy, they assume a ferocious attitude and aspect, seize hold of, and brandish their weapons of war, in precisely the same manner as they would do if they were in their presence, and about to engage in a deadly conflict. The wampum and pipe are handled in conversations on peaceable subjects, and everything connected with them is diametrically reversed. Speaking of men, game, birds, fish, trees, marching, hunting, swimming, &c., &c., the peculiar habits or character of each, individually, is imitated in so happy a manner as to be readily understood by those acquainted with the qualities of the subject intended to be described, although they should be entire strangers to the language. Independent of the above, they use many signs, which convey ideas of entire sentences: such, for instance, as a circular motion of the extended arm in the direction of the sun's course, to represent a day or a half day; the rapid sweep of the hand represents a violent wind; the uplifted hands and eyes, an invocation to the Great Spirit, &c. They also use significant emblems, such as the wing of the swan and wild goose, wampums and the pipe, for, or as overtures for peace: the arrow, war-club, and black and red paintings, for war, or as indications or declarations of it. Any article, but in general a skin painted black, or the wing of the raven, represents the death of friends; and when colored or striped with red, that of enemies . . . .

MODES OF WRITING AND DELINEATION. In their writing and correspondence, the Indians make use altogether of hieroglyphics; to which they are forced by their ignorance of characters which admit of a series of methodical combinations. Even if this were not the case, it is doubtful whether their languages would permit the application of such a knowledge; at any rate, it would be exceedingly arbitrary, and to understand it would require great and constant efforts of the imagination.

They inscribe their correspondence, and such subjects as require to be recorded, on the inner bark of the white birch *(Betula papyracea)*, or on skins prepared for the purpose.

Styluses of iron, wood, or stone, and brushes made of hair, feathers or the fibers of wood, are used to delineate or paint the most prominent objects embraced in their subjects; the remainder is to be supplied by the imagination of the reader.

If, for instance, they wished to describe the surprise of a party of their hunters by their enemies, and their rescue by white people, they would first imprint the tracks of the buffalo in advance; next, as many footsteps as there were hunters, provided the number was small, [or] if not, they would draw as many large footsteps as there were tens, and smaller ones for those of the fraction of that number, the whole arranged in disorder; then the number of the assailing party would be imprinted in the same manner, and the nation to which they belonged, be pointed out by some emblem of its chief, as that of a wolf for a Pawnee chief; finally, in the rear of the Pawnees, which should also be represented in disorder, the number of the rescuing party would be drawn as before, and their national character distinguished by the representation of its flag. The number of their own, and that of their friends slain, would be indicated by the number of footsteps painted black, and the wounded by those partially so colored: while that of their enemies would be distinguished by red paintings, in precisely the same manner. If they thought it necessary, the description would extend to the country, or even place where the surprise happened; as for instance, if it was either in a prairie, or in woods, or on the margin of a river, prairie grass, trees, or a stream, would be represented according as the occurrence happened; and the place would be characterized by the presentation of some generally known object, at or in its neighborhood.

In fine, the Indians experience little or no difficulty in describing or understanding any incident or subject, in this way. The chiefs, especially if any misunderstanding had previously existed, constantly wear on their robes the delineated boundaries of their hunting grounds, according to stipulations entered into by the disputing parties. These boundaries are also drawn on skins, and deposited in their public lodges, as records to be referred to on necessary occasions. They likewise design very correct maps, in which the rivers, hills, trails, and other circumstances worthy of notice, are very correctly laid down; they also very readily do the same on the sand or earth, for the information of strange travelers. In their marches, they inscribe instructions or any other information deemed necessary, for the spies or detached parties, on smooth-barked trees. Their distinguished warriors register on skins all the remarkable incidents of their lives: which, with the exception of those they are buried in, are uniformly kept by their relatives as sacred relics and testimonies of honorable descent for many succeeding generations. They sometimes cut with hard stones emblematical representations of remarkable events, &c. on soft or friable rocks, which, as their mode of computing time is very imperfect, soon cease to be interesting, and are forgotten. And the same skill is extended to ornamenting their pipes, and various domestic utensils.

I have seen many of those engravings, which, though in part apparently intelligible, could not be identified with any of the circumstances or traditions of the present population of the country; and I have no doubt, more correct information, respecting the origin of the Indians, might be obtained from a comparison the hiero-

Physical and Moral Condition of the Indians   89

glyphic characters of different nations and eras, than can possibly be arrived at from the analysis of their respective languages. The former are the delineations of truth, and probably have been imitated respectively by all the Indian nations from the remotest antiquity. The only objection to this source is the extreme scarcity of incident; while the latter, in the intermixtures, separations, and destructions, that slowly but surely happen, and the liability of their languages to change, as before remarked, presents clearly to my mind insurmountable difficulties to the acquirement of the desired knowledge. As well might the *debris* on the seashore be traced back to their primitive locations, by means of their external or chemical characters, as the Indians to their progenitors by their languages. What, let me inquire, would have become of the Greek and Roman languages, had not letters preserved their knowledge to after times? and changes, not of the same magnitude, but of equally the same importance, connected with their idioms, frequently take place among the Indians.

Besides, where the very best means exist to maintain or preserve the unity of language, how many new terms are constantly adding to it! How many old ones have become, or are becoming obsolete! It may be replied, that these changes do not extend to the radicals; and perhaps they do not, to any considerable extent, wherever registers exist; but the Indians are not provided with any means to arrest the oblivious effects of the changeable circumstances to which they are subject; and, therefore, have frequently to exercise their inventive faculties to give names to things which are not only altogether new, but also to such as had been forgotten. To confirm this position, it is only necessary to observe the great difference that at present exists in the languages of the different Pawnee tribes; which, there can be no doubt, were, originally, precisely the same.

Those living in villages speak fluently a much more copious and intelligible language than those do who lead wandering lives. Indeed, I am persuaded I hazard nothing, by saying that any person, a stranger to the circumstance of their origin, would without hesitation take them for different nations.

The great trait of character, which more particularly distinguishes the Indians from every other people on our globe, except the Jews, is their religion; which is so different, as to place the period of their descent from any other people, necessarily remote; because, from the best information extant on this subject, all the various races, from which there seems any probability of their having descended, have been from immemorial time involved in the grossest superstition and paganism. This circumstance of remoteness involves the subject in still greater obscurity; because it allows of proportionately extended chances for the very changes which, I contend, have taken place in their languages. However, if any similitude in their worship could be traced out, I would place more reliance on it, in attempting to establish their origin, than I can now consent to on any or all the circumstantial proofs and hypotheses that have been suggested; because, without referring to divine authority, I believe the whole human family, left to the exercise of their rational faculties from infancy, would in the process of time, and in accordance with those faculties, first adopt the doctrine of Theism, and that they would not be likely to deviate from it only in proportion as the means for indulging the baser passions increased.

From a resemblance to the Jews in their worship, and in some of their laws and cusfoms, particularly as respects murder, anointings, and places of refuge, some have attempted to show that the Indians originally descended from that people; while others, with greater plausibility, perhaps ascribe this conformation to accident.

This subject has excited much interest, and many ingenious hypotheses have been suggested without producing any satisfactory results. And I am persuaded that every step we take in pursuit of this truth, on the data we now possess, must terminate in the same way.

STRUCTURE AND COMPLEXION. The whole family of mankind are generally regarded but as one species; and the difference that exists in it, according to the influence of climate, or the regions they inhabit, constitutes only varieties: while some others, comparatively few in number, think the difference between the several races sufficiently marked to justify their arrangement into distinct species. But in regard to correctness in either of these opinions, it does not belong to me to discuss.* I shall, therefore, give only a brief outline of the most striking characteristics of the North American Indians.

Notwithstanding the countries they inhabit are nearly similar in respect to climate, supplies, and other circumstances, calculated to produce like results, a considerable difference in the size and color of the different nations does actually exist.

The Patawattomies, Shawanees, Osages, and Cherokees, are tall; the Ricaras, Mandans, and Kickapoos, are short; while the Kansas, Mahas, Pawnees, Ottowas, Quapaws, and Delawares, who are remarkable for their full chests and broad shoulders, are all intermediates to the two former. In their size and structure, considerable difference prevails among all the nations I have visited, both on this and on the other side of the Rocky Mountains.

According to the taste of the white people, the persons of the Indians generally are well proportioned: I ought, however, to except a general muscular deficiency on the calves of their legs, and, in some of the tribes, the disproportional increase of the integuments on the femores. and about the pelvis of the females; the latter, however, I observed only on the Pacific side of the continent.

Malformation is very rare among them; but, when an instance happens, it is thought to be influenced by the Great Spirit to punish, or by the Evil Spirit to torment them; and the individual, in either case, becomes the peculiar subject of their superstitious regard, under the hope that such conduct will appease the one, or propitiate the other.

Their foreheads are rather flat, and not generally very high and jutting; their eyes are small, black, and set somewhat deep in their sockets, with the external angles a little elevated above the internal; their noses long and prominent, and their cheekbones full, high, and generally broad, so as to terminate the inferior oval curb of the face, between the nose and mouth. The hair on their heads is naturally long and black, and much pains are bestowed by the women, to preserve it as an ornament to their persons; the men pluck all out, except a small tuft that covers the crown of their head or scalp, which they preserve with the most studious attention, with a view to meet their enemies on a fair footing, or with honorably corresponding objects for contention on the field of battle. The hair on the other parts of their bodies would, I am persuaded, be as abundant as it is on those of any other variety of the human family, were it permitted to grow; but all the Indians, except lunatics, or such as suffer from derangement of mind, extract it with great care, whenever it appears. I name this more particularly, because I have heard it suggested that they are naturally deficient in this respect; and because of the repeated inquiries addressed to me on this subject.*

The color of the Indians approaches a tawny copper; the shades, however, differ in the different tribes, and even among the individuals of the same tribe; but not sufficiently to change the characteristic trait. This does not appear to proceed from the influence of climate, so much as one would, on a cursory view of the subject, be led to suppose: for we find many of those located northwardly to be more swarthy or darker colored than their more southern neighbors, or even than some that are more remotely situated in the same direction. I shall pass by the philosophical disquisition as to the causes of this variation, because I feel incompetent to do the subject justice, and merely notice the facts as they occurred to my observations. The Patawattomies, inhabiting the headwaters of the Illinois River; the Sioux on the Missouri and Mississippi; the Pawnees on the Platte; and the Ricaras on the Missouri; are, I believe, more deeply shaded than any other nations with which I am acquainted. Next to the above in deepness of color, are the Osages, Kansas, Ottowas, and Cherokees, all more southwardly located; and the Mandans on the Missouri, and the Choctaws, and Creeks of the state of Mississippi, are among those of a still lighter cast.

Under this division, arbitrary as it is, all the tribes on the eastern side of the Rocky Mountains may be arranged conveniently enough for description, though it must be acknowledged that the shades of color of the extremes of each, approximate so closely, as perhaps to bring in question its propriety.

Those on the western side of this boundary, as far as my knowledge extends, are not so dark as the lightest above described. While a particular tribe, situated near the headwaters of the Mult-no-mah River, are of a pale ash, and very much resembling that of the African albinos, though somewhat darker.

The lips, which in some of the tribes are very thick, as I ought before to have noticed, are colored similar to the other parts of their bodies, while the palms of their hands and the soles of their feet are almost white.

The children, when first born, are of a dusky cream color, with the exception of spots under the eyes, and along the spinal ridge, which are more deeply shaded. They gradually become darker from exposure, and finally assume the complexion of the older Indians; which varies in a slight degree on the different parts of their bodies, accordingly as they may be more or less exposed to the action of the air and solar rays.

The Indians call themselves red men, in contradistinction to the whites and blacks, wherever such are known to exist. Generally they pride themselves much on their color; its coppery darkness being considered a peculiar mark of excellence.

The chiefs and influential men in some of the tribes object to intermarriages with the whites, on account of the aberration from this standard color, which is exhibited in the offspring: white being regarded characteristic of effeminacy and cowardice, and all the shades between it and their own as naturally influenced by those qualities, in proportion as it preponderates. They nevertheless think these traits may be corrected by rigid discipline and strict attention to early education: and I have no doubt the many battles I fought in my boyhood were countenanced in conformity to this opinion and their tuitive policy.

The Indians universally believe that the Great Spirit, when he created all things, exercised a partiality in their favor, which was indelibly registered in their color.

Next in order to themselves some class the whites, while others suppose the blacks to be superior to them: they generally believe this partiality extended to the whole descending series of organic and inorganic things, according to the perfections they respectively display.

The circumstances incidentally connnected with the wandering life and precarious condition of the Indians are not very favorable to procreant habits, and the cares they entail. Instances of a sanguine temperament seldom occur, though when they do, they are less frequent among the males. They do not arrive at puberty at so early a period of life as is common in civilized society; the difference may be estimated at two or three years. The particular time is similarly influenced by climate and other causes, and is equally various in different individuals.

Custom, with them, as with the whites, regulates the intercourse of the sexes, but not with so close a rein in respect to consequences; for a female may become a parent out of wedlock, without loss of reputation, or diminishing her chance for a subsequent matrimonial alliance, provided her paramour be of respectable standing. But, notwithstanding, instances of the kind seldom happen; not that the Indian women are over rigidly virtuous; but because abortives are sometimes resorted to as well in celibacy as in married life; though the practice is discountenanced by the men, except when on long marches or pressed by their enemies. The women seldom raise more than three or four children; I have known a few to have five, and, very rarely indeed, one or two more. They suckle them from two to three years, and sometimes even longer. This practice has, no doubt, grown out of the difficulty of procuring nutriment suitable to the digestive organs of infancy; though it is continued by some, under the belief that it promotes sterility;* an entire instance of which I have never known among Indian women. Their gestative, parturient, and travailing affections are so slight as scarcely to admit of any comparison with those experienced in civilized life, except in name and circumstance.

Of the proportions of male to female births, I cannot speak with precision; though it appears to me, from what I have observed, that the former are rather more numerous. The proportion of the men to the women is comparatively small, in consequence of the frequent and destructive wars in which the former are engaged, and their greater liability to disease.

This disparity is scarcely perceptible in early life; but, among those arrived at maturity, and still farther advanced in life, it is very obvious, and varies in the different tribes from two or three of the former to four of the latter, according as the causes above named prevail. In some tribes the extremes differ considerably from this average . . . and, as previously remarked, they are sometimes without men sufficient for the chase.

I am unable to say much in relation to the proportion

of the births to deaths that occur in the natural way; because the natural operations of disease and decay are interrupted, or rather anticipated, by their desolating wars. I may observe, however, from comparisons made since my arrival in the United States, that the births, in proportion to the population, are not more than half so numerous as they are among the white people; while the deaths by old age, apart from the causes above noticed, and regard being continued to numbers, are considerably more numerous. So that, if my observations have been correct, and the Indians were to desist from their belligerent habits, and lead regular and temperate lives, their chance of arriving at great age, and dying by decay, would be much greater than that of any people devoted to the pursuits and habits of civilized life.

The death of an Indian woman, aside from casualty, is a rare occurrence, except from the ordinary wane of the functions of life. The same cannot be said of the men: their frequent exposure to all varieties of temperature and weather, fatigues from long marches; and long abstinence from food, followed by an inordinate indulgence of the appetite; give rise to many diseases, from which death oftentimes ensues. Both the men and women that survive to old age, retain all their senses much more perfectly than is common to civilized life.

Disease, particularly the smallpox, has deprived some few of their vision; otherwise I have never known a single instance of total blindness: the same may be said of total deafness; though dimness of eyesight and difficulty of hearing are not uncommon to very aged persons; but they are not so frequent as among white people.

They also retain their mental and corporeal powers in greater vigor and perfection. When old, they usually depart from the taciturn habits of early life, become garrulous, and frequently discourse with an astonishing minuteness and accuracy, on the events of their past lives, and on circumstances calculated to inspire patriotism, and the love of glory, in younger minds. An ardent love for the chase continues with the men to the last. When too old to carry the rifle, they employ the boys or young men for that purpose, and frequently take long marches in pursuit of game. I have myself accompanied them till nearly worn out with fatigue, though ashamed to complain.

The men sometimes arrive at a very great age; though the proportional number of old women is much the greatest. I have known many whose ages were computed severally to be from ninety to one hundred years. The women generally live the longest, and retain their mental faculties more remarkably than the men.

They are not much afflicted with diseased teeth; I may truly say that I have never known a half dozen instances, in which they have been entirely decayed. The toothache, and swelled faces proceeding from it, are exceedingly rare; and it may be generally observed of the Indians on the eastern side of the Rocky Mountains, that they retain their teeth entire, to the close of their lives. It is not however the case with those on the western side. Nearly all the old ones there are without; and many middle aged, and some quite young, are exceedingly affected by diseased and decayed teeth. This difference in their condition and liability to decay, no doubt arises in the difference of their modes of living. Nearly all the Indians which subsist chiefly on animal food, are exempted from this misfortune and suffering; while those who are more confined to a vegetable diet, are peculiarly subject to them. None of the Indian tribes is, however, so much and so generally disfigured by decayed and lost teeth, as are the people of the United States, who, as I have been informed, are not in this respect singular among civilized nations.*

This effect [of dental caries], no doubt, generally results to the [Western] Indians from their want of cleanliness, and the acidity contained in their food, which is mainly vegetable, and often taken without the slightest preparation by cooking.

Education and habit disqualify the Indians for [the] laborious pursuits of civilized life; but the extraordinary performance of such as they are accustomed to, shows that they are not deficient in activity and strength.

I have known Indians, when much enfeebled by hunger, to carry loads of buffalo meat, deer, and elk, for miles to the camps of their party; which very few laboring white people, in perfect health and vigor, would have willingly undertaken, Besides, their greater ability to perform long journeys in shorter times than those less accustomed to this exercise could possibly do, is another proof, if one were wanting, to the same effect: and to these might be added the known capacity and cheerful compliance of the women to perform all their laborious duties, and that sometimes too under circumstances that would not be tolerated in civilized life.

So that no doubt remains in my mind, if we average the perfections and imperfections, that the Indians will bear a comparison, in their physical conditions, with any other great division of the human family.

MORAL CONDITION. In regard to the *moral condition* of the Indians, very little requires to be said; because, it will be admitted on all sides, if history may be credited, that they display, according to the opportunities presented by the circumstances and modes of their lives, as great energy of mental powers, and capability of accommodating it to particular exigencies, as any other people ever have.

The causes which operate against their increase of numbers, and the facilities with which they are in general able to supply all their wants, very much restrict, and I may say, prevent their moral advancement. Were these causes and facilities to cease or become considerably limited, it would be absurd to suppose the Indians would not resort to grazing and agriculture for a livelihood. Fixed residence would follow as a necessary consequence; and these objects once obtained, all the arts and policies connected with the wants and comforts of civilized life, would as necessarily be developed. And then, as population and wealth increased, science and refinement, and perhaps, disease and crime also, would commence their rapid march; never, from the constitution of the human mind, and the organization of things, to terminate, except in the wreck of universal nature.

In weighing or estimating these probable results, the long period of the aggregate of human existence, the slow development of the mental faculties, and of the arts and sciences, as they have actually occurred in the progressive condition of the world, should be constantly and prominently kept in view.

I have ventured to make the foregoing observations, from the progress which most of the Indian nations had made in such arts as are essentially connected with their manner of life, previous to their acquaintance and intercourse with the white people. Their manner of dressing skins into leather, either with or without preserving the hair, for many purposes far exceeds those in general practice in the United States. For, besides the pliant softness which is imparted to them by their process of dressing, and which, though ever so frequently wet, is retained to a considerable degree, they are neither so liable to stretch, nor to be destroyed by worms.

They also succeed in making very good pottery; though the forms are neither various nor elegant; nor do the uses to which it is applied, require that they should be; but they resist the effects of fire very well, and till lately were the only implements used in their cookery. They make mats from grass and rushes, and very warm and durable, though not very sightly, blankets from the hair of the buffalo, and other animals. They form stones into various shapes, as the pestle and mortar, tomahawks, pipes, and knives; construct various kinds of canoes, as from trees, the barks of trees, and the skins of animals; and, sometimes, comfortable and spacious lodges, though they are not generally very particular in this respect. They cultivate such plants for food and medicine as they have found by experience to require it; and, in a few instances, where the advantages were favorable, irrigated their fields, and conveyed water to their lodges, in drains, or the barks of trees. They boil, roast, bake, and broil their meats, and cook their vegetables generally in an appropriate manner.

They sketch general resemblances of men, quadrupeds, &c., delineate maps of countries with considerable accuracy, and chisel hieroglyphic figures in massive rocks. Of their proficiency in music, little can be said: they, however, have instruments resembling the tambourine, drum, and pandean pipes; on which they perform to a regular cadence, and they well understand their effect on the passions, either in the festive pastime, or tumultuous din of battle.

They observe some of the heavenly bodies, as the north and seven stars, and direct their way by them, across the trackless prairies, with as much accuracy in general as the mariner steers his ship by means of the compass.

In reasoning, their judgment and perceptions are clear and quick, and their arguments ingenious and cogent.

They resort much to figures, which are generally poetic, bold, and appropriate: in fact, if I am a competent judge, their eloquence is more persuasive, lofty, and commanding, and their orators far more numerous, in proportion to numbers, than is common among any class of people on the globe.

Their fundamental laws are few in number, and traditionary, but are as fixed as the reputed ones "of the Medes and Persians" [and] they are in general well adapted to their condition; and some of them are precisely similar to those of the justly celebrated Jewish Lawgiver, as, for "Thou shalt not kill," they require blood for blood. Their minor laws are subject to modifications; they may generally be denominated common, for they result from public opinion.

Their diseases are comparatively few, though some of them are acute and complicated; nevertheless those in general incidental to their modes of life, readily yield to their modes of practicing medicine; and indeed most of those for which they are indebted to their intercourse with the whites are treated with a like happy success. So that they may be said to have made greater proficiency in the healing, than in any other art or science. In general their knowledge and skill are adapted to the occasion, in as striking a degree as they are in societies, which, in other respects, have greatly preceded them in the march towards perfection. It must, however, be allowed, that in some tribes, the knowledge of medicine is exceedingly limited, and its practice amounts to very little more than the hocus-pocus of conjuration.

They are, so far as my acquaintance extends, universally Theists, and have, according to their traditions, from immemorial time worshiped only the Deity. This circumstance alone, whether it originated from comparative inquiries, or was an especial gift of Heaven, entitles them to a high grade in the scale of intellectual and moral beings. . . .

Many other circumstances might be deduced, were it necessary, to establish the claim of the Indians to be classed with those races of mankind, which have already developed the higher intellectual faculties of their natures. But enough, in my opinion, has been said on the subject, to convince all unprejudiced and reflecting minds; and for those who think differently, if volumes were to be written in support of this position, it is probable their opinions would remain unaltered.

As an illustration of the capacity of the Indians for moral improvement, it appears necessary to make some general observations on their present state of society, their tenor, and modes of their education, &c., before the more particular details on these subjects are attempted.

Their multiplied division into tribes or nations; the want of well-defined natural boundaries to their respective territories; added to a domineering disposition, natural perhaps to man; their zeal for the chase, and ardent love of independence [—all] have an extraordinary influence in forming their character, which is essentially warlike. Nevertheless, it undergoes modification according to climate, abundance or scarcity of game, feebleness, strength, disposition, and habits of neighbors.

Those which inhabit the warm regions where game is plenty, are naturally of a peaceable turn, but are forced to become warlike, to defend their hunting grounds. Those which have retreated to the mountains while weak are, from policy, of the same disposition; but, as they grow strong, they almost uniformly change in character, and become offensively active. Those who till the earth, and fish for a livelihood, and those who are feeble, and border on powerful neighbors, generally cultivate social and friendly relations; while those who live on poor hunting grounds, and are formidable, are as generally hostile in their avocations and character. There are some exceptions to the foregoing, particularly along our frontier settlements; and where they do exist, they arise from the prejudices the Indians entertain against the customs and habits of the white people, and their reluctance to gratify the ambitious views of speculators, by parting with their lands. These motives with some others not named, operating on the almost endlessly varying condition of the Indians, produce a suspicious, watchful, and disturbed society, in almost all the different tribes and nations, and exact the most rigid and constant performance of duty from every individual capable of bearing arms. In this state of things, the high object of their education is, to constitute the able and fearless warrior; and all the duties of life connected with their preservation, matrimonial alliances, and amusements, are subservient and directed to it. The love of their tribe or country, the individuals of their own family scarcely more than that of any other, and above all, that of real self-excellence, is unceasingly impressed on their youth, first by the women, and then by the old men, in the narration of traditions and remarkable events, till they enter, and distinguish themselves in the *arena* of mature life. In addition to this, they are the spectators of their boyish quarrels and amusements, and award censure or praise, as it is merited.

I have already noticed this subject in my narrative at considerable length, as practiced among the Kansas, and as is much conformed to by the other Indian nations, with which I am acquainted, and I shall in consequence treat it very slightly in this place. The youths are taught, both by precept and example, to reward a benefit, and resent and punish an injury; to love and oblige a friend, and to hate and persecute an enemy; and a dereliction from either, would subject the delinquent to reproach or ridicule. They are instructed to regard and reverence age, and, so careful and punctilious are they in the observance of this lesson, that the passives frequently become the subjects of great error and inconvenience.* The young are always silent in the presence of the aged, and counsel which, from an equal or middle-aged person, would not be listened to, would, on coming from an old man, be regarded as oracular, and most scrupulously followed. They are also taught to condemn falsehood, and never to practice it; but even with them this wholesome lesson is not always regarded; though its violation, especially if often repeated, is certain to involve the offender in a loss of character. Slanderers are reprobated to the same punishment. Theft, except when practiced on enemies, is esteemed execrable, and is indeed seldom known among them. Adultery and murder are strictly prohibited. The former, without the consent of the husband, is generally punished by separation; though I have known one instance, in which the outraged put the offender to death. For the latter, the blood of the offender, if it can be obtained, must atone.

By what I have before stated, it will readily be perceived that their crimes are few, and their punishments in general very appropriate, and, I can assure my readers, not less effective than those which have commonly been resorted to in civilized society. In general their virtues are limited in the same ratio with their vices; but, it must be understood that I allude to those which are uncontaminated by any intercourse with the white people. Where the fact is otherwise, the proportion is hideously altered; for the Indians readily adopt, in an aggravating degree, their examples in respect to the latter,

---

*That is, the unquestioning acquiescence of the young frequently led to great error and inconvenience. (RD)

while from necessity they remain strangers to the former. I say, from necessity; because mankind in all ages have been the creatures of example; and the Indians, with a very few exceptions, have only had an opportunity for imitating the most abandoned of their [white] species. Besides, from education they have been taught to pursue that course of life which would present the most extensive means for their sensual gratification. Vice, in all its various forms, is the concomitant of their intercourse with the dissolute portion of civilized life; and it is cultivated with great zeal by a majority of the traders who visit them, because it most effectually breaks down the lofty notions of independence and superiority, entertained by the Indians, and renders them the unresisting dupes to cupidity and fraud. And, I repeat, the benevolent of our race trust their hopes of benefiting the Indians, on a "sandy foundation," so long as this kind of intercourse is tolerated.

Beyond what has been said, the education of the Indian youth is derived from imitating their superiors, or from experience derived from a more extended observation and intercourse. The means of acquiring knowledge being thus limited and defective, and the pupils at perfect liberty either to improve by, or neglect them, it is not a subject for surprise, that their range of ideas should be much circumscribed, and their information in general extend no farther than is made necessary by their convenience and safety.

It should be kept in mind, that all the comparisons presented in this chapter between the white people and Indians, have relation to respective conditions and proportional numbers.

For the information of the reader I ought to mention that it will be necessary to dwell more at large on some of the subjects which have been hurried over in the preceding considerations on the physical and moral circumstances of the Indians, when I come to treat of particulars in the subsequent parts of my work.

2
Views of Theocracy, Religion, Agency of Good and Bad Spirits; of the Soul and Its Migration; Religious Rites; Prophets, Priests, and Physicians; Dreams, &c.

In respect to the origin of their religion, the Indians themselves are altogether ignorant. It is certain, however, that they acknowledge, at least so far as my acquaintance extends, one supreme, all powerful, and intelligent Being, *viz.* the Great Spirit, or the Giver of Life, who created and governs all things. They believe, in general, that, after the hunting grounds had been formed and supplied with game, he created the first red man and woman, who were very large in their stature, and lived to an exceedingly old age; that he often held councils and smoked with them, gave them laws to be observed, and taught them how to take game and cultivate corn: but that in consequence of their disobedience, he withdrew from, and abandoned them to the vexations of the Bad Spirit, who had since been instrumental to all their degeneracy and sufferings.

They believe him of too exalted a character to be directly the author of evil, and that, notwithstanding the offenses of his red children, he continues to shower down on them all the blessings they enjoy: in consequence of this parental regard for them, they are truly filial and sincere in their devotions, and pray to him for such things as they need, and return thanks for such good things as they receive.

On the other hand, when in affliction, or suffering under any great calamity, in the belief that it will appease his wrath or mitigate his chastisements, they pray with equal fervency to the Evil Spirit, who, they conceive, is of a character directly the reverse of the Good Spirit, to whom he is inferior, but, nevertheless, has sufficient power, and is constantly employed in devising means to torment and punish the human family.

By the term Spirit, the Indians have an idea of a being that can, at pleasure, be present, and yet invisible: they nevertheless think the Great Spirit, like themselves, possessed of a corporeal form, though endowed with a nature infinitely more excellent than theirs, and which will endure forever without change.*

Although they believe in a future state of existence, as before noticed, they associate it with natural things, having no idea of the soul, or of intellectual enjoyments; but expect, at some future time after death, to become in their proper persons the perpetual inhabitants of a delightful country; where their employments, divested of pains and troubles, will resemble those here; where game will be abundant; and where there is one continued spring, and cloudless sky.

They also expect that their sensual pleasures will be in proportion to individual merit: the brave warrior, expert hunter, and those slain in battle in defense of their country, having the highest claims, will be the most distinguished; while those of subordinate pretensions will occupy subordinate stations.

They have no particular days set apart for devotional purposes, though they have particular times; such, for instance, as the declaration of war, the restoration of peace, and extraordinary natural visitations. They also have rejoicings, which assume something of the pious form; such are their harvests, and the return of the new moon. In general, however, a day seldom passes with an elderly Indian, or others who are esteemed wise and good, in which a blessing is not asked, or thanks returned to the Giver of Life; sometimes audibly, but most generally in the devotional language of the heart.

This ceremony is particularly observed after allaying their thirst at the fountains, but is not confined to circumstance nor place. It is practiced by individuals, parties, and even by whole tribes, when they break up their encampments, as was noticed in my narrative. (Page 47.)

Their manner of worshiping the Deity differs, however, on different occasions. Shortly after a council has determined on war, every individual that is able to walk, and the old men sometimes borne by others, assemble in a grove, or some other place rendered sacred by the occasion, and offer up their prayers to the Great Spirit for success against their enemies.

Sometimes the devotional exercises are pantomimic and profoundly silent; at others, ejaculatory and vociferous. At the conclusion, some one of the old men or prophets addresses the assembly; states the cause of their grievances; and enjoins the warriors to merit success, by being brave, and placing their confidence in the Great Giver of Life. Afterwards all return to their homes. These meetings vary in their duration from three hours to a whole day.

Similar meetings are generally held on the conclusion of peace, or the attainment of a victory, though their devotions assume more or less of the character of rejoicing or mourning, according to the success that has attended their arms. When triumphant, they dance and sing songs of victory, in which the name of the Great Spirit is frequently introduced with great reverence; if vanquished, or having suffered great losses, the women and children weep immoderately, pull their hair, beat on their breast, and pray for the destruction of their enemies. The men for the most part of the time maintain a sullen and mournful silence, beat on their breasts, and occasionally pray for their lives to be spared till they have revenged themselves on their enemies. These meetings never take place till after the burial of those who have fallen in battle; a particular account of which will be given in its proper place.

Meetings similar to the above are also convened on any extraordinary natural occurrence, or on the prevalence of any fatal epidemic. On such occasions, some one of the old men, or a prophet, if one should be present, addresses the Indians in an authoritative tone of voice, and assures them that the calamity which threatens is a visitation from the Great Spirit, to chastise them for their ill-spent lives and willful offenses against him; he then commands them to be penitent for what has passed, and to reform for the future. Silent prayers are now offered, accompanied by promises to become more obedient to their Great Father; the meeting is then dissolved, all amusements and recreations cease, and individual prayers and fastings are frequently observed for many successive days. All their serious devotions are performed in a standing position.

At the ingathering of the corn, they observe general rejoicings at which all who are able join in appropriate dances, songs, and feasts, and in thanks to the Great Spirit, for his munificence towards them. On these occasions, as also at the new moon, at the commencement of hunting the buffalo in the spring, lamps, constructed of shells, and supplied with bears' grease and rush wicks, are kept burning all the night preceding and following these joyous festivals; but for what particular purpose the practice is kept up, or from what circumstances it originated, I could never learn; and it is probable the history is lost, as the Indians themselves only conform to it in obedience to usage.

They in general, on discovering the new moon, utter a short prayer to the Great Spirit, to preserve them from, and make them victorious over their enemies; and to give them a cloudless sky, and an abundance of game.

Their addresses to the Evil Spirit are only made on particular occasions, as before observed, and then not uniformly by all such as are generally esteemed subjects of his tormenting visitations: for, in regard to his agency, there are some among the Indians, as well as the white people, who entertain doubts, and others, though this number is small, who altogether discredit it, and pay all their adoration to Him, who, under whatever name he may be worshiped, is alone worthy.

Their ideas of good and evil spirits, the agents or minions of superior powers, are exceedingly various. There are some exceptions to the belief of their existence, though these are rare. Some believe that they invisibly hover around and influence all their conduct, and are on ordinary occasions the immediate executors of rewards and punishments. Others believe that they perform only the offices of exciting to good and bad actions; and others again, that they only officiate on great and important occasions. They also believe that these good and bad spirits are at perpetual war with each other; that their power is much limited, and not transferable to human beings in general, though in a very limited degree so to those who are remarkable for their wisdom and goodness, or for qualities of an opposite nature. The former constitute their prophets or priests, and the latter their enchanters, or practicers of witchery, as is believed, to the injury of inoffensive Indians.

In all the tribes I have visited, the belief of a future state of existence, and of future rewards and punishments, is prevalent; though this in many respects is various, and generally confused and indistinct, as might reasonably be supposed would be the case among any people possessed of no better opportunities or advantages for acquiring or perpetuating information. This belief in their accountability to the Great Spirit makes the Indians generally scrupulous and enthusiastic observers of all their traditionary, tuitive, and exemplary dogmas; and it is a fact worthy of remark, that neither frigidity, indifference, nor hypocrisy, in regard to sacred things, is known to exist among them, excepting occasionally [among] the young and inconsiderate, some of their prophets or priests, and all their conjurers. This conduct, with most of the Indians, is founded on a perfect conviction that the cultivation and observance of good and virtuous actions in this life, will, in the next, entitle them to the perpetual enjoyment of ease and happiness, in delightful and abundantly supplied hunting grounds, situated at a vast distance beyond the Great Waters, where they will be again restored to the favor, and enjoy the immediate presence, counsel, and protection of the Great Spirit. While a dereliction from it, or the pursuit of an opposite course, will as assuredly entail on them endless afflictions, wants, and wretchedness; barren, parched, and desolate hunting grounds; the inheritance and residence of wicked spirits, whose pleasure and province it is to render the unhappy still more miserable. Others again think, that the pleasure or displeasure of the Great Spirit is manifested in the passage, or attempted passage, of the good and bad, from this to another world. On this eventful occasion all are supplied with canoes; which, if they have been brave warriors, and otherwise virtuous and commendable, the Great Spirit, either directly or indirectly, guides across the deep to the haven of unceasing happiness and peace. On the other hand, if they have been cowardly, vicious, and negligent in the performance of their duties, they are reprobated to the evil fantasies of malign spirits, who either sink their canoes, and leave them to struggle amidst contending floods, or feed their hopes with delusive prospects, and bewilder them into inextricable errors, or strand them on some shore, and there transform them into some beast, reptile, or insect, according to the enormity of their guilt.

This latter opinion, omitting the sea voyage, prevails to a considerable extent among some of the tribes. Indeed, the metamorphosis is supposed sometimes to take place in a varying and alternating series in the same individual, according to his culpableness, till he has atoned for all his offenses, and, in his proper character, merited a residence in the elysium of the good.

Every Indian of any standing has his sacred place, such as a tree, rock, fountain, &c. to which he resorts for devotional exercise, whenever his feelings prompt to the measure; sometimes many resort to the same place. Preceding any public meeting, held either for religious or festive purposes, or the assemblage of a council, they uniformly retire to their respective places of private worship, and solicit the counsel and protection of the Great Spirit. No compulsion is ever exercised to procure attendance at any of these meetings; but those who omit to attend are thought less of, and their conduct is ascribed to an indifference to holy things, and a want of solicitude for the national welfare.

The religious opinions entertained, and modes of worship observed by the several Indian tribes, with which I have any acquaintance, vary in their general character but little. My knowledge, however, is limited to very few; and what I have above stated applies particularly to the Osage and Kansas nations. There are some in all the tribes who do not subscribe in opinion, or conform in conduct to the general dogmas and modes of worship: of this number I regard Clermont, the chief of the Great Osages. I have several times, both in public and private meetings, heard him observe, that all good actions would be rewarded, and all bad actions punished by the Great Spirit; that the evil actions of those whose lives were generally good were the causes of the afflictions they suffered, the losses they sustained, and the more painful death that followed; their offenses would, however, be finally forgotten. [Clermont believed] that such would not be the condition of those whose lives were generally wicked, for in this life they suffered much greater evils and afflictions than the good, which in the next would continue to be their lot; [and] because then they would not have it in their power to reform, and merit a happy state.

Tut-tus-sug-geh,* another distinguished Osage, entertains opinions very similar. At first, one might be led to suppose that this belief was a modification of doctrines taught by some of the missionaries; but such is not the case; for, antecedent to my leaving those people, they had been held in such discredit, as to render all arguments and discourses on religious subjects suspect and of no avail. Besides, Clermont had been celebrated for the singularity of his opinions, before any of this class, I believe, visited his nation; and we might as reasonably expect a disciple of the Cross to preach up the worship of idols, as that an Indian trader would have attempted to unfold the doctrine of future rewards and punishments to the benighted Indians. This opinion, therefore, must have originated in the versatility of some reflecting mind among the Indians.

It may be remarked here, that a general opinion prevails among them that the disquietude produced by, or the misery attendant on bad conduct, is always greater than the pleasure afforded by the transaction—which, say they, independent of their obligations to perform what is agreeable to the Great Spirit, is a sufficient motive, and should always stimulate to the performance of good actions. The Indians generally conform to this; not, however, from selfish views, but from principle, to which they in general accommodate their conduct with greater zeal, in my opinion, than any other people on the globe.

They are scrupulous observers of their engagements, prompt and steady friends, active and inveterate enemies, sincere in religious things, and, in fact, perform all their duties, after the manner in which they have been educated, "heart in hand."

Among the Indians there is no difference in the character of their prophets and priests: one performs the duties of both offices, if two can be said to exist. They also, in general, officiate as physicians, but the practice of medicine is by no means confined to them and we often see persons applying themselves to it, without any regard to age or sex; though experience and success are thought to be essentially requisite to entitle them to the character.

The power of holding communication with invisible agents, and thus of being able to foretell future events, is pretended to, and practiced, to a greater or less extent; but the sacerdotal office, in the strict sense of the word, is, in general, unknown among the Indians. I, however, witnessed an instance, while at the Ricara villages, wherein the priest burnt tobacco, and the offals of the buffalo and deer, on a kind of altar constructed of stones on a mound. The ceremony was accompanied with signs and incantations, addressed to the Great, or some other spirit, which, from my ignorance of their language, were altogether unintelligible to me. During the performance, a large concourse of people was assembled round the mound, but no one, except the priest, was permitted to tread on the spot consecrated to religious purposes.

The only thing further connected with this circumstance, as worthy of remark, was the dress or habiliments of the priest. His cap was very high, and made of a beaver skin, the tail of which was curiously ornamented with stained porcupine quills, and hung down on his back; his robe was a buffalo skin, singularly decorated with various colored feathers and dyed porcupine quills; and he wore on his breast, suspended from his neck, a dressed beaver skin stretched on sticks, on which were painted various hieroglyphic figures, in different colors. His forehead was painted black, his cheeks blue, with stripes of red obliquely out and downwards from the alae [bridge] of the nose. All his beard was plucked out, except two small bunches on the upper lip, midway between the nose and angles of the mouth, and two other bunches, of about the same size, on the sides of the chin, directly under those on the upper lip. These bunches were all painted of different colors, and helped, as I then thought, to constitute one of the most singular and grotesque figures I had ever seen.

The Indians speak of similar characters being among some other tribes, but the above described is the only one that ever came under my observation. The prophets, as before noticed, are more numerous, though the number of those who are, or have been much distinguished, is comparatively small. Some of them are wise, good, and pious men, who found their pretensions to a knowledge of the future on careful observation, and on their dreams, which the Indians generally suppose are inspired by invisible agents, of either good or evil qualities, according to the nature of the sleeping effusion, and believing them the faithful foreboders of unavoidable events, they are happy or wretched, cheerful or gloomy, in conformation to whatever they may portend.

The title of prophet is sometimes awarded by the Indians to individuals who have rendered themselves remarkable by their wise sayings, clearness of judgment, and virtuous lives; but, for the most part, it is assumed by pretenders, and supported by juggling tricks, and impostures practiced on unsuspecting credulity.

They are not distinguished by their dress from the rest of the Indians.

On ordinary occasions they retire secretly to their sacred places, and invoke the assistance of the Great Spirit, and make the most solemn vows to him, which they never fail to perform, should he vouchsafe to lend an ear to their prayers; or, in other words, should events correspond to their predictions or prayers. But at times more momentous, such as the declaration of war, conclusion of peace, or the prevalence of epidemics, &c. they impose on themselves long fastings and severe penance; take narcotic and nauseating drugs, envelope themselves entirely in several layers of skins, without any regard to the temperature of the season; and, in a perspiring and suffocating condition, are carried by the people into one of the public lodges, or to some sacred place, where they remain, without the slightest interruption, in a delirium or deep sleep, till the potency of the drugs is exhausted. After the performance of this ceremony, while the body is much debilitated, and the mind still partially deranged, they proclaim their dreams or phantasms to the astonished multitude as the will or commands of the Great Spirit, made known to them through their intercourse with his ministering agents. These pretended oracles are always unfolded in equivocal language, or are made to depend on contingencies, so that if they should not comport with the events which follow, they can charge it to the ignorance or misconduct of the Indians themselves; which is often done with an assurance and cunning that secures their reputation not only against attack, but even suspicion.

They usually predict such things as in the natural order of events would be most likely to take place: such, for instance, as changes in the weather, abundance or scarcity of game, visits from strangers, marriage, sickness, death, &c., and it is perfectly consistent with the doctrine of chances that they should, as they often do, turn out correct. The Indians, however, never take this view of the subject, but in general give full credit to the pretensions or absurd ability of their prophets. Sometimes they predict so falsely as to be detected: in such case, they totally lose their character and influence in the tribe, and are contemned as the abusers of sacred things, and offenders against the goodness of the Great Spirit.

When they are possessed of popular qualities, such as bravery and skill in war, great strength and vigor of body, eloquence, &c. they exercise an almost unlimited power over the minds and actions of the Indians, not only in their own, but in other tribes, their allies or friends. Such, for a time, were Tecumseh and Francis, the celebrated Shawanee prophets,* whose patriotic and magnanimous designs, connected with their own country, were too vast for their means of execution, and involved them and many of their abettors in consequences too generally known to require any detail in this place.

The opinions of the Kansas and Osages are very similar on this subject; though some difference prevails in their various ceremonials, which, however, is not sufficient to bring in question their common origin. The Shawanees, I have understood, dispense with many of these ceremonies, and are much more credulous to their soothsayers and fortune-tellers, who are much more numerous, and are held in higher estimation among them, than is usually the case in any of the other tribes. They are also in great credit among many of the white people on the frontiers; and some of them travel, and make a living in the practice of their arts among them; but such generally become dissipated and lose their standing, both abroad and at home.

I have before mentioned that the Indians place great reliance on dreams. When any difficulty arises in regard to their interpretation, recourse is had to the prophets or old men, who generally aim to put a favorable construction on all, but particularly on those which excite the greatest apprehensions. The motive for this conduct no doubt grows out of a sympathetic feeling; and it ought to be regarded commendable, on account of the relief thus extended to anxious and highly perturbed minds, which, in violation of these sleeping inspirations, could hardly be brought to cooperate with the body for their mutual preservation, or for that of any of their dependents. Indeed, I have known several instances in which an Indian has postponed his hunts for several succeeding nights, notwithstanding his family were in want, rather than go without the auspices of a favorable dream. They sometimes dream of combats with the wounded buffalo, elk, or buck; which serve to make the Indians more cautious; and should they afterwards experience any danger, whether resembling them or not, they are sure, in the fertility of their imaginations, to trace out a connection which, they conceive, lays them under very particular obligations to their invisible protector.

Should their dreams be partially or wholly verified, the horn of the animal, or something connected with the circumstance, is consecrated among their sacred things, and preserved with the most assiduous care, as an amulet possessed of the occult power of procuring safety to its proprietor against evil spirits, and every kind of disease and danger.

On some occasions the more artful avail themselves of imputed dreams to secure their right to valuables against the solicitations of others, and, at the same time, to avoid the reproach of being avaricious, a quality uniformly unpopular among the Indians.

It is considered a moral crime to part with anything which has been so consecrated. Almost every lodge contains something of the kind; and whenever any suffering does befall its inmates, the cause is ascribed to their own misconduct, which, they say, has been so great as to paralyze their efficacy.

That the Indians should regard their prophets as the oracles of mysterious Heaven to benighted man, and dreams or sleeping reveries as divine visitations, cannot be regarded as extraordinary, since every nation and people on the face of the earth, of which history has taken any notice, have, in a greater or less degree, entertained and conformed their conduct to similar notions. It is true, the progressive march of reason has very much dispelled the ridiculous and absurd opinions of supernatural agency, and pointed out the causes of the delusion; nevertheless, I think I may say, without the fear of contradiction, that nearly one half of the population, in countries where the mental faculties have been most perfectly developed, still advocate and believe in their existence, and virtual influence.

3
Courtship, Marriage, Widowhood, Polygamy, Divorcements, Continuance of Families, Adoption of Children, Indian Names, Disposition of the Infirm and Poor

The young Indians are led, both by precept and example, to adopt the married life; and instances of celibacy very rarely continue, more particularly on the part of the males, much beyond the period of mature puberty. Old bachelors, settled in their towns and villages, are a race of beings altogether unknown. I have, however, known a few, who led a wandering life, sometimes attaching themselves to one tribe, and sometimes to another, accordingly as they happen to be engaged in war. They were renowned warriors, and on that account much sought for whenever any hostile operations were to be carried on against the enemies of their country or its allies.

The Indians ascribe the cause of their not marrying to their love of glory, which is only to be acquired, in their opinion, by deeds of valor in the deadly combat: "the possession of a family and fixed home," they say, "would restrain their inclinations and fetter their movements." The squaws are not so liberal in their apologies for such anomalous conduct but ascribe it either to moral or physical imperfections.

Early marriages are more frequent in the tribes bordering on the white settlements, than in those which are more remotely situated; and the practice is encouraged by the old men, with a view to diminish the tendency to habits of intercourse with the traders, &c. which is frequently followed by virulent diseases, that occasionally baffle all their skill in the healing art, and produce the most distressing consequences. The old Indians say, when they were young, that they did not marry, nor even think of being called men, till they were upwards of twenty winters old, and had distinguished themselves in encounters or engagements with the enemies of their tribe; that this innovation on their ancient customs, together with the use of ardent spirits, and their intercourse with the whites, had introduced many diseases among them that formerly were altogether unknown, enervated the warriors, caused the Indians to be more indolent, quarrelsome, and wicked, and materially shortened the period of their existence.

There is very little difference in the circumstances of the Indians generally, and as polygamy is tolerated to any extent commensurate with the means which the husband may possess for subsisting his family, an unmarried Indian woman over the age of twenty-three or four years, is very seldom to be met with in any of the tribes which I have visited. The females commonly marry at about the same age as the males, though sometimes much earlier in life. They esteem celibacy as a misfortune and disgrace, and indeed for a squaw to live perpetually single among the Indians, she must be possessed of a very forbidding person, as sometimes is the case from the effects of the smallpox, or some other deforming disease, or of a demoniac disposition, which tallies with the fact, whenever instances of the kind occur.

There is less restraint among the sexes in savage, than in civilized life: the Indians generally reside in towns, and the young men, when not engaged in war, hunting, traveling excursions, &c., have it in their power to, and do associate with the females; and although some of the tribes are more particular, and provide separate apartments for those of different sexes to sleep in; yet, among the largest portion, no arrangements of this kind are made; and the custom of males and females sleeping indiscriminately together in the same lodge, prevails without the thought or association of an idea of impropriety, or a breach of decorum. It was thus with the amiable Ruth of old, who lay at the feet of Boaz; and no doubt the same practice prevailed in all countries in the infancy of civilization. As this advanced, the contaminating influence of luxuries and refinement polluted the simplicity and purity of primeval manners, and deranged their harmony with the most atrocious crimes.

The custom which tolerates this intimacy among the Indians, exists without producing any criminal desire; and we find chastity as common a virtue among those Indians who have not been corrupted by an intercourse with the whites, as it is, or ever has been, among any people on earth. Indeed, the reason why travelers, who have visited the Indians, so liberally accuse their females of an opposite trait of character, is not because they are less virtuous than the females of civilized life, but because their innocence and artlessness render them more liable to become the dupes of accomplished villains; and because when they have transgressed, they do not become outcasts, but retain their standing in society, thus inducing the appearance that the practice is generally tolerated. Such, however, is not the fact among tribes remote from, and holding very little intercourse with the traders, &c., and but in a very limited degree so, where some of this class have exercised full sway to the extent of their power. Wherever such has been the case, great allowance ought to be made for the demoralizing effect of ardent spirits,, which, no doubt, have been a more potent negotiator, than all others combined, including even their own natural propensities or desires; which, notwithstanding all that has been written by various authors, who pretend to be well acquainted with the subject, I do not believe are as great in general among the Indians, as are incident to civilized life.* The difference in the modes of living, including food, amusements, and intercourse, I think, will support my opinion satisfactorily, in the minds of all who will take the trouble to investigate their influence.

Seduction is regarded as a despicable crime, and more blame is attached to the man, than to the woman, when instances of the kind occur: hence, the offense on the part of the female is more readily forgotten and forgiven, and she finds little or no difficulty, as before noticed, in forming a subsequent matrimonial alliance when deserted by her betrayer, who is generally regarded with distrust and avoided in social intercourse.

Formerly, if what the Indians say may be relied on, illegitimate births seldom occurred in any of the tribes. But, since the white people have appeared among them, the character of their females has suffered a modification, and instances have become more frequent.

Though this is a subject for regret, it is not much to be wondered at, since base and profligate men successfully practice their seductive wiles, in all the various walks of civilized life; and since the patients [i.e., victims] to these artifices among the Indians have not had their minds fortified with those wholesome axioms that keep pace with crime in civilized society, no matter how rapid and bold it may stride.

It is considered disgraceful for a young Indian publicly to prefer one woman to another, until he has distinguished himself either in war or in the chase; though attachments between the sexes are frequently formed during childhood, which are as lasting as life, but are never made generally known until the candidates are thought fit subjects for, and about to enter into, the matrimonial state.

When a young Indian becomes attached to a female, he does not frequent the lodge of her parents, or visit her elsewhere, oftener, perhaps, than he would, provided no such attachment existed. Were he to pursue an opposite course before he had acquired either the reputation of a warrior or hunter, and suffer his attachments to be known or suspected by any personal attention, he would be sure to suffer the painful mortification of a rejection; he would become the derision of the warriors, and the contempt of the squaws. On meeting, however, she is the first, excepting the elderly people, who engages his respectful and kind inquiries; after which no conversation passes between them, except it be with the language of the eyes, which, even among savages, is eloquent, and appears to be well understood.

The next indication of serious intentions on the part of the young

Indian, is his assumption of more industrious habits. He rises by daybreak, and, with his gun or bow, visits the woods or prairies, in search of the most rare and esteemed game. He endeavors to acquire the character of an expert and industrious hunter, and whenever success has crowned his efforts, never fails to send the parents of the object of his affections, some of the choicest he has procured. His mother is generally the bearer, and she is sure to tell from what source it comes, and to dilate largely on the merits and excellencies of her son. The girl, on her part, exercises all her skill in preparing it for food, and, when it is cooked, frequently sends some of the most delicious pieces, accompanied by other small presents, such as nuts, moccasins, &c., to her lover. These negotiations are usually carried on by the mothers of the respective parties, who consider them confidential, and seldom divulge them even to the remaining parents, except one or both of the candidates should be the offspring of a chief, when a deviation from this practice is exacted, and generally observed.

Instances sometimes happen wherein the parties themselves negotiate; but then, it is generally believed, the maternal parents are consulted. and are privy to their progress.

After an Indian has acquired the reputation of a warrior, expert hunter, or swift runner, he has little need of minor qualifications, or of much address or formality in forwarding his matrimonial views. The young squaws sometimes discover their attachments to those they love, by some act of tender regard; but more frequently through the kind offices of a confidant or friend. Such overtures generally succeed but, should they fail, it is by no means considered disgraceful, or in the least disadvantageous to the female; on the contrary, should the object of her affections have distinguished himself, especially in battle, she is more esteemed, on account of the judgment she displayed in her partiality for a respectable and brave warrior. With such, the squaws generally deem a connection highly desirable and honorable; and it often happens, that the same individual finds himself favored with an opportunity of making choice from several, which is seldom suffered to pass unimproved; indeed, I have known instances of their having accommodated the greatest part, and even the whole number of applicants, who entered upon their new relations, and discharged their respective duties, in the most perfect harmony and good fellowship.

A state of widowhood is extremely unpleasant among the squaws. I have repeatedly known them to meet a returning war party, at a considerable distance from their villages, and, finding their husbands had fallen in battle, after pulling their hair, tearing their flesh, and beating themselves in the most frantic manner, to lay siege to some favorite warrior, and not suffer him to depart till he had promised to revenge the death of their deceased husbands. Promises given in this manner, are considered as matrimonial engagements of the most sacred kind, and are never violated. After the death of her husband, the sooner a squaw marries again, the greater respect and regard she is considered to show for his memory; and should the subject of her recent connection be able individually to retaliate the promised revenge, it is considered the greatest possible mark of attachment, and a much greater favor than though her enemy had fallen by the same individual totally disconnected with her, or by the hand of some other person. Such a female courtier feels the mortification of a refusal much more sensibly than a maiden applicant, and laments it sincerely and deeply, because it deprives her of the opportunity of demonstrating the strength of her attachment to her deceased husband.

I have known mothers greatly advanced in years make interest for their daughters on such occasions, and generally with success.

Indeed, nothing can exceed their solicitude at such times, particularly if the deceased was their own son.

These suits are generally soon terminated: if the warrior approves of the overture, he readily and cheerfully assents to the proposal; and if otherwise, he postpones the consideration of the subject for another time: the meaning of which is, that the proposed alliance is not agreeable. Sometimes these offers are renewed through different channels, and the first decision is reversed; but in case it finally fails, the party making the offer usually sends presents to the rejecting one, as a token that no enmity exists, and that they wish for a continuance of friendly relations. Intermarriages between families that are not on friendly terms seldom take place: so that the opposition of parents is an obstacle not often experienced in the formation of these alliances. . . . The chiefs generally bestow their children, particularly their daughters, in marriage, on such as they prefer. Sometimes they form alliances with the families of the chiefs of some of the neighboring friendly tribes, but more frequently with the distinguished warriors and families of their own.

They, however, are never peremptory, and, when the proposed marriage is disagreeable, the parties are generally governed by their own inclinations.

When the preliminaries for a marriage have been agreed upon, which amount to nothing more than the conviction of the parents that a suitable attachment exists between the parties, and that they are qualified, competent, and willing, to perform their respective duties in the new relations they are about to form, the connections and friends of the parties are invited by the parents to attend the ceremony at the residence of the bride.

On this occasion, after the guests are assembled, the young Indian takes his intended by the wrist; occupies a central situation in regard to the party, and, in a standing position, candidly proclaims the affectionate attachment he entertains for her, promises to protect her and provide her with game, and at the same time presents her with some comparatively imperishable part of a buffalo, elk, deer, &c. as a pledge of his faithful performance. The female, on her part, makes a similar declaration of attachment; promises to cultivate the corn, &c., transact the other offices of her station, and pledges the faithful performance, by presenting her husband an ear of corn, or some other article to which it becomes her province to attend. The new married couple are now greeted with the kind wishes of all present; and the remainder of the day, and a part, or the whole of the following night, is passed in feasting, mirth, and festivity.

The party separates as suits their inclination, leaving the young couple to receive the visits of those friends who could not attend, or were not invited to the wedding; a ceremony usually observed, to show, at least, that no hostile or inimical feelings exist. These visits are next returned, and, in fact, extended to all their relations and friends. After a few days have elapsed, more or less of the warriors or hunters, according to the respectability and standing of the recently married Indian, assemble and construct him a house or lodge, which is soon furnished with presents from their particular friends. The parties now remove to their new home, and enter upon the discharge of their respective duties.

No people enjoy more unalloyed pleasure at such meetings; and, though they frequently indulge to excess, they suffer less from their irregularities than the white people settled along their frontiers do on such occasions. Where they have no ardent spirits, they usually retire more orderly, and in better time.

In the marriage ceremonies there is considerable difference in the same tribe; and this difference is very much influenced by the age and condition of the parties. Sometimes it is performed by merely an exchange of pledges or tokens, similar to those above described, which, it may here be remarked, are carefully preserved as a record of their marriage. At other times, particularly where there is considerable disparity in the age of the parties, or where an Indian already has several wives, little or no ceremony is observed. The parties having come to an understanding, the new wife is provided with a separate lodge, as is uniformly the practice on such occasions, and the Indian makes as kind and provident a husband, as though the whole tribe had witnessed their union in the most formal manner.

It has already been remarked that the tribes bordering on the white settlements are anxious for, and encourage early marriages; by this, however, I do not mean to be understood that any relaxation of disposition exists among the tribes more remotely situated; but only that this disposition is procrastinated, till, in fact, the young men assume the character, and discharge, or are competent to discharge, the duties of the warrior. The motives which lead to it, also, spring from a widely different source. It is the strength, importance, and character of their tribe or nation, their ambition for a superior ascendancy in dominion and war, or the policy of those who are really weak to attempt to match the more powerful, that cause their old men particularly to advocate the early entrance into, and the continued maintenance of the marriage state, through all the changes to which they are liable, either from custom or the chances of war.

These motives have been so long adhered to, that the habit has assumed the character of a sacred duty or obligation.

Experience has taught the Indians that this mode of life is most conducive to individual happiness, and to the objects to which they aspire; therefore, all who adopt it, are regarded with moral and natural feelings of pride. The squaw is esteemed in proportion to the number of children she raises, particularly if they are males, and prove brave warriors; otherwise, she attracts no marked respect, and, should any of them act cowardly, she is openly charged with having been remiss in her duty as a mother, respecting their early education. When instances of this kind happen, disgrace is certain to follow, and the mother would a thousand times prefer to hear of the death of her son, than that he had acted cowardly in battle.

POLYGAMY. The Indians, regarding themselves as the lords of the earth, look down upon the squaws as an inferior order of beings, especially given them by the Great Spirit, to rear up their families; to take charge of, and, with the exception of game, to provide for the household: and the squaws, accustomed to such usage, cheerfully acquiesce in it as a duty. To become the legitimate mother of a warrior, and to discharge the offices of a wife, are objects of the greatest solicitude with them; and to be disappointed in these respects is to them a subject of deep distress. This circumstance, joined to their warlike disposition and the necessity that consequently exists in the opinion of the Indians for constantly repairing the losses to which they are always liable, and which they frequently sustain, probably gave rise to the toleration of polygamy; at least, they appear to be proximate causes; though remotely, no doubt, it originated in arbitrary inclination or caprice.

The Indians in general have but one wife; though they, as well as the chiefs and distinguished warriors, may have more according to their inclination and ability to support their different families. They frequently amount to two or three, and sometimes to more.

Clermont and Was-saw-be-ton-ga, each had four, and O-kon-now was remarkable for having six or seven. The wives of the former had about twenty children, and those of the latter seventeen or eighteen.

They construct lodges at a short distance one from another, for the accommodation of their different wives, who fulfill the respective duties of mother and wife separately, occasionally visit each other, and generally live on the most friendly terms. The chief or warrior takes up his residence with the one he most esteems, and only leaves her, to reside with the next in favor, during the periods of her pregnancy and lactation. The one with whom the husband resides, considers it her duty and interest, and is ambitious, to discharge all the offices pertaining to a wife, so far as regards his comfort and convenience; and any interference with her on the part of his other wives, except in case of sickness or inability, is regarded as a just cause for offense.

Where any difference exists between the wives of an Indian, he is sometimes appealed to by the offended party; he does not, however, interfere in their affairs, but leaves them to settle their own disputes, which oftentimes terminate in his separating from some one of them.

DIVORCEMENTS. As the Indians enter into the marriage state for the mutual happiness and comfort of the parties concerned, no obligation exists for remaining in it for a longer period than these objects are secured. They say, whenever a continuance in this state becomes disagreeable to either one or both, the purposes of the original contract are defeated; and instead of its being a source, it is the very bane of happiness, and renders the parties miserable. wIt isE a result contrary to the design of all contracts, which are, or ought to be, made for their mutual benefit, instead of the reverse.

They, therefore, neither feel any compunction, nor find any difficulty from their companions or connections, in effecting a separation whenever such a measure has a tendency to gratify their inclinations, or promote their happiness. But, independent of these notions, they possess, and are governed in these transactions by more elevated motives. They generally regard every circumstance of their lives as influenced by two orders of supernatural beings, *viz.* Good and Bad Spirits, which have already been noticed under an appropriate head. To these they ascribe the immediate agency of all their happiness and misery, all their pleasures and pain.

Therefore, whenever the men or women, for in instances of this kind there is no exclusive privilege, are dissatisfied or unhappy with their matrimonial companion, they place it to the account of some malign spirit, which, they say, takes delight in tormenting them, and will not cease so long as they continue to maintain their present condition, and hence do not suffer much time to elapse before they effect a separation.

An Indian, when about to leave his wife, conducts himself very distantly towards her; goes on his hunting or other excursions without naming them, or the time of his return; maintains a sullen silence towards his own connections, but most generally hints his dissatisfaction to those of his wife. During this time, if a separation should be disagreeable to his companion, she appears exceedingly solicitous to atone for any misconduct of her own, and uses every possible means in her power to conciliate her husband, and regain his affections and regard, which very frequently are attended with the sought-for result. But should she fail in her endeavors, her husband, after burying the pledge he received at their marriage, deserts her altogether, and never after is heard to mention her name. She is branded as a bad squaw, but, nevertheless, soon finds another husband, to whom she usually proves an excellent wife, to avoid, perhaps, the repetition of a similar mortification and suffering. Repudiated squaws are more anxious to marry than any others, in order to do away the disgrace they are conceived to labor under. On occasions of this kind the squaw is left in possession of the lodge, &c., and generally of all the children, though the husband sometimes takes one or two of the boys, provided they are of a sufficient size not to require the further care of a mother.

Separations are, however, very rare, especially after the parents have much of a family. After separating, the husband usually goes on a long hunting excursion, or visits a neighboring tribe. And even thus late I have known successful overtures to a reconciliation, made either by the wife or some of her friends, and the husband to return again to his family. Such instances, however, do not often occur; he most frequently returns to his tribe, and forms a new connection, though sometimes he intermarries and incorporates himself with some other.

When a chief or distinguished warrior parts with his wife, attempts at reconciliation are not frequently made; because the wife having in the discharge of her duties exhausted every effort to obtain or maintain a preference in the good opinion of her husband, has few resources left to bring into operation on these extraordinary occasions. Nevertheless, there are some exceptions, in which they have been known to restore their repudiated wives to favor. Usually they exercise less ceremony, and appear to feel less, than the other Indians do on similar occasions.

These circumstances may be plausibly accounted for, in the greater facility they find in procuring wives, and in the greater number they possess.

When a female is disposed to leave her husband, she burns or destroys the pledge she received at her wedding, deserts his lodge, and returns with her family and effects to her parents, or some of her near relations. Under such circumstances she finds no difficulty in marrying again, and in general she soon commences the duties of a wife, under the protection of another husband.

Jealousy is a passion but little known, and much less indulged, among the Indians. Their principal causes for divorcements are indolence, intemperance, cowardice, impotence, and sterility. I have never known a single instance of either the two last, and their existence must be exceedingly rare.

OF CONTINUING FAMILIES, AND ADOPTION OF CHILDREN AND OTHERS. Whenever a distinguished warrior falls in battle, or otherwise, it is considered a great privilege to marry his squaw; and whoever does, is obliged to assume the name of her former husband, and to sustain, as far as possible, his reputation and character. This custom of continuing families is indulged to a considerable extent; sometimes the brother of the deceased becomes the husband; but the most frequent source of continuance is from the prisoners taken in battle, who, but for this kind of preferment, are generally condemned to suffer tortures and death.

The squaw who has lost her husband, makes the election herself; the warrior thus chosen generally accedes to the offer, assumes the name of the deceased, and attaches himself to his new wife, and to her tribe: sometimes, however, he rejects the overture, and in preference magnanimously, as he supposes, submits to the tortures and persecutions of his tormentors, among the foremost of which the slighted and offended squaw is often found.

The motives of the Indians for keeping up families, originate in part in the respect entertained for the deceased, but much more in policy; for by the custom fecundity is promoted, and a kind of provision secured to the sufferers, which does not in any way encroach on the public interests or solicitude: besides, it removes all apprehensions for family welfare and happiness from the mind of the warrior, who thus circumstanced, and otherwise conformably educated, goes to battle under the strongest belief that no change, except that of disgrace, can possibly happen to him for the worse. But, nevertheless, they are as sincerely attached to, and feel as great interest and solicitude for their families as any other people whatever; and I am convinced would, were it not for their customs, be influenced on their account in times of peril, so as materially to alter their warlike characters.

The young Indians are regarded as national property; as the source from which all their losses in war, or otherwise, are to be repaired, and by which they are to maintain their importance, or arrive at greater distinction. Hence, they engross the most earnest attention and care of those who have entered upon the active duties of war and the chase. In fact, a solicitude is manifested even before birth, in respect to sex; and this increases according to circumstances, till the character be developed in manhood. This interest for the young males, connected with the objects above noticed, has many important bearings on the customs of the Indians. It removes from obloquy those females who become parents out of wedlock; it prevents, in a great degree, the procurement of abortions; and it is also the reason why the children and women taken prisoners are preserved, and adopted, especially into such families among their captors as have lost any of their numbers, either by sickness or war.

This is done without much ceremony; some trifling presents are generally made them, and in common they receive names similar to those for whom they have been substituted.

They mutually make promises of love and regard for each other, which in general they faithfully perform, and appear to become as sincerely attached, as though they were really connected by consanguinity. The adopted warriors nevertheless sometimes abscond, but should they afterwards be taken in arms fighting against their adopted tribe, their lives most generally atone for the offense.

OF INDIAN NAMES. Since the Indians are so scrupulous in keeping up families, it appears somewhat singular that they should all be distinguished by their maternal names, till some act of prowess, intrepidity, or skill, entitles them to others of their own choice.

But, apart from the natural propriety, it must on reflection be acknowledged judicious; because it elicits a very early ambition in youth, to create by their own efforts meritorious names for themselves; which are generally changed for others on the occurrence of some remarkable incidents, and serve as so many records of the bravery and worth of respective families—circumstances that are particularly regarded by the chiefs and respectable warriors, when they make choice of wives.

In the cowardice or bad conduct of an Indian, his mother, sister, or daughter suffers in a degree, and their chances for a respectable marriage are diminished; because the Indians think that good and bad qualities may be both inherited and entailed, though, as before observed, with proper management, they think that their faults may be wholly corrected. The blame in such instances is charged on the squaws, who are accused with a negligence of duty towards their children in early life, and, probably, on pretty good grounds. For the Indians, who are nice observers, say, that a squaw who loves her country and reputation, and does her duty, can never be the mother of a bad Indian.

The Indians, as just noticed, are known frequently to change their own names as they grow older, and incidents of sufficient consequence occur to justify the measure; and sometimes names are bestowed by common consent, on characters either notoriously good or bad. But in all cases they are intended as representations or remembrances of the particular events, qualities, or actions, of particular individuals, and in general they are appropriate and judicious.

DISPOSITION OF THE INFIRM AND POOR. Each warrior makes provision for the aged, infirm, and needy, which are nearly related to him; and, where it is not wholly beyond his power, for those also more remotely connected. This, in general, is not a severe duty, since the hunters divide their game, when this form is observed, in proportion to the individuals of each family.

They are very assiduous and attentive to the wants and comforts particularly of the aged, and kind to all who require their assistance. And an Indian who failed in these respects, though he otherwise merited esteem, would be neglected and despised. To the credit of their morals few such are to be found, except where debauched by the vices of the white people.

Whenever the helpless are too numerous for their natural protectors, they are distributed in the same manner that is observed in respect to their orphans, as will presently be noticed.

Women who have not been married, and those who have separated from, or lost their husbands, live with or return to their parents or connections, where they assist in the ordinary duties of the females. The children of such generally accompany their mothers; but orphan children are adopted into other families, and virtually become constituent members of them.

Whenever a widowed mother sickens and is considered to be in danger, the warriors, immediately related to her, exhibit great concern for her children; take them to their lodges; and, in case of her death, adopt and bring them up. But should there be no relations, there is always a sufficient number of applicants, and generally from the most respectable of the tribe, who adopt and bring them up as their own.

Where such individuals are adopted into families, a mutual confidence is sure to follow; and the same respectful attentions, obedience, and affections, appear to exist between the factitious [i.e., adoptive], as is common among the natural members.

4

Family Government, Occupation, and Economy; Birth, Nursing and Education of Infants; Education and Amusements of Youth; Games of Chance, Modes of Salutation; Treatment of Strangers; Forms of Visits, Feasts, Festivals, &c.

In the government of their families, the management of their lodges, and in the transactions of all their duties, the squaws are sole mistresses. Whenever the husband requires anything, he has but to name it, and his squaw immediately complies with his wishes. These intimations, however, only extend to his own or his friends' individual wants and comforts, and are often anticipated. The slightest deviation from this line of conduct on her part, would be considered a just cause of offense, and, if not corrected, lead to a separation. Although the women, especially in their towns and villages, are employed in attending to their children, cultivating their fields, collecting wood, water, &c., they do not think their task more severe than that of the men.

However, in civilized life, where people are educated differently, and conform to different regulations, a concurrence with them in opinion is not very likely to prevail: but, before final judgment be passed, regard should be had to the two modes of life. Those qualifications which render their possessors ornaments in civilized life would be esteemed altogether useless, not to say contemptible, in the views of the savages. While nothing but the most urgent necessity could induce civilized man to submit to an almost continual state of warfare, to long marches, fastings, and exposures, to procure a subsistence. But relatively, each conform to the peculiarities of their own respective modes of life, with a zealous preference. The white people commiserate the Indians, on account of their thousand misfortunes and sufferings, and congratulate themselves on the superior privileges and blessings they enjoy. The Indians reverse the position, and thank the Great Spirit for not having made them white, and subjected them to the drudgery of civilized life.

In order to maintain their existence, the Indians are obliged to become skillful and expert in war and the chase; and, to qualify or accomplish themselves for these pursuits, becomes an avocation both of pleasure and duty; and until they acquire celebrity, no people on earth pursue the objects of their ambition with greater zeal and industry. As they become older, and their characters are established, habits of indolence succeed; and nothing but the most stimulating and urgent incidents, such as revenge, war, or hunger, can rouse them to action. To this trait there are occasional exceptions, in which the warriors, from a playful condescension, are seen to mingle with, and assist the squaws in almost all their varied occupations; or when grown old, to devote themselves to the education of the youths.

The course of life pursued by the Indians is necessarily attended with exposure and loss of life; with mutilations and peril; and with great deprivations and fatigue, which lay the foundation for, and are frequently followed by many distressing diseases, from which the women are comparatively exempted. With these circumstances, and their particular bearings, the squaws are well acquainted; they also know that they are not physically qualified to contend with the men for the prize of distinction.

Therefore they cheerfully submit, and from necessity must, at least so long as the present sentiments of the Indians prevail, to till the ground, perform the menial offices, and content themselves with acquiring as respectable a standing in their tribes, and in the esteem of the men, as a life of obedience and submission can procure. Custom has sanctified this, and nature has kindly furnished them with the means and ability to perform their task, which, as before observed, they neither think severe nor difficult, particularly where game is abundant, and the soil productive, and of easy cultivation. Nor, in fact, are they: for except in planting and harvest times, which only last a few days, they have more than half their time leisure, which is devoted to visiting and instructive amusements, in which their children generally are conspicuous agents.

The women of some tribes, however, have much more to perform than in others. This is particularly observable of those who live in towns and villages, where wood is scarce, the earth cultivated, and game has to be brought from a distance; while those who rove, generally encamp in the neighborhood of wood and water, and follow and subsist on game.

The latter, however, where horses are scarce, carry great burdens, perform long marches, and experience many more privations, and fewer comforts.

In some of the tribes, the men pack in the game; while in others, the task is imposed on the squaws, and is cheerfully performed by them as a part of their duty. This practice, no doubt, had its origin in necessity: the greater exertions of the men being required in hunting, and defending their territories from the encroachment of their enemies.

The women and children, both male and female, plant, cultivate, and gather in the crops; collect the wild rice, nuts, roots, &c.; procure wood and water; dress buffalo robes, and other skins; manufacture sugar, pottery, mats, waistcloths, moccasins and leggings; pound the corn; and prepare or cook the food, &c., &c.; and to intermeddle in any of their concerns, to wrangle with, or inflict a blow on any of them, the warriors think is disgraceful, and descending from their own elevated character to the degraded one of the squaw. But, notwithstanding, since whiskey has been introduced among them, a great portion of the Indians disregard, or forget to maintain this distinctive dignity; and, while under its influence, are often guilty of beating them most severely.

Wrought on by the same magic, the squaws as often retaliate on their inoffensive children; and when an abundance of this article is attainable, and freely distributed among them, these scenes of castigations extend widely; and are accompanied with such a medley of shrieks and jargon, that a spectator, in his sober senses, might, without any extraordinary efforts of his imagination, suppose himself in a community of bedlamites. (See page 25.) In common, however, the women, to whom, as I have previously noticed, the government of the children is submitted, are judicious and wise disciplinarians. And to do justice to the character of the Indians, there are many among them, particularly their chiefs and old men, who observe the strictest regimen in their food and drinks, and never indulge in any species of excess. In fact, I have known them first to exercise persuasion, and then authority, to prevent intemperance among their people; and finally, when these failed, and the traders persisted in selling their liquor, to demolish the vessels which contained it, and thus, for the time, effectually to arrest a propensity that they could not otherwise control.

But to return again to our subject. The squaws raise for the consumption of their families, corn, tobacco, pumpkins, squashes, melons, gourds, beans, peas, and, within a few years past, potatoes in small quantities. They collect hazelnuts, hickory nuts, walnuts, chestnuts, pecan nuts, grass or ground nuts, various kinds of acorns, wild licorice, sweet myrrh, or anise root, and Pash-e-quah, a large bulbous root somewhat resembling the sweet potato in form, and very similar to the chestnut in flavor, though more juicy.

They also collect, in their seasons, crab and may apples, Osage oranges, three or four kinds of plums, strawberries, gooseberries, whortleberries [huckleberries], black- and dew-berries, and a great variety of grapes.

All their various products, as well as those of the chase, are, in general, distributed in proportion to the members of each family concerned in their acquirement; though sometimes no distribution takes place, but all draw, as they want, from the supplying source, as a common reservoir, till it is exhausted.

After a distribution has taken place, the various articles are carefully preserved by the respective proprietors; the corn in cribs, constructed of small poles and bark of trees; potatoes in the ground; tobacco on small rods; nuts, &c., either in sacks or cribs; and oil, honey, &c., in skins; all [of] which are contained in their cabins or lodges.

Whenever a scarcity prevails, they reciprocally lend, or rather share with each other, their respective stores, till they are all exhausted. I speak now of those who are provident, and sustain good characters.

When the case is otherwise, the wants of such individuals are regarded with comparative indifference; though their families share in the stock, [which] becomes otherwise common from the public exigency. Under such circumstances, the warriors cheerfully surrender their whole share of eatables to the women, children, and infirm, and submit without complaint to privations, which often materially affect their health, and sometimes threaten their very existence. Such instances, however, rarely happen, and when they do, it is either in the winter, early spring, or during the prevalence of long-continued tempestuous weather. I have known the warriors forced to subsist for days together on roots, and the bark and sap of trees. The Indians generally are good providers, though the duties of the chase are from choice usually performed by the youth, or young men.

If they took sufficient care in preserving their animal food, a scarcity would seldom, if ever, be experienced. But, once engaged in their hunts, their feelings are too much engrossed to attend to so subordinate employments, as those of drying and smoking their meats.

This essential operation being neglected, or too much hurried, occasions great losses, especially as the warm weather comes on in the spring; and I have known a severe scarcity to prevail from this very circumstance. In cooking, they resort to various simple modes. The most prevalent is that of roasting, which is effected by enveloping the meat first in leaves, and then in ashes and burning coals: dressed in this way, it possesses a juicy sweetness not rivaled by any other process with which I am acquainted. They frequently broil it on embers, and sometimes roast, by suspending it by a vine before the fire. But, next to baking, the practice of boiling their meats with vegetables most generally prevails. From their unripe corn recently gathered or dried, other vegetables, and bear's oil, buffalo's fat or marrow, they also prepare a very nutritive, and when meat and spices are superadded, as is frequently the case, a very savory and palatable food.

When the days are long and their supplies abundant, the grown people generally eat daily three meals; when the days are shorter, two; and when provisions are scarce, only one; and sometimes not even that.

The usual times of taking their meals, are at sunrise, noon, and sunset.

The children eat whenever they are hungry.

I have already remarked that the warriors suffer most during periods of scarcity; though from their deportment, their most intimate acquaintance might be led to suppose, that they feasted daily from the stores of plenty.

It is the common practice of the Indians, however closely pressed their appetites may be, to exercise patience; and I have frequently known them to return from long marches, in an almost famished condition, and sustain conversation with their friends for hours together, without giving the slightest intimation of their pressing exigencies.

In the summer, they usually cook their food in the open air; but in cool and wet weather, in their lodges; which are heated by fires built either on rocks, or in excavations of the earth, situated directly in their centers. Every individual supplies himself or is supplied with a separate dish and eating utensils, which are used on all ordinary occasions, and even taken to their feasts by them, and they are never exchanged or used by any, except the rightful owners. Their cabin furniture is very limited; they use neither stools nor tables, but generally sit cross-legged on mats or skins placed on the earth; in which position, when the weather is cold, they eat their meals around their fires; but when it is otherwise or tolerable, they take their food in the shade of trees, or in the open air. In general, the men eat by themselves; during their meals, they observe the most profound silence. They prefer their own articles of food, and modes of cooking, to any other; and even the traders, after they have become accustomed, are generally fond of, and also frequently prefer them.

In general, they are moderate eaters; but, when plenty succeeds a scarcity, they are too apt to indulge their appetites to excess, though the old men, and those who have suffered from such conduct, commonly exercise more forbearance or self-denial. Their usual drink is pure cold water; though sometimes they mix maple sugar with it, or honey, which they procure in considerable quantities from the stores of the honeybees, deposited in hollow trees; and at others they make agreeable teas from the leaves, roots, and bark of various spicy plants, which, unless they are indisposed, are suffered to cool before drunk.

Fermentation, in their opinion, spoils them, and whenever that takes place, they are always thrown away.

Their cooking utensils are few in number, and not various in form: they consist of pots and pans made of clay, and since their intercourse with the traders, of some castings. They make use of some tin pots, knives and spoons, also obtained from the traders; but in general, earthenware of their own make, gourd shells, and wooden spoons, bowls, and mortars, make up their stock of cooking and eating apparatus. In addition, however, each village has one or two large stone mortars for pounding corn; they are placed in a central situation, are public property, and are used in rotation by the different families. Their lodges, as before noticed, answer the purpose of storehouses: they also smoke their skins, and frequently their meats in them; and very little order is observed in the arrangement of their contents.

They sleep on skins, usually stretched on poles, and elevated a little above the ground, though sometimes they are laid directly on it.

They go to rest whenever nature prompts, which commonly is within an hour or two after sunset; and they rise about daybreak.

When not excited to action, they also sleep in the daytime; but, when watchfulness is necessary, they recline in nearly the same position without sleep, for forty or fifty hours at a time. The old people and young children sleep about one half, and those who perform the home duties perhaps one third of their time. . . .

When a young Indian woman, for the first time, is in travail, it is common for her mother, or some aged or experienced person to be in attendance. Afterwards, they commonly retire to lodges constructed for the purpose, and there patiently submit to natural operations, which, as before noticed, with regard to duration and suffering, scarcely deserve to be mentioned in comparison with what are commonly experienced in civilized life.

The performance of their duties is seldom interrupted for more than a day on such occasions; nevertheless, instances do sometimes occur in which they are confined for days and weeks together, by the milder forms of some diseases incident to labor.

Their infants, wrapped in skins, are secured with belts to a small thin piece of board placed along the back. As they grow older, should the weather be mild, the skins are removed altogether, and no other dresses are substituted for them, except in very cold weather, till near the period of puberty.

When traveling, the mother places the board to which the infant is secured on her back, and supports it in this manner for the whole distance of the journey. While resting, or at work, she suspends

Family Government, Birth, Education, Festivals, &c.   129

it perpendicularly from the side of her lodge, the arm of a tree, or a post she has erected for the purpose. She administers food to it when she thinks it is hungry, disregards its crying, and seldom unbinds and soothes it to rest, except when she herself retires for sleep.

When the temperature of the weather is mild, they bathe their children daily from their birth till they are able to walk alone, in order to make their skins hardy, and capable of resisting the extreme changes of the weather, to which they are more particuarly exposed in early life. When sufficiently old and strong, they wean and suffer them to run about: this is generally between the age of two and three years. They would, no doubt, deviate from this practice sometimes, did they not apprehend that such conduct would be stigmatized by a pair of bowed legs, which would bear witness against their parental care and good qualities to the whole tribe.

Should the child be a boy, this period is to the mother peculiarly interesting. She now takes it with her in all her visits, witnesses its playful, impassioned, or vindictive emotions and conduct, with its infantile fellows; and feels her soul bowed down with mortification and grief, or swelled with pride and joy, as she discovers the ignoble traits of cowardice, or the innate characters of courage, unfold themselves in the offspring of her hopes. Boys are seldom long together without quarreling, and pretty generally make a bold fight, though they are not permitted to continue it. Should the case be otherwise, the disappointed mother soon returns to her lodge and commences a very extraordinary discipline. She begins by placing a rod in his hand, assists him to beat and make flee the dog, or anything else that may come in his way, and then encourages him to pursue. An adept in this, she teases and vexes him, creates an irritable temper, submits to the rod, and flees before him with great apparent dread. When skilled in this branch, she strikes him with her hand, pulls his hair, &c., which her now *hopeful* boy retaliates in a spiteful and *becoming* manner. Some time having passed in this way, by which her pupil has learned to bear pain without dread, she takes him again on a visit, and I have never known an instance of a second disappointment in these trials of courage. They are then permitted to play with the other children of the village, and to quarrel and make up as well as they can.

After this conceived salutary course of discipline, the parents bring them back to their accustomed subjection, by a steady and determined course of government.

There is nothing connnected with the education of the female part of the children that requires to be noticed, except it be their early entrance with the boys into sports and amusements in imitation of the grown people. . . . Those in which they most frequently engage are the dances, which they soon learn to perform with accuracy, and with the same variety as practiced by the older ones. Running races, wrestling, jumping, and swimming, also engross much of their time. They perform these sports in a manner very similar to what is practiced among civilized people and therefore I shall not attempt their description. Playing the hoop is performed on an oblong level piece of ground, prepared for the purpose. Three parallel lines run the whole length of the plot, at about fifteen yards' distance from each other. On the exterior ones, the opposing parties, which generally consist of from twelve to eighteen persons, arrange themselves about ten paces apart, each individual fronting intermediate to his two opposite or nearest opponents. On the central line, extended a few paces beyond the wings of the two parties, stand two persons facing each other; it is their part of the play alternately to roll a hoop of about the diameter of a common hogshead, with all their strength, from one to the other. The object for triumph between these two is, who shall catch his opponent's hoop the oftenest, and of the contending parties, which shall throw the greatest number of balls through the hoop as it passes rapidly along the intervening space. Judges are appointed, usually from among the old men, to determine which party is victorious, and to distribute the prizes, which, on some particular occasions, consist of beaver and deer skins, moccasins, leggings, &c., but more usually of shells, nuts, and other trifles.

Throwing the tomahawk, and shooting with the bow, are practiced with great perseverance and zeal, and form no inconsiderable or unimportant part of their amusement. In regard to the first, the whole art consists in strength and precision, and in accommodating the motions of the arm and hand to the distance, so as invariably to cause the edge of the tomahawk to strike the mark, and it is attained to an astonishing degree of perfection by the Indians.

In sham battles, another of their amusements, all the feelings of the warrior are excited. The contending parties secrete themselves in the woods and prairie grass, and reciprocally practice on each other surprise and open attack, before or after which, as the case may be proper, the war-whoop is raised, and the feats of real warfare are imitated.

Councils are afterwards held, the pipe of peace smoked, and as much gravity observed as though the fate of the nation depended on their deliberations. These sports are finally terminated in the dance of peace, and other rejoicings, in which the young squaws usually take a part. All these various sports are encouraged and promoted by the older Indians, with the avowed purpose of qualifying the minds and habits, and preparing the bodies of the younger for the more important offices of war and hunting, to excel in which constitutes their first duty, and is the acme of their ambition.

The rest of the Indian's education, apart from what is acquired by experience, is obtained from the discourses of the aged warriors, who, from the services rendered their country, have high claims on its gratitude and respect. Such was Tshut-che-nau, as mentioned on page 15, and similar to his are the doctrines they generally teach. The elderly women also frequently perform these offices, more particularly as they relate to narratives and traditions, of which they are by the consent of custom the unerring and sacred depositories.

The young warriors, to the age of twenty-five or thirty years, occasionally amuse themselves with the boys in their plays; and sometimes they form parties entirely from their own numbers, bet high, at least for Indians, and contend with astonishing activity and skill for the mastery. This is one of their modes of gambling. But those commonly practiced by the older Indians are altogether different. In common, they merely burn on one side a few grains of corn or pumpkin seeds, which the stakers alternately throw up for a succession of times, or till one arrives to a given number first: that is, counting those only that show of the requisite color when he wins. A very similar game is played with small flat pieces of wood or bone, on one side of which are notched or burned a greater or less number of marks, like the individual faces of a die. It is played and counted like the preceding.

Besides these, they shoot the rifle and bow, and throw the tomahawk at marks, and perform various feats, frequently for no other purpose but to vary the chance or mode of their bets.

Some are extravagantly fond of games of chance, and play at them till they lose everything they possess, except their war accoutrements and consecrated things. In fact, a large majority of the Indians are fond of them, while there are a few to be met with who contemn, and are neither agents in, nor spectators of the practice.

The warriors are of taciturn and rather unsocial habits, which do not, however, proceed from any want of respect for those with whom they associate—as has often been charged to them by persons imperfectly acquainted with their character—but altogether from their education.

They say, to be garrulous and familiar is unbecoming the warrior and hunter, and only sufferable in old men, women, and children, whose duties are more trivial and relaxed.

In compliance with this custom, either at home, or on hunting, or war excursions, they observe an almost uninterrupted silence, and never condescend to become familiar, even with each other, except it be in their amusements with their particular friends, or at meetings of a public nature. I have already observed that great attention is paid to marked seniority, and this custom no doubt materially influences their taciturn dispositions.

Their usual mode of salutation is to take hold of the wrist, and give it a gentle shake. When there is a difference of age, it is performed first by the eldest, who always approaches for the performance of this ceremony with much confidence. When the individual first saluting is venerable from age, irreproachable character, and the achievement of many great actions, those but little inferior to him accompany theirs with a slight inclination of the body, while those who are young and more removed from him in their claims to respect, merely take hold of his robe, or some other article of his dress.

But in regard to their modes of salutation, as well as visits, custom is very indefinite as to forms. There are many ways in which respect may be shown by one to another, which cannot well be described, but which are daily practiced among the Indians; and for one to fail in courtesy where there are just claims for a demonstration of it, is generally regarded by them as a personal insult, or as characteristic of a vulgar mind.

When a stranger arrives among them, their first object is to ascertain whether he is friendly. In doing this, they do not so much rely on professions, as conduct. They therefore talk very little, eye him at first closely, and then observe all his movements and looks with apparent carelessness, till convinced of his sincerity and good will.

Satisfied in this respect, the Indians welcome him with a respectful and friendly attention, and make him a joint partaker in their comforts and pleasures. This conduct is particularly observable towards those who are in distress; I have known them to accompany those who have been indisposed, or had lost their way, for two or three days together. In fact, for a friend or a friendly stranger, they have no measure for their kindness and hospitality. The same may generally be said of their hatred and persecution of those whom they esteem their enemies, though instances have occurred in which their active sympathies have been awakened in favor of known enemies, who had become incapable of doing them any injury.

An Indian who has promised protection, or who feels himself obligated by the relations of friendship or hospitality to afford it, will assuredly do so; or at any rate, his lifeless body must be trampled under foot, before it can be violated, or the safety of his guest be disturbed.

One warrior seldom visits another, unless he has business, or is on very intimate terms. On entering a lodge, he is welcomed by the proprietor with the usual salutations. He then speaks a word or two to the individuals of the family, beginning with the eldest, and continuing downwards frequently to the younger branches; but, contrary to the forms observed in civilized life, the men engross his first attentions, and afterwards the women. He next mentions the individual his visit is for, sits perhaps half an hour engaged in conversation, has food offered, which he commonly eats, and then takes a general leave. During these visits the men commonly speak slowly, and are very dignified, though complaisant, in their demeanor.

The visits of the women are more frequent, continue longer, and are not often particularized. Consequently the conversations on these occasions are more general and brisk; otherwise they do not materially differ from those of the men. Their conversations, as in civilized life, turn in general on the incidents of the day, and their deviations from them relate mostly to subjects calculated to attract the attention, excite the curiosity, and stimulate the ambition of the germinating warriors, whose education, as repeatedly remarked, seems constantly to engross their solicitude. They are very emulous of excellence; hence to praise everything relating to themselves is one of the favorite topics of conversation among female visitors. I have frequently known them dispute who had the bravest husbands, whose sons were the most valiant in war and the chase, or the swiftest runners and most able to bear fatigue and hunger. They also frequently boast that they can carry the heaviest burden, make the best canoe, and raise the best corn. These conversations, as well as those of the men, are generally confined to those present, and when they do speak of those who are absent, it is of such as have recently lost friends, or experienced some other misfortune which appropriately calls forth an expression of their sympathies. Backbiting, or talking ill of those not present, is ranked by them amongst the blackest of their crimes and is never practiced or listened to by any who have claims to a good character.

Whenever a misunderstanding does occur, they never employ second-hand agents, but either secretly or openly chastise the aggressor. A contrary course of conduct would subject the insulted or aggrieved party to reproach and ridicule. Even the profligate look with contempt on the slanderer; while he is singled out with the finger of scorn by the more respectable, who shun him as they would the poisonous serpent, and hold no kind of intercourse with him. None will venture to traduce those who sustain a fair and honorable character, and as for the worthless, they never condescend to talk about them.

Slander, therefore, the most pitiful vice of little and malicious minds, is beneath the notice even of the Indian women, without reference to the men, whose notions of propriety are still more elevated. This noble trait in their character is highly worthy to be imitated by many of both sexes, who pretend to much higher claims in the scale of rational beings.

Another trait in the Indian character equally admirable and worthy of general adoption is, "never to meddle or interfere with the business of another."

Hence they have very few confidential stories or injunctions to secrecy to impose on their friends, and hence that freedom from broils and quarreling which so frequently disturb more complex societies.

The respect paid to the aged is not wholly confined to the men. On the contrary, the women come in for their share but then it is somewhat different in character. The aged warrior, who, by the prowess of his deeds, and the wisdom of his conduct, has acquired high reputation among the counsellors of his nation; who, bowed down with years, infirmities, and disease, is rapidly hastening to mingle the mechanism of his greatness with its parent earth; but who, nevertheless, is solicitous only for the happiness of his people, founded on the correct education of the rising generation with which he is constantly busied, receives as a just due the spontaneous homage of their highest respect and veneration. On the other hand, the aged female's claim to admiration and esteem rests on her having been an industrious, faithful, and obedient wife, and the parent and instructress of a race of valiant and distinguished warriors.

They are, in general, looked upon by the young females as patterns for imitation; but on some occasions, as, for instance, that of the corn feast, they exercise almost unlimited authority. The oldest and most respectable mother in the tribe prepares for, and conducts the ceremony. She also claims and exercises the privilege of informing her children, as she calls her tribe, when they may commence eating the green corn. Nor do the younger ones ever anticipate this permission.

She frequents the fields, daily examines the silks of the young spikes, and, when they become dry, plucks and prepares some of them in different ways, and then presents them to her friends.

Afterwards she decorates the doorway leading to her lodge with the husks of the recently gathered corn, which are regarded as signals for the approaching feast. The intelligence spreads rapidly, and the whole tribe, as it were, pass in review before her lodge to witness the welcome invitation.

Forthwith the young and the old, without regard to sex, are seen joyfully skipping and dancing to their respective fields, and the whole atmosphere resounds with shouts and songs appropriate to the occasion; they return in the same manner loaded with ears of green corn, which they either bury in the embers, still enveloped in their husks, or roast before the fire. When sufficiently done, they season it with bear's oil, buffalo's suet, or marrow, and partake of the rich though simple repast with joyful gratitude.

No occasion with which I am acquainted, displays in a more manifest degree its social effects than the corn feast. The heart dilates with pleasure even to overflowing, and the guests give utterance to their joys in songs and dances, and continue the hilarity for the remaining part of the day and night, and frequently for the whole of the succeeding day. No people, I am persuaded, experience the mirthful scenes of life in a higher degree than they do. In fact, the old gray-headed men and women are seen to commingle in the sports, and seem to re-enjoy with increased zest the scenes of their youth.

After this breach upon their new crops, they are permitted to gather without restraint whatever their wants require; but the Indians, both old and young, look upon it as upon their game, as the gift of the Great Spirit, and never wantonly destroy either, except as before remarked, while in the territories of their enemies.

The harvest feast, and that observed at the appearance of the buffalo, are conducted so very similar to the foregoing, as to render any description of them altogether unnecessary. The songs are different; but the dances and other enjoyments are nearly the same.

I have already remarked, that the appearance of the new moon was a subject for rejoicing among the Indians; but such is not uniformly the case, and they are somewhat capricious amongst themselves about it. Should it be discovered in the daytime, the youth of both sexes, and frequently the young warriors and married women, join in the dance and song, which are equally gay and animated with the before-described, but are not as exclusively appropriate. When the discovery is made in the evening, the parties are more numerous, especially if the weather be fine; but these occasions are far more generally noticed when they happen on the approach of the hunting season, or at the planting or ingathering of the crops, or antecedent to contemplated hostile operations against their enemies.

Hunting, Fishing, Agriculture, Manufactures, Currency, and Trade

5

Hunting, next to war, is thought by the Indians to be the most honorable employment they can pursue. As it is essential to their mode of existence, they are trained to it from the time they are able to bend the bow, and become familiar with every art and cunning that can be devised to destroy such animals as are necessary for food, or valuable for their furs. Though naturally indolent, nothing can exceed their industry when engaged in the chase. They rise early, hunt late, fast during long marches, and pursue game through forest and prairie grass by trails, which none but themselves would be able to discover.

In general, their hunting parties are not numerous, and are conducted according to the caprice of the individuals composing them, the majority commonly governing. But when they hunt for their winter stores, they are large, take different routes, and generally follow the directions prescribed before starting by a general council.

They are all composed of volunteers, who respectively yield obedience, for the time, to the chiefs they have assisted to elect for the occasion. Before they start on these expeditions, whether their number be few or many, it is customary to await the favorable omen of dreams, which, if not forthcoming when wished for, are encouraged or forced by prayers and long and painful fastings, oftentimes to the inconvenience, and sometimes to the manifest injury, of all those concerned. This conduct frequently disconcerts the previous arrangement of the councils; for should the dream of the chief, or one of the principal hunters of a party, and those only are much depended on, happen to the contrary, they generally resign their appointments, or abandon the old and form new parties, in which their friends generally support them.

These changes are not thought of any consequence, and are only named to present the peculiarity of their characters.

The Indians of different tribes pursue different methods in taking their game. Some effect it on horseback, others on foot, and occasionally the hunting parties are made up promiscuously of both. The hunting implements, where an intercourse with the traders admits of it, consist of rifles; but, under different circumstances, of lances five or six feet in length, armed with pointed stones, iron, or bones, and of bows with arrows pointed in the same manner.

The hunters from experience become acquainted with the habits of the animal they pursue; and, indeed, their success depends very much on this knowledge. They always approach from the leeward those which are naturally gifted with an acute sense of smell, as it were to guard them from danger; they resort to ambushes to take such as depend on vision and flight for their safety; and to decoys and imitations to circumvent others not peculiarly discriminative. In hunting the buffalo with rifles, no great difficulty is presented; precaution in the approach, and in aim, which is always at or near the ear, or just back of the shoulder, being all that is required.

The lance is used on horseback, but not till after the partial success of the bow and arrow, which are promiscuously resorted to, as occasion requires.

The mounted parties for hunting are usually numerous. They approach the herds through ravines, or under cover of mounds, &c. till they are discovered, when each pursues a separate buffalo, at an accommodating speed, apparently as well understood by the horse as his rider, and continues to shoot his arrows till he inflicts a mortal wound; or should there be any doubt in this respect, and circumstances admit, he resorts to his lance. He then attacks another, and sometimes a third and fourth, though it is very seldom their horses are able to continue the chase so long. The individuals who kill the greatest number, through a series of hunts, are of course esteemed the best hunters, a distinction which all are exceedingly ambitious to acquire and strive to, with a zeal and intrepidity almost bordering on madness. These observations are universally applicable in respect to all the different modes of hunting. When the bow and arrow are used by hunters on foot, they usually resort to the salt-licks and watering places, where they secrete themselves among bushes or excavations of the earth, frequently arranged or constructed for the purpose. On the arrival of a herd, they simultaneously discharge their arrows at some one, or more, occupying different places, that had been previously fixed on, and generally with success.

The hunters in some tribes surround large herds of buffalo, elk, and deer, and drive them either into impassable ravines, or upon the precipitous confines of rocky cliffs, where they take with their lances, bows and arrows, as many as their necessity may require.

I have never known a solitary instance of their wantonly destroying any of those animals, except on the hunting grounds of their enemies, or encouraged to it by the prospect of bartering their skins with the traders.

When an opportunity for a choice is presented, and their wants extend no farther, the Indians kill the calves, on account of the preference they have for their meat; and on the same account they select the fallow cows when they lay in their stores. However, when such cannot be conveniently obtained, they shoot promiscuously at such as chance presents. But as the buffalo is a difficult animal to kill, unless shot in particular places, and as the Indians are no ways remarkable for the use of the rifle or gun, they wound very many more than they are able to take.

The wounded bulls, in particular, become fearless and ferocious. [They] roar terribly, pitch against trees and rocks, tear up the earth, and frequently attack, and sometimes destroy, the hunters.

Many are destroyed by the hunters and panthers; but a much greater number, in my opinion, perish in the burning prairies, or are drowned by the breaking away of the ice in their attempts to pass over streams, or by the devastating floods which sometimes deluge the alluvions [bottoms], and bear off immense herds. Notwithstanding the great extent of this sweeping destruction, there is no apparent diminution of their number, the increase being, at least, equal to the waste. Such are the opinions of the old Indians, who have had good opportunities to judge, and such, I have no doubt, is the fact, from the existence of so many circumstances favorable to their propagation.

The sense of smell with the elk and deer is remarkably acute. They also see quick, are very cunning, and run with great rapidity; hence they are exceedingly difficult to be taken. They are hunted in the same manner as the buffalo, excepting the pursuit on horseback, and the decoys that are sometimes resorted to at particular seasons of the year.

For a decoy the Indians use the head of a buck elk, or deer, nicely preserved with the horns attached, with which, having previously secreted themselves, they beat the bushes, and at the same time imitate the wooing bleat or defying snort of the real animal. This maneuvering generally produces the intended effect. The males or females, as they may happen to be near, are attracted to the spot, and, if in proper condition, shot by the hunters.

The Indians seldom eat the flesh of either of these animals, while that of the buffalo can be obtained. It is, nevertheless, excellent in its season, particularly that of the deer, and they preserve it in considerable quantities.

The tendons of the deer are wrought into a sort of twine, with which they sew their leggings and moccasins. The tips of their horns are applied to point their arrows, perforate skins for sewing, and the like.

They seldom hunt purposely either for bears or small game; but kill such as come in their way, and for which they have occasion. When on their hunts, at a distance from their villages, they cut their meat in pieces of greater or less thickness, according to the temperature of the weather, suspend it on poles, smoke and dry it, and finally convey it home, either on their pack horses, or in canoes, which they construct for the purpose. When in the neighborhood of their settlements, the meat is conveyed home fresh, in which condition they greatly prefer it.

Formerly, the Indians almost venerated the beaver, on account of the high rational faculties it revealed, in damming creeks, and building houses for its own accommodation, and particularly in educating its young, and avoiding dangers.* But, latterly, since they have become acquainted with the value and consequence which the white people attach to the fur of this animal, they hunt it with an avidity and industry that threaten in the course of a few years to eradicate them from their hunting grounds. They are commonly taken with traps and snares, or falls; though sometimes they are killed with rifles, lances, or arrows.

Their haunts soon attract the notice of the hunters, who bury their traps, or suspend large logs in such a manner that the beaver, in attempting to obtain the baits, springs them to his own destruction. Sometimes holes are made in the ice formed on their ponds, to which the beavers, when driven from their houses, resort to breathe, and are despatched with spears or lances. They also break down their dams, and having previously prevented their retreat, take them by destroying their cells. Their skins form a very important item in the Indian trade.

The turkey is not much valued, though, when fat, the Indians

---

*The young beavers often begin to cut down trees, for the purpose of making dams, before they are capable of judging of the directions in which they would be likely to fall. In such cases, the old ones not only interrupt their progress, but take them to such as, when felled, will answer the sought-for object. This trait in their character is well known to the Indians, who could not travel over their haunts without observing numerous trees thus partially cut off, and judiciously abandoned. I have heard it suggested that these appearances had been produced in their playful frolics, or to acquire experience. But, if such was the fact, we might suppose that they would cut those nearest to their cabins first; that they would be found fresh cut in the neighborhood of their ponds, and sometimes remote from the water; but I have never seen them except in situations well calculated in every other respect for the construction of their dams.

I have repeatedly seen traps which had been sprung with sticks and robbed of their baits, and evidently by beavers, as their footsteps were traceable in their vicinity, while those of no other animal could be discovered. (JDH)

frequently take them alive in the following manner. Having prepared from the skin an apt resemblance of the living bird, they follow the turkey trails or haunts, till they discover a flock, when they secrete themselves behind a log, in such a manner as to elude discovery, partially display their decoy, and imitate the gobbling noise of the cock. This management generally succeeds to draw off first one and then another from their companions, which from their social and unsuspecting habits, thus successively place themselves literally in the hands of the hunters, who quickly despatch them, and wait for the arrival of more. This species of hunting, with fishing, is more practiced by the boys than the older Indians, who seldom, in fact, undertake them, unless closely pressed by hunger.

They take fish with a kind of hurdle net, made by weaving bunches of brushwood or sticks together with grape vines. They are of considerable length, and are used nearly in the same manner practiced for taking shad, herrings, &c. in the United States. They are not, however, extended into deep water, and the lower ends of the brush are loaded with stones, and the rear of the net is lined with boys, who constantly beat the water with rods, to prevent the escape of the fish. In this way, considerable quantities are taken, and oftentimes merely for sport. But in such cases, the fish are always suffered to escape uninjured, a usage strictly enjoined by the older Indians, to prevent their unnecessary and wanton destruction.

AGRICULTURE. The Indians chiefly depend on the chase for a subsistence; therefore what little progress they have made in agriculture, ought rather to be ascribed to incident, than to any settled design.

There are many, besides the roving tribes, that do not practice tillage; and it is highly probable that those which do inherit what of the art they possess from remote antiquity.

Otherwise, in a country so well supplied with game as theirs generally is, it appears to me, it would have received no attention, or else have been carried to a much greater degree of perfection. Observation, in which they are by no means deficient, must have unfolded to their knowledge the fecundifying powers of the earth, at as early a period (supposing their progenitors the same) as it did to any other race of men; and, had a similar necessity existed, they, no doubt, would have made as great proficiency. Even circumstanced as they are, they raise, in the neighborhood of many of their villages, excellent though not very abundant crops of corn, beans, tobacco, pumpkins, squashes, &c., as before noticed. In effecting this, they usually till the prairies; when otherwise, they clear their grounds by building fires at the roots of trees, or by stripping the barks from them, and, with hoes procured from the traders, plant their various kinds of seeds promiscuously, that is, without regard to sorts or arrangement. They carefully remove the weeds; keep the soil loose; and when occasion requires, hill it, to prevent the fragile vegetation from being injured by the winds. In dry seasons they irrigate their fields occasionally, and at their harvests preserve all the refuse as a common stock of food for their horses, which, with the dogs, are the only animals they have in a state of domestication. The former are much more abundant in some tribes than others, and, where most so, constitute the principal wealth of the Indians. They are valued in proportion to their fleetness and ability to continue the chase; and those that can run down three or four buffaloes at a hunt are esteemed almost invaluable, because, to their owners, they are the certain passports to distinction. Among the Osages and Kansas, they are common property, and are rarely used, except as pack horses in their hunting excursions.

Their dogs are all similar in their qualities and appearance, and seem to be intermediates between the fox and wolf.

They are with the Indians, as elsewhere, generous, faithful, and devotedly attached to their masters, who, in return, caress and provide for them with almost as much care and assiduity as they do for their own families.

They are trained to guard the corn fields against the depredatory encroachments of the horses; to pursue game, especially after it has been wounded; and, when collected, to defend it from the wolves, which seldom have the courage to dispute with them the propriety of their trust. In some tribes they are eaten, and esteemed a great delicacy; but this practice does not prevail where the buffalo, elk, and deer, are found in any considerable numbers.

According to tradition, the Great Spirit, when he became offended with the Indians because of their malpractices, particularly one towards another, gave them the dog, as a pattern of fidelity for their imitation. From which, and from their own accounts of these animals, I infer that they were in a state of domestication among the Indians, very long before the American continent was known to, or even thought of, by the Europeans.

MANUFACTURES. I have already noticed the progress the Indians have made in geographical delineations and hieroglyphic writings, as proofs of their capacity for further and more important improvements, even though wholly insulated from the civilized world. And, were others wanting, I might add the knowledge they have acquired in such branches of manufacture as are essential to their comforts.

These attainments have principally originated in necessity, and they unquestionably would have been extended to more positive demonstrations to the point, provided the exciting causes essential to such improvements had existed.

But the case is far otherwise; the means of procuring a comfortable livelihood are generally at command, and opposed to them; besides, the men are taught to regard every kind of labor and fatigue, apart from war, the chase, and the construction of implements connected with these several pursuits, as servile, and unbecoming the lofty character of the warrior. Hence, they can claim but very little if any credit for the proficiency to which some of the arts have arrived among them. It is true, they construct cabins and canoes, and manufacture for their own use, besides what I have mentioned, wooden bowls and spoons from the protuberances of trees, and pipes from clay and indurated boles. But the dressing of skins, the construction of pottery, and the fabrication of blankets and mats are left for the performance of the women, notwithstanding their other engagements, and supposed inferior intellectual endowments. In consequence of this state of things, added to the roving and belligerent lives they lead, and the disadvantages they labor under for want of working tools, the very limited knowledge they have acquired ought not to excite our surprise, and I am persuaded will not, when all the circumstances of their lives have been considered.

Their mode of dressing skins is very simple. When they wish to preserve the hair, they first extend the skins in the shade, and spread a thin covering of the recent ordure of the buffalo mixed with clay, on the fleshy sides, which for two or three days are kept constantly moistened with water. In the next place, they are thoroughly cleansed, and subsequently rubbed in the brain of some animal, till they become dry, soft, and pliant.

They are then washed in water thickened with corn bran, dried, and finally scraped with bones, sharp stones, or knives, or sometimes they are worked soft, by drawing them backwards and forwards over the rounded end of a piece of timber, fixed permanently in the ground. When sufficiently dressed, in the manner above described, they are hung up to be smoked, either in the smoke aperture of the lodges, or in places constructed exclusively for the purpose.

Dressed skins are generally kept in this situation, except when required for use.

Should the hair at any time become loose, they cover the hairy sides of the skins with finely cut oak bark, and sprinkle water on them three, four, or five times a day, till it becomes fixed.

When skins are to be dressed without the hair, they are covered with ashes, and kept in a trough of water, till the action of the lye readily admits of its being scraped off. Then the same processes, as above described, are performed with brains, bran, smoke, &c.

The former are used by the Indians for bedding, robes, and dresses, and, in some instances, for lining their lodges; the latter are made into leggings and moccasins, and in some of the tribes into coverings for their tents or lodges. Those used for constructing their canoes are never dressed.

While traveling, the hunters preserve their skins by simply rolling, or placing leaves in them. This, it should be understood, is only done in cool weather, for they seldom attempt to save them in the summer months; or if they should, it is by drying and smoking them over a fire. The skins are generally dry when put into the hands of the women for dressing, though this condition is not considered as a requisite in the process. It is a fact worthy of notice, that skins dressed by the Indians, that is, those which have been smoked, are never injured by worms, and are not so liable to become hard, or to stretch, after having been wet, as are the pliant ones of the professed leather-dressers among the white people.

In manufacturing their pottery for cooking and domestic purposes, they collect tough clay, beat it into powder, temper it with water, and then spread it over blocks of wood, which have been formed into shapes to suit their convenience or fancy. When sufficiently dried, they are removed from the molds, placed in proper situations, and burned to a hardness suitable to their intended uses.

Another method practiced by them is to coat the inner surface of baskets made of rushes or willows with clay to any required thickness and, when dry, to burn them as above described.

In this way they construct large, handsome, and tolerably durable ware. Though latterly, with such tribes as have much intercourse with the whites, it is not much used, because of the substitution of cast-iron ware in its stead.

When these vessels are large, as is the case for the manufacture of sugar, they are suspended by grapevines, which, wherever exposed to the fire, are constantly kept covered with moist clay.

Sometimes, however, the rims are made strong and project a little inwardly quite round the vessels, so as to admit of their being sustained by flattened pieces of wood, slid underneath these projections, and extending across their centers.

The hair of the buffalo and other animals is sometimes manufactured into blankets. The hair is first twisted by hand, and wound into balls. The warp is then laid of a length to answer the size of the intended blanket, crossed by three small smooth rods alternately beneath the threads, and secured at each end to stronger rods supported on forks, at a short distance above the ground. Thus prepared, the woof is filled in, thread by thread, and pressed closely together, by means of a long flattened wooden needle. When the weaving is finished, the ends of the warp and woof are tied into knots, and the blanket is ready for use. In the same manner they construct mats from flags and rushes, on which, particularly in warm weather, they sleep and sit.*

In districts of country where the sugar maple abounds, the Indians prepare considerable quantities of sugar by simply concentrating the juices of the tree by boiling, till it acquires a sufficient consistency to crystallize on cooling. But, as they are extravagantly fond of it, very little is preserved beyond the sugar-making season. The men tap the trees, attach spigots to them, make the sap troughs, and sometimes, at this frolicking season, assist the squaws in collecting sap.

The men occasionally amuse themselves with making bowls and pipes of clay, for their individual use, which are burned as before described.

They also make bowls and pipes of a kind of indurated bole, and of compact sand and limestone, which are excavated and reduced to form by means of friction with harder substances, and the intervention of sand and water. They generally ornament them with some figure characteristic of the owner's name; as for instance with that of a buffalo, elk, bear, tortoise, serpent, &c., according to the circumstance or caprice that has given rise to its assumption. In the same way they manufacture their large stone mortars, for reducing corn into fine meal.

In specifying the employments of the Indians, although the subjects do not properly come under this head, I ought not to omit giving some account of their cabins or lodges, which are always constructed by the men. They are usually formed of split poles, in the shape of an equilateral, quadrangular, obtusely truncated cone, with an aperture through the top, for the egress of the smoke. They are generally about twenty feet square, and from twelve to fourteen in height. The apertures between the poles are closed either with prairie grass and clay, turf, or the barks of trees. They have no windows, and but one door, which is generally on the south side. In cold weather they close it with a curtain of skins, and it is not unusual, as I have already remarked, for the cabins of the chiefs and principal warriors to be partially, and sometimes wholly lined with the same materials.

From the loose manner in which they build their fires, their lodges are intolerably smoky, especially in windy weather; and, in fact, whenever artificially heated, they are sufficiently so to render them exceedingly uncomfortable to all except Indians, who, from being accustomed, scarcely experience any inconvenience from it.

Considerable difference prevails among the different tribes, and even among the individuals of the same tribe, in the construction of their lodges.

Sometimes they are built principally of clay or turf, and at others of bark or brush, sustained by poles, and covered first with prairie grass, and then with loose earth.

This difference particularly distinguishes the Indians settled in villages from the roving bands, which always construct their huts in the most temporary manner; nevertheless, they are generally very comfortable, being covered with skins, which, for the especial purpose, make up part of their baggage.

The lodges for public purposes are much larger and vary considerably in the forms of their structure. Sometimes they are octagonal, at others oblong, or square, and, as the case may be, are otherwise pyramidical.

They are the depositories of all public records and property, and are never entered by any of the individuals of a tribe, except on public occasions. Even enemies, when they have it completely in their power, deem it sacrilegious to enter them, or in any way to molest their contents, unless the proprietary nation should have been wholly cut off or vanquished.

Their canoes are made promiscuously by either men or women, and sometimes conjointly by both, according to the exigency for which they are wanted. The skeletons or frames are made of osier or flexible poles, lashed together with bark or some other materials, and are covered generally with the skins of the buffalo sewed together, and to the frame, with the sinews of the deer. They vary in size considerably according to the service for which they are wanted: sometimes a single skin covers one, and, at others, a half dozen are required. The hair is left on the outside. However, it soon wears off, when the boat moves rapidly in the water, and is easily managed.

The Indians smoke, oil, and preserve them with great care, which makes them very durable. When traveling, they often remove them to the land, invert and use them for shelters against the rain. Being exceedingly light, they are carried without inconvenience over the longest portages. The Indians also construct canoes from the bark of the birch tree, and from cottonwood trees, and such are more or less in use among most of the tribes.

CURRENCY AND TRADE. From the nature and origin of society among the Indians, it may readily be supposed, and correctly too, that trade among themselves, and even with strangers, is conducted on a very limited scale, and by precarious standards.

Their currency standard of value is different in different tribes. Among the Osages, Kansas, Ottowas, Mahas, and their neighboring tribes, the beaver skin is as much the aggregate of fractions, as the dollar is in Spain and the United States, or as the sovereign in Great Britain.

In general, two good otter skins are valued equal to one beaver skin; from ten to twelve racoon, or four or five wildcat skins, at the same rate; and so on for other skins, or materials for traffic. The standard among the Mandans is a skin full of corn.

These skin measures are of different dimensions, and are kept in the council lodge. The Ricaras use a stone mortar for the same purpose, and it is kept in the same public place; while some of the tribes situated on the western side of the Rocky Mountains make use of various colored shells, ground to an oval or nearly round shape. Belts of wampum are also used, not only as standards of value, but as records of important transactions. According to these various standards they exchange property among themselves, and with the traders, for such articles as they fancy, or may really want; but, as the Indians are not generally acquainted with the value of foreign commodities, it frequently happens among some of the tribes, that councils are convened to establish the rate of exchange, which is afterwards publicly promulgated, and pretty strictly adhered to. In most of the tribes, however, the traders are left to fix their own prices, and they generally avail themselves of the privilege to the extent of the credulity and ignorance of the Indians; but I have already named this circumstance, together with the consequences that sometimes follow [see p. 25].

When two of the Indians have entered into a contract, and a credit is given, the time of payment always extends to the termination of the next hunting season, and the number of beaver skins due, is registered by a similar number of marks or notches cut on the inside of the great council lodge, at the first subsequent public meeting. On the final settlement, it is exceedingly rare that any disagreement takes place; though, should any exist, the affair is referred for adjustment to some of the most respectable old men or counsellors, much after the manner practiced in civilized life. The decision is final, and, though it should be disapproved, is very seldom reproached. Nothing, indeed, could give greater offense to the referees, than an opposite line of conduct: the offended parties would never afterwards sit at the same council fire, nor hold any other intercourse with the offender.

Breach of contract is very seldom known among them; but, when one does occur, coercion is out of the question. In fact, they are strangers to all systems of the kind. When told by the traders of the practice of imprisoning for debt, which prevails among the whites, the motive, unless it be for revenge, appears to them altogether paradoxical.

Should an Indian be unable to meet his engagements, in consequence of sickness or ill success in hunting, the creditor never duns him, nor even so much as mentions his individual wants in his presence, but the same friendly relations subsist between them, as though no disappointment or delinquency had taken place. But if the inability of the debtor originates in his indolent or intemperate habits; or if he willfully omits to pay when he has the means in his power, and otherwise applies them, he then suffers a greater penalty than imprisonment. He is abandoned by his friends, characterized as a bad Indian, and his creditor would esteem it dishonorable to receive from him afterwards even his just demands. Such instances have occurred within my knowledge, but they are exceedingly rare. These methods of negotiation and trade answer very well among the Indians. They suffer no inconvenience from the absence of a specie currency. In fact, many Indians are ignorant of its use, and, when in possession of coin, apply it solely to decorating their persons. They are generally strangers to exclusive property, except as regards their lodges and furniture. It is true, after their hunts and harvestings they make divisions, but they are for the convenience of disposition. As before remarked, no one of respectable standing will be allowed to experience want or sufferings of any kind, while it is in the power of others of the same community to prevent it. In this respect they are extravagantly generous, always supplying the wants of their friend from their own superabundance. In this equality of condition and privilege enjoined by natural laws, the Indians, where they understand how different people in civilized life manage their affairs, feel themselves supremely happy, in being exempted from the evils which avarice, pride, and folly entail on them.

Crimes and Modes of Punishment

6

There happen but very few occurrences among the Indians which are regarded as criminal. I have never heard of an instance of treason, or conspiracy against any of their communities, and know of no punishment for such an offense. But, if I understand the Indian character, an individual detected in holding a correspondence with the enemies of his country, would, I venture to assert, suffer instant death at the hands of the detector.

Murder, ingratitude, cowardice, adultery, stealing, and lying, constitute nearly the whole list of their crimes.

The first is punished "blood for blood," as according to the Mosaic law, by the relations of the deceased, without regard to the justification of trial and condemnation.

Ingratitude is certain to involve the offender in a loss of character; and this offense, and cowardice, are represented in more hideous colors, and dwelt on with more pointed emphasis by the squaws and old men, in their lessons to the youth, than any other, with the exception of murder, in their whole catalog. It is sometimes punishable with death: should an Indian, who had been taken prisoner, accept grace by being adopted into the family of his captors, and afterwards abscond and be retaken fighting against them, he would forfeit his life, without the possibility of a second reprieve.

Loss of reputation is not the only consequence of cowardice. Among the Kansas, when it cannot be corrected, they destroy cowards, probably with a view to nerve the young warriors in the practice of the opposite quality.

I witnessed one of these executions, which originated in the following circumstances, and was conducted in the following manner.

The Kansas had returned from a successful war excursion, in which one of their party, who had on a former occasion been culpable, behaved in a very cowardly manner. The whole nation, except those who had lost relations, and Te-pa-gee, the subject for chastisement, was engaged in rejoicings appropriate to the occasion of victory. Te-pa-gee, probably without the least suspicion of the destiny that awaited him, had withdrawn from the public ceremonials, and sullenly seated himself on the trunk of a tree adjacent to the river. Shortly after, and apparently without design, the squaws and children in their dances approached the river, near the place occupied by him. Then E-gron-ga-see walked carelessly through the festive groups, presented himself before the astonished culprit, and proclaimed to him, in a voice audible to all present, "Thy cowardice has forfeited thy life." The sports instantly ceased. All was silence and consternation. E-gron-ga-see drew his knife from beneath his robe. Te-pa-gee bared his bosom, received a thrust to the heart, and died without scarcely uttering a groan. The warriors then assembled with the witnesses of this tragic scene. The executioner, addressing his audience in a few words, stated the reprehensible conduct of the deceased, and the necessity that existed for inflicting so signal a punishment. After which [they] all returned to their respective homes.

I need not attempt to describe the feelings which this event occasioned in my mind, and those of the young Indians generally. We all concluded, that, in preference to suffering such ignominy, we would die a thousand deaths, if it were possible, in defense of our country; and the old men and squaws availed themselves of the occurrence to confirm and strengthen our resolutions.

The Indians claim the sole disposal of their wives; and although, in many instances, they devote them to the sensual gratification of their friends, without associating the least impropriety to the transaction, yet they regard a voluntary indulgence of the passions, on their part, as an unpardonable offense.

Incontinency after marriage, apart from that tolerated by custom, as above noticed, can scarcely be numbered among the sins prevalent among the Indians. The men reprobate lasciviousness, as unbecoming the character of the warrior. Hence, though their temperament may be as ardent as is common to any particular race of the human family, they affect a phlegmatic disposition, to which the love of reputation and glory forces them to conform their habits.

The women are not less ardent than the men, but the love of character, the apprehension of suffering, and the continency of their husbands, combine in general to establish similar habits.

This is not uniformly the case, however, more particularly with those who have adjuncts to participate in the favors of their husbands. With such, dereliction from duty occurs much more frequently than it does where the conjugal relations are more consistently balanced between the sexes.

Repudiation is the punishment most generally inflicted for this offense. It is resorted to both by men and women, especially when an ex-parte attachment exists. On the part of the men the punishment is, however, discretionary. They sometimes cut off their hair, slit, or cut off their noses or ears. At others, when they have many children, they merely discontinue all intercourse with them, and substitute other wives in their stead. I knew of an instance in which the outraged husband took the life of his light-footed squaw. He was himself an eye-witness to her offense. He loved, and had never suspected. Anger, for the moment, triumphed over reason: he directed his tomahawk, and the blow was unerring. This circumstance produced some excitement among her relations, but no attempt was ever made, within my knowledge, to revenge her death.

Among the individuals of some tribes or nations, theft is a crime scarcely known. They have neither fastenings to the doors of their lodges, nor any secret place for the security of their effects; and they leave them for days together, or retire to rest, without entertaining the least apprehension for their own safety, or that of their property. They however are taught from infancy that it is not only right, but a duty, to depredate on the goods and effects of their enemies, and such as maintain equivocal relations with them. But these observations will not apply universally. In some [tribes] which have become more settled, a distinction of, and desire to accumulate property exists in a limited degree. Under such circumstances, the means of obtaining a livelihood are more difficult, and the indolent are more apt to become dishonest. The offender is sometimes punished by banishment; but, in general, he is made to restore the stolen goods, and, if able, sometimes threefold.

Falsehood they esteem much more mean and contemptible than stealing. The greatest insult that can be offered to an Indian is to doubt his courage. The next is to question his honor or truth, then to doubt his ability to hunt and travel, and [finally] to slight his proffered hospitality and friendship. But insults are not accounted crimes, except against individuals.

Lying, as well as stealing, entails loss of character on habitual offenders. Indeed, an Indian of independent feelings and elevated character will hold no kind of intercourse with anyone who has been once clearly convicted.

For the commission of all crimes, insults, and offenses, the party or individual injured is the executor of his own revenge, except in the case of bloodshed, when, as before remarked, it devolves on the nearest relations of the deceased, who seldom relax in their resentments short of obtaining the most ample satisfaction.

In general they are just one towards another, and inculcate and practice the moral duties, no doubt because experience has taught, that such conduct is the most conducive to their own and the public happiness. Nevertheless, difficulties sometimes occur, which cannot be accommodated even by the interposition of the influence of the national councils. In such cases, one or other of the parties, with its adherents, separates from the nation.

While I lived with the Kansas, a young girl who had been adopted into the Wolf family, was insulted by a young Indian, belonging to the family distinguished by the name of the Panther.* The girl entertained a strong antipathy for this would-be gallant, and, in retaliation for offered violence, or rather in self-defense, inflicted several dangerous wounds with a scalping-knife. At first the parents of the parties sided with their respective children, and afterwards the entire families became involved in the quarrel, and some lives were lost on both sides. The affair assuming a serious aspect was carried before the councils, which at first, from the motives before noticed, refused to give it consideration. Nor did their final decision satisfy both parties: the more feeble one abandoned the village and established a settlement considerably farther up, on the Kansas River. After I left them, the parties became reconciled in consequence of a war with the Pawnees, and the discontented returned to their former habitations.

In common, the councils do not intermeddle with private disputes. As the Indians say, it would have a tendency to increase the evil, by increasing its consequence.

When complaints are preferred, their answer generally is that "none but squaws become involved in troubles and disputes, from which they cannot extricate themselves."

7

Policy, Councils, Transaction of Public Business Generally, Election of Chiefs, Reception of Ambassadors, Peace-runners, &c.

The Indians individually acknowledge no superior, nor are they subordinate to any government, except such as they find by experience to be essential to their preservation, triumph, and success in their war and hunting parties.

On such occasions, and even where the most urgent necessity exists, they only become voluntarily so, and can at any time withdraw themselves from all self-imposed restrictions. Nevertheless, as the object of their government is almost wholly connected with their foreign relations, the dread of their enemies perhaps more than their patriotism commands their services, and, while on actual duty, renders them obedient to their chiefs.

Some of their chiefs, from extraordinary qualifications, exercise at all times an influence which falls very little, if anything, short of absolute authority. In general, however, the warriors, while in their villages, are unyielding, exceedingly tenacious of their freedom, and live together in a state of equality, closely approximated to natural rights.

Whenever they deviate from this conduct, it is out of respect for their chiefs, or because they believe that a much greater degree of success will crown their efforts when united under, and controlled by a single efficient head, than otherwise possibly could.

Hence it will be seen that their governments depend on caprice or circumstances, and that although they somewhat resemble the democratic form, still a majority cannot bind a minority to a compliance with any acts of its own.

The convocation of their meetings, except immediately after a council, is rather capricious and arbitrary. Any individual may notify one, but unless the occasion be highly important, it will be attended more or less numerously, according to the respect entertained for the convocator. They are usually held at the request of some one of the aged, however, who, if in a village, goes from house to house, and mentions his wishes; if the population be more scattered, the notice is promulgated by runners. Preparatory to holding a council, the chiefs and principal warriors generally hold private meetings, at which the propriety of the contemplated business and the assemblage of the counsellors is considered. The eldest person always enters a council lodge first, and is followed by the other counsellors much according to seniority, and in the most perfect order. They next seat themselves in a cross-legged position on mats, which are arranged circularly around the lodge. The chief then lights the national pipe, takes three whiffs, and passes it to the individual next to himself, of the greatest consequence in the nation. In this manner it is passed round, till the whole have smoked. The chief then rises, and in the midst of the most profound silence, tells them that he is ready to hear their talk.

The council thus organized, the eldest orator rises and addresses his audience on the subject for debate. After he has finished, another rises, and turns by seniority are observed, till every member of the council so disposed has spoken. On these occasions, the subjects are debated with much gravity and often with nervous eloquence, and the orators listened to with deep interest and attention.

During this time not a breath of censure or applause is uttered, and the speaker can judge of the effect of his eloquence only by the countenances of his audience, and the turn of the subsequent votes.

They do not speak long, nor irrelatively; neither are they interrupted by calls to order, nor in any other way. It is a maxim amongst the counsellors to make short and pertinent speeches; "chattering," they say, "is the privilege of the squaws; but it is not characteristic of wise and brave warriors, for they think and act without much talk."

In their councils a majority generally determines all their important concerns. It is commonly ascertained by a division and subsequent count. Every individual determines for himself as to the propriety of his vote, and no greater insult could be offered than an attempt to bias it.

In voting, the counsellors sometimes divide, part arranging themselves with their chief as *pros,* or *cons,* as the subject may conform with his ideas. At others, they express their approbation by merely rising, or by smoking the national pipe, and not infrequently by depositing their respective badges, which as counted, are reclaimed by them. On some occasions they arrange themselves on the sides of particular chiefs, as will presently be noticed. Discussions on the expediency of war, and the declaration of it, are often conducted with closed doors, or, in other words, with secrecy. Opinions in favor of this subject are often expressed when the final question is taken by the war-whoop, as the warriors pass in succession by the chief.

When the majority is large, the minority generally join it; but should the division be nearly equal, and the subject of much moment, great obstinacy frequently prevails, more particularly should the disagreement extend to their chiefs. The young men, and even boys, are permitted to attend these assemblages; but they are not suffered to take any part in them, till they have arrived at puberty, and distinguished themselves either in war or the chase. If this were not the case, deference for the aged, and respect for superiors, which are so strictly enjoined and universally practiced in youth as almost to become a natural habit, would alone operate as a sufficient restraint.

When an election for a chief takes place, the candidates go by turns to the public lodge, or some mound near it, and there recount all the deeds they have achieved; exhibit the trophies they have obtained, and the scars they have received while fighting for their country; and promise to be the fathers and protectors of their tribes, and to watch over their welfare, and promote their happiness.

The preference is generally given to those who can exhibit the greatest number of trophies. Age has great weight, however, especially if accompanied by other commendable qualities. It sometimes happens that the elderly warriors receive this mark of distinction, to the exclusion of more equitable rights, if graduated to the scale of actual merit. After these harangues and exhibitions are concluded, the warriors respectively assemble round the candidate to whom they give the preference, and whichever has the greatest number of adherents is commonly acknowledged as the chief.

Sometimes, however, these elections give rise to quarrels or misunderstandings, which result in the separation of the nation either into friendly or hostile tribes, though instances of this kind are very rare.

On some occasions their elections are conducted in a different way. The counsellors assemble and nominate a candidate, who separates from the electors, carrying with him the national pipe. Such as are friendly to the nomination join him and testify their approbation by smoking the customary number of whiffs. Should his partisans be a minority, a new candidate is named, and the same course pursued till an election is effected. This mode is generally consented to by the candidates when considerable excitement prevails with a view to preserve the union and strength of their tribe.

On others, the candidates decorate themselves with some particular badge, as that of the buck or beaver's tail, which they wear for several days preceding the election. In the meantime, their respective partisans decorate themselves in the same manner, and when the period for determining the choice arrives, as in the former instances, it is awarded in favor of the greatest number, to which the others generally consent by joining in the public rejoicings.

Whenever these elections take place in a nation composed of different tribes, or in tribes composed of different villages, which are somewhat remote, the respective families constituting them often depute their chiefs to attend, who exercise an influence at them, in proportion to the number of warriors they represent.

Individuals sometimes exercise the duties, and receive all the respectful attentions which the Indians are accustomed to bestow on chiefs who have been regularly elected to the station. This occasionally happens on account of real merit, but more frequently from the various deceptions and artifices practiced on their credulity, with a view to secure this particular influence. Such, for instance, are some of the prophets. Electioneering for oneself is thought to be very disgraceful, and is seldom if ever resorted to, but much intrigue is practiced on these occasions by the immediate friends of the candidate. They are sly, cunning, and oftentimes deceitful; sometimes they buy articles at an extravagant price from one, and gratuitously part with them to others, with a view, no doubt, to secure the reputation of being generous. At others, they pretend to have had remarkable dreams, or to predict future events, dependent on contingencies connected with their own advancement.

The candidate elected next receives presents from his subordinate chiefs, or rather, from the chiefs of families, consisting of trophies obtained from their enemies, or of badges of national distinction. After this he is conducted to the council lodge (provided the election was held without it, as is commonly the case) where all the records and public property are inscribed with an additional hieroglyphic, characteristic of the new chief. This ceremony is followed by public feasts and rejoicing, which, in general, are of short duration, and close with the day.

The candidates spurn with contempt the aid of those Indians who do not support good characters. Cowardice and mean habits constitute their principal disqualifications. Should persons of this trait join in the proceedings, they are studiously avoided, and not infrequently insulted.

The chiefs and candidates for public preferment render themselves popular by their disinterestedness and poverty. Whenever any extraordinary success attends them in the acquisition of property, it is only for the benefit of their most meritorious adherents: they distribute it with a profuse liberality, and pride themselves in being estimated the poorest men in the community. Valor, intrepidity, and liberality, are the passports to popular favor, while the contrasts are the damning sins of Indian politicians. In general, each family elects a chief to overlook and attend to its interests. He is its orator, attends the councils, and is, whenever occasion requires, an aid to the principal chief.

The preference in these elections is always given to the aged, victorious, and brave warrior. Although their chiefs have great influence, they are obliged to hunt for their own support, with as much industry as their warriors, and frequently, when their wives are numerous, with much greater. It should be recollected, however, that this can only happen during the recess of the general hunts. As at other times the products of the chase are then divided in proportion to the size of their families. Their squaws and families enjoy no particular privileges, but submit to perform the same duties as are common to the rest of the tribe.

These heads of the nation receive no emolument for their services. The honor attached to the situation is considered a most enviable and satisfactory reward.

The ambassadors from friendly nations are received with much ceremony. Usually the chiefs appropriate a lodge and one of their squaws to each of them; and while they remain, they exercise the same control as though they were permanently invested in the proprietary. These tokens of regard are, however, extended to all distinguished friends. On entering the council lodge, the chief conducts them to the most honorable situation, and after the ceremony of lighting the pipe has been performed, takes the customary number of whiffs from it himself, and then offers it to his foreign guests. They then unfold the object of their mission. In the course of a day or two, they receive a reply and take their departure, accompanied perhaps by half a dozen of the most distinguished warriors, who sometimes escort them to their homes.

Messengers from hostile nations are not permitted to enter their villages, unless they bring proposals for peace that can be honorably accepted. They communicate through a deputation and are dismissed without having become acquainted with any of the opinions or circumstances of their enemies.

Should their negotiations terminate favorably, they are then placed on the footing of friends, and treated accordingly.

Messengers of peace, on entering an enemy's country, secrete their arms, and decorate themselves with the feathers of the white swan, belts of wampum, &c. They are sacred personages and no violence is ever offered them.

Patriotism, Martial Character and Propensity, War Implements, Preparations for, and Management and Termination of War, &c.

8

No people are more enthusiastically attached to their country than the Indians. This does not originate, in any considerable degree, from those local circumstances which influence the feelings in civilized life, but from the love of national distinction and glory. Each nation is divided into families or sub-tribes, which are taught to become competitors for the meed of excellence, in whatever relates to their mode of life. This honorable strife exists among all the members of their respective families. But it, together with ambition and self-love, is strenuously cultivated as subservient to national attachment and devotion. It is this which constitutes their union and strength. To an Indian, when his country is to be benefited by it, death has no terrors: self is never taken into the account and he submits to his fate, under the impression that he has done his duty, with a magnanimity not to be appreciated by worldly minds. Nevertheless, the Indians have their attachments for particular places. They sometimes go for miles out of their way, to visit the site of an old encampment, or situations where they have escaped imminent dangers, or anything remarkable has occurred. But such conduct appears to be primarily connected with their devotional exercises.

The mode of life peculiar to the Indians exposes them to the optional encroachment of all their hostile neighbors. For their security they are therefore indebted to personal bravery, and skill in attack and defense. That is, in their active warlike operations, they obey only general instructions; each warrior accommodates his maneuvers according to his own judgment on the exigency of the occasion. Hence, the cultivation of martial habits and taste becomes essential, and constitutes the chief employment of every individual in their respective communities: first of the squaws and old men, in relation to precept, and then of the warriors, in respect to example.

Under such guidance, the love of war becomes almost a natural propensity. Besides, they are taught to believe that their happiness here and hereafter is made to depend on their warlike achievements.

Daily example confirms it as a fact, so far as the indulgence of their affections is concerned, for the females, both young and old, affect to despise the Indian who openly becomes the lover, without the authority of having acquired distinction, either in the chase, or in fighting against the enemies of his country.

It is not, therefore, extraordinary that they should love war, since so many and important results are believed to depend on their success in it: their happiness, their standing in society, and their sexual relations, make it necessary that they should excel, or at least strive to, in whatever is connected with their mode of existence. Hence they court opportunities for self-distinction, and, in fact, when wanting, often make them, in opposition to justice, and the welfare of their nation. The indulgence of this disposition is one of the principal causes of the frequency of war among the Indian nations.

They regard their hunting grounds as their birthright, defend them with the most determined bravery, and never yield them till forced by superior numbers, and the adverse fate of war. They are exceedingly tenacious of their rights, and chastise the slightest infringement. Hence, they are almost constantly engaged in warfare with some of their neighbors.

Their instruments of war were formerly the scalping-knife and tomahawk, formed from flinty rocks, the bow and arrow, the war-club, and javelin or spear, and, among some tribes, shields made of several folds of buffalo skin. Latterly those have been pretty generally superseded by the rifle, steel tomahawk, and scalping-knife, procured from the traders.

When a sufficient cause for war is thought to exist, it becomes the subject of private conversation, till the opinions of the warriors are pretty well understood. A council is then convened and it undergoes a thorough discussion. If determined on conditionally, the offending tribe is made acquainted with all the circumstances. Otherwise, they generally keep the affair secret, at least so far as respects the subject of their hostility.

On some occasions, when the chiefs from prudential motives think it advisable not to go to war, and omit to convene a council to try the question, the discontent of the warriors reminds them of their duty. They demonstrate it by planting painted posts, blazing trees, ornamenting their persons with black feathers, and omitting to paint, or painting their faces after the manner practiced in war. These symptoms are discoverable among the young and uninfluential warriors but nevertheless produce the intended effect, and lead to a formal expression of the public feelings.

On adjournment of the council, the warriors repair to their respective homes, and, having painted their necks red, and their faces in red and black stripes, they reassemble at some place previously fixed on, and discover their hostile intentions in the dances and songs that follow. They next prepare their arms, and provide the munitions for war and then follow the ceremonials of fasts, ablutions, anointings, and prayers to the Great Spirit, to crown their undertaking with success. They take drastic cathartics, bathe repeatedly, and finally anoint themselves with bears' grease, in which yellow root has been steeped. They abstain from sexual intercourse, eat sparingly from their military provisions, and take freely of the Kut-che-nau, a plant which operates on the human system something like opium, without producing the same comatose effects.* They then perform the war dance, which is not less appropriate to this occasion than are all their festive ones to the events for which they have been adapted. Whole days are sometimes spent in making preparations for it. Robes, stumps, posts, &c. are painted red or black. Every movement and appearance bespeaks the interest and solemnity that are diffused through the tribe.

At a proper signal the warriors, arrayed in their military habiliments, assemble and commence the dance. It consists in imitating all the feats of real warfare, accompanied with the alternate shouts of victory and yells of defeat. In short, they perform everything which is calculated to inspire confidence in themselves and to infuse terror into their enemies. They are celebrated only at the dawn of a campaign. After this dance, they commence their march to the cadence of the shouts, songs, and prayers of the old men, women, and children, who usually attend them a short distance on their way.

Their equipments and stores amount merely to indispensables, which consist of their arms, buffalo suet, bears' oil, parched corn, anise and wild licorice roots, and pipes and tobacco.

Their progress differs according to the make of the country, the prevalence of woods, or hiding-places, &c., through which they have to pass. It sometimes amounts to fifty or sixty miles in a day but usually to about thirty or forty. This difference arises in general from the circumstance whether they are the pursuers or pursued. They use great precaution in traveling so as not to leave traces for their enemies to follow them. They march by families, or small parties separated from each other, within hearing distance, in single file, and step high and light.

They make various kinds of whoops, by which they communicate intelligence one to another, to any distance within hearing: such as those of war, which are to encourage their own adherents, and intimidate their foes; those of alarm, which advise secrecy or flight, as the exigency may require; those of the chase, &c. They imitate the barking of the fox, the cry of the hawk, or the howl of the wolf, at short intervals of time, so as to maintain their regular distances, and give each other notice in case of danger. These imitations are varied, and accommodated to circumstances previously agreed on, and are as well understood as the telegraphic signals practiced among civilized nations.

When arrived within the neighborhood of their enemies, a whispering council is held, which is constituted of the principal and subordinate chiefs, and their deliberations are guarded by sentinels, secreted at convenient distances, to prevent a surprise. They then separate and remain hidden, till intelligence from their spies authorizes an attack. . . .

They generally aim at surprising their enemies and, with such views, secrete themselves, and wait patiently, for many days together, for an opportunity. During such times they neither visit nor converse with each other, but lie the whole time, without varying their position more than they can possibly help.

They are implacable in their enmities, and will undergo privations that threaten their own existence, and even rush on certain death, to obtain revenge; but they are grateful for benefits received, and ardent and unchangeable in their friendship. When battle rages, and death is in every aim, the Indian, at the risk of his own life, will save his friend, though arrayed against him in the combat.

Shin-ga-was-sa, while young, visited the Kansas during a hunting excursion. The wife of a distinguished warrior paid him some attentions without the approbation of her husband, which resulted in her repudiation, and threatened the existence of her gallant. Pa-ton-seeh, a young Kansas, secretly interfered, and Shin-ga-was-sa made his escape, without coming in collision with his justly irritated foe. Many years afterwards, the Grand Osages and Kansas were involved in war. A battle followed, in which an Osage had shot down Pa-ton-seeh, and was in the very act of taking his scalp, when Shin-ga-was-sa arrested his hand, and preserved his friend.*

In another instance, a Pawnee, who had rendered himself an object of public resentment to the Kansas, and was about to expiate his offenses by suffering torture, was, to the astonishment of the whole tribe, preserved by the daring intrepidity of his friend. The circumstance was as follows: The Pawnee had on some former occasion laid his preserver under particular obligations, by an act of which I am now ignorant. In return for it, Sha-won-ga-seeh, the moment he knew of the captivity of his friend, intrigued with the young warriors, who, with some of his friends, interrupted the ceremonials that had been authorized by a national council. He cut the bonds of the prisoner, mounted him on a fleet horse, and commanded him to fly for his life.

This daring Kansas had previously so disposed of their horses, that pursuit was out of the question. The boldness of the measure so completely paralyzed the volition of the Indians, that a single effort was not made to arrest its success. The excitement produced by this affair at first threatened tragic consequences, but Shawon-ga-seeh's friends rallied to his defense. An explanation ensued, and he finally was much commended for an act that might have cost him his life, without the propitiation demanded for murder on all other occasions. . . .

In taking a scalp, they seize the tuft of hair left for the purpose on the crown of the head in the left hand, and, raising the head a little from the ground, with one cut of the scalping knife, which is held in their right hand, they separate the skin from the skull.

During an engagement quarters are very seldom asked or given; but should a combatant throw down his arms, his life is spared, and he is placed in charge of those who are entrusted with the wounded. When it is over, the prisoners are all assembled, and marched to the villages of the captors, either slow or fast, according as they apprehend danger from pursuit. Should this, however, be pressing, they destroy all, sparing neither the aged, women, nor children. When arrived within hearing distance of their homes, the warriors set up the shout of victory and after a short pause utter as many distinct whoops as they have taken prisoners and scalps. At this signal all the inhabitants tumultuously proceed to meet them, and, after the first greetings and salutations are over, commence an attack, with clubs, switches, and missiles, on the captive warriors. The women are exceedingly barbarous on such occasions, particularly if they have lost their husbands, or any near relatives, in the preceding fight.

Every village has a post planted near the council lodge, which is uniformly painted red, on the breaking out of a war. It is the prisoner's place of refuge. On arriving within a short distance of it, the women and children, armed as above, and sometimes even with firebrands, place themselves in two ranks, between which the warriors, one by one, are forced to pass. It is in general a flight for life; some, who are sensible of the fate that awaits them should they survive, move slowly, and perish by the way. Those who reach it are afterwards treated kindly, and permitted to enjoy uninterrupted repose, under the charge of relief guards, until a general council finally determines their fate. The women and children are at once adopted into the respective families of the captors, or some of their friends.

Such warriors as are exempted from their vengeance, generally marry among them, and constitute members of their community.

They, however, have it in their power to return to their relatives and nation whenever a peace has been concluded; but, as such conduct would be esteemed ungrateful, instances of the kind very seldom occur. Those who are condemned to death, suffer with great magnanimity the most cruel tortures which revenge can invent. They are generally bound hand and foot, sometimes together, and at others to separate posts or trees, and burned with small pieces of touchwood, pierced with goads, and whipped with briars or spiny shrubs, at different intervals, so as to protract the periods of their tortures.

These victims to a mistaken policy, during their sufferings, recount, in an audible and manly voice, and generally with vehement eloquence, all their valorous deeds of former times, and particularly those which they have performed against their persecutors. They contrast the bravery of their own people with the squaw-like conduct of their enemies. They say that they have done their duty; that the fortune of war happened to be against them; and that they are only hastening into more delightful hunting grounds than those they possess here, by squaws who are incapable of appreciating the merits of brave warriors.

They speak of their own deaths as a matter of no consequence; their nation will not miss them; they have many fearless warriors, who will not fail to revenge their wrongs.

As they grow feeble from suffering, they sing their death songs, and finally expire, without betraying the slightest indication of the pains they endure. Indeed nothing can exceed the indifference with which the Indians apparently suffer the tortures and protracted deaths, inflicted on them by their relentless and unfeeling foes.

In these executions the prisoners often make use of the most provoking language, with a view, no doubt, to shorten the period of their tortures. They generally succeed, for the outraged party, unable to resist the desire of revenge, dispatches them at once with the tomahawk, or some other deadly weapon.

I have known an instance, and others have occurred, in which a female had the temerity to risk the public resentment, by interfering in behalf of the captive. It was at the Kansas village. The subject was a young Maha, who had rendered himself particularly odious, from having taken the scalp of one of their distinguished warriors. He had been bound, and his tormentors had just commenced their dances, and fiend-like yells, as the prelude to his destruction, when Shu-ja-he-min-keh, a beautiful girl of eighteen, and daughter of one of their chiefs, abandoned her countrywomen, and, as it were, her country. Clasping the destined victim in her arms, [she] implored his life, and would not be separated till her prayers were granted.

Attempts of this kind are not, however, always successful. The

Indians are governed somewhat by the number of those condemned and by the respective standings and character of the supplicants.

In these instances, the sufferers believe that to die courageously will entitle them to the particular favor and protection of the Great Spirit, and introduce them into the councils and society of the brave and good, in the delightful regions of perpetual spring and plenty, where, under a cloudless sky, they are destined to enjoy with heightened zest the consciousness of this life, unalloyed by its anxieties, pains, and afflictions.

With the Indians, the passion of revenge ceases with its object. These tragic scenes close with the burial of their victims, which are universally respectful, and attended with very nearly the same exterior ceremonials that are observed in the interment of their own dead. [This happens] especially if their conduct at the closing scene had been brave and consistent.

In their campaigns the Indians are always accompanied by some who officiate, when necessary, in the character of surgeons and physicians, but who ordinarily perform the warrior's duty. They do not, however, attend to the wounded till the battle is over, unless they should be in imminent danger, or it should prove of long duration, and the number of sufferers or prisoners becomes considerable. In such cases they become noncombatants and perform the twofold duty of surgeons and guards. . . . The wounded are borne off on litters to some place of safety. In cases of retreat they are sometimes abandoned, but in general they are kept in the advance, and defended with the most obstinate bravery and resolution. They observe the same pertinacious courage in regard to their dead. When obliged to abandon them, they do not, if they can possibly avoid it, permit their scalps to fall into the possession of their enemies, and always return and collect their bones, as soon as they can do it with safety. When at a great distance from home, they inter their dead temporarily, but always return, when the proper period has arrived, for their skeletons, and pay them the same honors as though they were enveloped in their muscular integuments.

Nothing can exceed the joyous exultations of the old men, women and children, who have not lost relations, on the return of the warriors from successful warfare. While with those who have, the expression of grief is equally extravagant.

The afflicted associate themselves on the occasion, apart from the festive circles, and the duration of their grief is generally in the inverse ratio of this violence: it does not last long, and they soon join in the rejoicings, which are continued for several days. They are consummated by the scalp dance—in which the squaws bear the trophies, such as scalps, arms, and apparel, won by their husbands from the enemy—by songs, by the torture of their enemies, and finally by feasts. In the performance of the scalp dance, the squaw usually attaches all the scalps that are in her family to a pole, which she bears on the occasion. As they dance round the council lodge or fire, they alternately sing and recount the exploits that were achieved on their acquisition. The one who sings is for the time the principal, and all the others obsequiously follow her. The men and children join in the whoops and rejoicings. During these festivities, marks of favor are lavished, particularly by the squaws, on all such as have distinguished themselves. The most worthy are seated by the old men and chiefs. The women dance round them, decorate their persons with dresses ornamented with feathers, and porcupine quills stained of various colors, and crown them with wreaths of oak leaves, fantastically interwoven with flowers, beads, and shells.

The reception of the warriors from an unsuccessful expedition is different in the extreme, from the reverse of the circumstance. The mournings are general, and last for several days. The men are morose and gloomy, and only break silence in their prayers to the Great Spirit for support in the revenge they meditate, or in imprecations denounced against their enemies. After the mournings are at an end, the women appear apprehensive and reserved, and do not generally renew their caresses for some time, unless invited to by the occurrence of more fortuitous [or fortunate] events.

Residence, Dress, Painting, Disposal of the Dead, Mournings, &c.   9

The Osages and Kansas live in villages, which, even during the hunting seasons, are never wholly abandoned, as is the case with several tribes settled on the Missouri.

Their lodges are built promiscuously, in situations to please their respective proprietors. They are arranged to neither streets nor alleys and are sometimes so crowded as to render the passage between them difficult.

Their towns are subject to no police regulations. Every individual goes and comes when, and does what he pleases. Consequently nothing can be said in favor of their cleanliness. Though, in general, I think them less filthy than many places met with in some of the large cities of the United States, which boast wise and rigidly administered municipal governments.

Those who rove, and sometimes those engaged in hunting, live in portable tents, which they pitch or strike at pleasure. Such generally follow the buffalo and other game, in their migratory routes.

When a village is large and crowded, and a division becomes necessary, they uniformly fix on a site for another as near the original or parent settlement as circumstances will permit, in order to secure the whole force of the nation against their enemies, and to maintain, by a constant intercourse, the relations of friendship and consanguinity.

DRESS. The ordinary dress of both men and women in warm weather, consists only of moccasins, leggings, and breechcloths, made from the skins of various animals, dressed after their particular manner. The last-named article is from twelve to eighteen inches wide, and its convolutions or folds are varied according to the temperature of the weather.

In addition to the foregoing, during the cold seasons, they wrap their shoulders and bodies in blankets procured from the traders, or in robes made of the dressed skins of various animals, and cover their heads with fur caps, particularly when exposed.

Some of the women wear stays to support their breasts, while nursing; the custom, however, is so restricted, as scarcely to deserve notice. On religious or festive occasions, the men generally exercise extraordinary pains and patience in decorating their persons. I have known them to pass a whole day at the toilet, and then to appear mortified at the necessity which obliged them to leave it before they had satisfactorily completed their dress.

All commence their preparations with ablutions, which in general are preceded by rubbing themselves in clay. They next anoint themselves all over with bears' oil or buffaloes' marrow, which is frequently scented with some odoriferous substance, as that of anise or sassafras. They then paint themselves in the style called for by the occasion. After these preliminaries have been performed, the men dress their heads in beaver or otter-skin caps, neatly ornamented with feathers, porcupine quills, and horsehairs stained of various colors, and variegated shells, beads, &c.

They encircle their arms above the elbow, and at the wrist, with beads, shells, beans, &c., fancifully strung; and their waist and necks with belts of wampum beautifully braided, from deer sinews and horsehairs, tastefully strung with beads of various shades and colors. Their waistcloths, leggings, and moccasins, omitting the feathers, are decorated in the same manner as their caps. They attach the tails of foxes, or other animals, to their heels, and also wear pendent from their caps behind the tails of the animals from which they have severally been made.

The dress of the females, omitting the belts of wampum, and the particular head and heel ornaments, resembles that of the warriors, though there is a considerable difference in the style of workmanship: that of the squaws distinguishes only the families to which they belong, while the warrior's always characterizes the nation, and is frequently the record of his own heroic deeds. On all occasions, where sanctioned, they fasten to their ankles and knees small tortoise shells, containing rounded pebbles, with a view to increase the variety and confusedness of their music. The married women suffer their hair to hang loosely on their backs, and decorate their head with feathers; while, by way of distinction, the unmarried only part theirs, and bring it forward over their breasts. In some tribes they roll it up, and fasten it on the top of the crown.

In cold weather the full dress is completed by the addition of skin robes, which are ornamented with hieroglyphic painting, characterizing either their nation, family, or exploits, and not infrequently all of them together. But here, as in the other parts of their dress, a sexual distinction, except under very extraordinary circumstances, is constantly maintained. A Kansas squaw, who, with two boys, had killed two Ottowas in the act of stealing their horses (see page 22), was permitted to wear a robe, and other articles of dress, emblazoned with symbols commemorative of the event. I once saw a Pawnee woman whose dress was characterized by masculine distinctions, but I am ignorant of the circumstance which tolerated it.

PAINTING. In peace, the custom of painting is resorted to with a view to ornament their persons; but in proportion as it resembles the natural color, the more it is admired.

To obtain this color they calcine clay, and mix it with pulverized charcoal and bears' grease in proper proportions. The more coxcombical sometimes use the purest red they can obtain, which is prepared from an earth found on the Vermillion River, and in some other places, and some vegetable colors. In war, they usually paint themselves red back of the ears, and in stripes of red and black on their faces. Sometimes they paint their faces wholly black, which indicates that no quarter is to be given to their enemies. Black is understood by them as emblematical of death, and red merely of war. Their black paints are prepared from pulverized charcoal and bears' grease.

The Indians in general paint themselves only on festive or religious occasions, or while traveling without their territories, or when actually engaged in war, or entertaining hostile feelings against their neighbors. The various modes they observe are always strictly emblematical of their feelings. The more hideous a warrior can render himself by these factitious means, the greater he conceives his claim to be to the martial character. When in complete military array, their appearance is in general truly frightful.

The practice of painting is universal among all the tribes, but less dispensable with some than others. With the Osages, an Indian who neglects it humbles himself very much in the estimation of the rest of the nation. Instances of this kind, however, rarely occur. When they do, the delinquents are not permitted to join in the ceremonials, or, in other words, are totally neglected.* The females paint as well as the males, but only after the manner tolerated in peace.

After bathing in warm weather, and generally towards evening, they anoint their bodies slightly with bears' grease. This practice is continued for no other purpose than to prevent the annoyance of insects, and it answers the object remarkably well.

FORMS OF BURIAL. When an Indian dies, the body is laid in an extended position on buffalo robes, and is thus kept until the incipient signs of putrefaction make their appearance. The friends of the deceased then convey it in a very silent, respectful, and solemn manner to the place of interment, where it is wrapped in a skin robe, along with a bow, furnished quiver, tomahawk, and such other things as it most valued while living, and finally buried.

This ceremony is performed differently, not only by different tribes, but by the individuals of the same tribe. The body is sometimes placed on the surface of the ground, between flat stones set edge upwards, and then covered over, first by similar stones, and then with earth brought a short distance. Occasionally this stone casing is only applied to the head, and then again it is altogether omitted. Others excavate the earth to the depth of two or three feet, and deposit their dead below its surface.

When at too great a distance from their villages to convey them home, they dispose of them temporarily, as I have before noticed, in some one of the modes above described, or they deposit them in caves, or on scaffolds, erected several feet above the ground, and secure them with skins, &c., against predatory animals. [There they remain] until the fugitive or more perishable parts have become detached from the bones, when they are placed promiscuously beside those of their fathers. The ceremony of removing and depositing such bones is, however, as formal and solemn, as it is in cases of recent death; and even more so, when they are the remains of their warriors.

They leave the face of their dead, after burial, uncovered for several days, according to the season of the year, with a view to facilitate the intercourse between the body and its good spirit, which, they suppose, continues till the latter has made ample provision for their entrance into the next world. It is then covered in presence of all the relations of the deceased, and the period of their mourning generally ceases.

The professed object for accoutring their dead with arms, &c. is, to provide them with the means to procure subsistence in their journey from this to the next world. It is complied with, by the intelligent Indians, merely on account of custom. For they teach, that the wants of this life extend no farther than to food, drinks, and clothing; that more than is essential for these objects is of no account. They can take nothing with them when they leave this world. If they could, it would not be necessary to do so, because their Great Father has made far better and more abundant provisions for them in the next.

The funeral ceremonies are conducted in various forms, according to the respect entertained for, or the circumstance of sex or age of the deceased. An old and able counsellor, distinguished chief, brave warrior, swift runner, and expert hunter, are the constant subjects of their highest esteem. The death of any such is therefore regarded as a greater misfortune than that of an ordinary warrior, or of a squaw or child, and is followed by an expression of grief, and display of funeral solemnities, proportioned to the supposed national sufferings.

At the burial of an aged Indian, who has often fought in their defense, and provided for their wants, and who, when disqualified by decay for these pursuits, has devoted all his faculties to instruct the rising generation, the greatest honors are paid; the deepest afflictions are felt; and the mournings continue for the longest periods. So, if their sorrows and ceremonies can be graduated, they decrease in intensity as the respectability of the deceased diminishes. Nevertheless, those exhibited at the death of their women and children are decent, pious, and solemn.

Their burying places are generally located at the distance of a mile or two from their villages, and are often resorted to by those who have recently lost relations, and by others during their public and private fasts, and self-imposed penances.

It is said some tribes at present bury their dead in caves. If such be the fact, it has escaped my knowledge, though, that such was the practice at some very remote period, I cannot doubt. I myself have seen dead bodies in such cemeteries, but they were in a high state of preservation. The circumstance or costume of appearance in which they were discovered, leaves no room to suppose that they were the remains of any people now existing in their neighborhood, or within the knowledge of the neighboring Indians.

MOURNINGS. The grief that is suppressed during the dangerous sickness of an Indian, bursts out with redoubled violence whenever death ensues. On these occasions, the men sometimes relax the rigidity of their muscles, swerve from their apparent constitutional apathy, which does not allow the escape of tears, and with heartfelt grief mingle their cries with the piercing lamentations of the women.

They consider tears as a just tribute to the memory of their meritorious dead. Their escape discovers neither a want of fortitude, nor an idle compliance with custom. No doubt their public mournings operate as powerful incentives on the living, in the discharge of what they conceive to be their moral duties. They continue for longer or shorter periods, according to the respectability of the deceased, or the prevalence of peace or war.

When a campaign is on foot that requires their attendance, the warriors only mourn while the obsequies of the dead are performed. Under other circumstances, they conform their grief to that of the nation. During their mournings all their operations are suspended, except in the above-named instance, or in the scarcity of food.

Extreme grief is sometimes revealed by plucking out the hair, tearing the flesh, fastings, and painting the face black. Whenever it is so violent, it is commonly of short duration.

When the loss of an individual is deeply felt, the mournings are continued for one, two, or three months, in audible lamentations or howlings, which begin daily at daybreak, and are continued generally till the sun makes his appearance.

The chief of the nation, or the most respectable warrior related to the deceased, commences the cry of distress. Shortly afterwards, those next in respectability or consanguinity join successively in the symphony, till all present may be truly said to personify grief.

Some travelers who have visited the Indians have ascribed this custom, as practiced on the most trivial occasions. My readers may rest assured that the above account of it is correct, and further, that they never practice it, unless urged by extreme and sincere affliction, arising from the decease of their relatives or friends. . . .*

Indian Anecdotes   10

The white settlements on the frontiers of civilized life . . . cultivate the greatest friendship towards the Indians, in order to prevent the vengeance with which they usually repay an affront. When the friendly Indians, therefore, pass through the white peoples' neighborhood, they are certain to call, to tell them they are friends: they "smoke the pipe of peace under the shadow of the same tree, and walk the same path to the spring."

Indeed, to pass by an old friend's house without calling to wish him well, and ask him how he does, an Indian would think this friend had sufficient reason to be angry, or to suspect his friendship. They commonly make some present of venison, or other fresh meats, as further tokens of their good will. In many instances, the white women have become quite reconciled to them, having had sufficient proofs of their peaceful intentions. Where the Indian calling happens to be an old acquaintance, and the man of the house be at home, he walks in confidently, and without ceremony. But should the man be from home, he lays his long knife and tomahawk by the door, and puts his gun behind it, or conceals his side-armor under his breechcloth, walks to the lady of the house, looks pleasing, handles his "calamut," or pipe, inquires for the welfare of the family, and usually asks for tobacco, which is a certain indication of his friendly disposition. The good woman immediately orders something to be got ready for her Indian friend to eat. On such occasions, the white women, as well as their husbands, become quite sociable with them. Indeed, there are many traits in the character of an Indian, who sustains a fair reputation, truly interesting. A life of hardships and adventure afford much experience, which they treasure up in memory, and for many years after will relate, with minuteness and accuracy. . . .

It happened, that the old warrior and counsellor, "Round Buttons," was traveling through a white settlement on the frontiers of the Illinois some years since. His road led him near the house of an old acquaintance, a gentleman of well-known respectability and friendship towards the Indians. Round Buttons was noted for his experience and intelligence. [He] had fought many battles, had several wives, and was a great hunter and runner. The gentleman and lady were happy to see their old friend: the usual expressions of friendship being over, the old guest entertained his kind host with many curious and interesting stories about his people, his hunting and running, killing his enemies, &c. The lady now commenced conversation with him. She interrogated him on many subjects relating to their manners and habits: How many snows he had seen? or How old he was? How the Indians lived? How many wives he had? The character of this Indian was such as to give him the title which we called a privileged character. After answering many of the lady's questions, he looked into the yard through the window very earnestly, where an aspen tree grew. The lady asked him what he was looking at so intently. He asked her what tree she called that in the yard? She said it was a quaking asp. He replied, in broken English,"Indian no call him quake asp." "What then?" asked the inquisitive hostess "Woman tongue, woman tongue," answered the sagacious warrior; "never still, never still, always go." He then turned away, in a very good humor, to enjoy the inspiring beverage, of which he was unfortunately too fond; and to regale, and be regaled in turn, by the gentlemen, with their favorite exploits of hunting, shooting, &c.

The same Indian, returning from a visit to the governor on his way to Kaskaskia, stopped at a tippling shop on the road. A number of half-civilized whites were at the place drinking and playing cards. In the language of the country, they were "rowdying," indulging low vices. Round Buttons was unfortunately "craving a dram" when he arrived. Having taken rather freely, and feeling its influence [he] began to relax from his native dignity of character, and to mix with the ruffians, who now began to think they might make more free with him. He did not choose to permit such liberty, however, for the Indians always think themselves above mean white people, even the most abandoned Indian you can find. They took this conduct as an insult. Some of the party proposed drenching him with whiskey, because he refused to drink any more with them. They would show him what it was to place himself above white people. The owner of the house wished him to take protection in a separate room and be shut up until the men got sober. They might kill him. But the brave warrior was not to be intimidated by threats. And besides, he too well knew human nature, in its savage state, to think of avoiding danger from ruffians by hiding from them. He assured the man he need not be uneasy on his account, though he very warmly thanked him for wishing to afford him protection. "No blood, when much talk," he said; "chattering belongs to women and wild geese! When men make themselves squaws," said he, "they are much beneath them."

The infuriated men cursed and abused the warrior at a horrid rate. Nothing can exceed the silence and secrecy an Indian observes, when he is about to execute some important enterprise. Nothing can exceed his contempt, therefore, for a person who makes harsh threats, and speaks much of what he intends doing. They say on such occasions, "Talk much, do little." Round Buttons, therefore, insisted Mr. Duke not exhibit the smallest symptom of uneasiness for his safety, supposing it would encourage those desperadoes to persist in their ferocity, or make them boast that they had alarmed him. He asked for a board, went deliberately to the fire, and charred one side black [and] then asked for a piece of white paper, which, pinned against the board, he placed by the side of a tree as a target. He deliberately stepped off one hundred yards, took aim, and shot the ball near the center. He reloaded and repeated with similar success. Having wiped his piece and charged it again, still keeping his eye on, and watching minutely the effect of his conduct on his adversaries, he asked his host how he liked his shooting. Did he think any of his neighbors could beat him? He then desired the little boy, son of Mr. Duke, the owner of the house, to run and fetch the tomahawk, as he was without his own. Having greased and dusted the handle, he threw it against a post with much accuracy and force. "Thus," said he, turning to his generous friend, "Indian man provide for his wife and little ones in peace; thus defend them in war." He saw the effect produced which he intended. His rude opponents were convinced they had best not interrupt him, for he was no "woman". . . .

The long and destructive war which had existed between the Mahas, Ottowas, and Kansas tribes, was at length compromised by a meeting at the grand council fire, of the Kansas towns on the Kansas River. Each nation sent its principal representatives, who, in conformity to their expression, came to "bury the tomahawk and scalping-knife, and to remove the sticks out of their path." The most unequivocal tokens of reconciliation were expressed, and the most dignified and decent deportment observed. The Red Scarf of the Ottowas arrived first, with two of his tribe, all with their national costume, but Ma-la-huk bore the wampum of peace. Later in the afternoon of the same day, Kas-ka-he-ga or Moonlight, of the Mahas, arrived with his attendants. The Ottowa and his suite stayed in the house of Mu-kea or Star,* and Kas-ka-he-ga lodged with Kos-hu-ka, and all became acquainted, but not social that evening. They were solemn and serious, which deportment they always observed just before any concern of national importance is to be transacted, or, as they term it, just at the *sleep* or night before they sit around their council fire. Any indulgence in sociality, or levity at such times, is deemed highly improper and inconsistent with the dignity of their high trust. Besides, they think that to show much levity at such a time but ill comports with the importance of the occasion, and discloses a want of sincerity. There is another reason for their retiring to rest very calmly just on the eve of a national "smoke." They commonly take a portion of the herb, heb-ri, and go calmly to rest, lest any irregularities should disturb the lessons or instructions of the Good Spirit, who is supposed to visit them at such times.

They arose early the next morning, and literally drank out of the same spring. They went, as usual on such occasions, and laid their peace wampums in the council lodge, and at the seat where they were to sit at the "smoking." They partook very temperately of roasted buffalo, hominy, &c., and at midday, when the sun was highest and the rays the warmest and the time weariness called for rest arrived, they smoked the "pipe of peace" in the name of their nation.

The sun is highest above the horizon at noon, which is emblematical of their highest friendship. His rays are then most sensibly felt, and that is expressive of the greatest sense of reconciliation. As it causes weariness and a want of rest, they show by this they now agree to bury the weapons of war under the tree of peace, and repose together under its shadow. Sometimes they do, but at this time they did not indulge in any extravagant expressions of pleasure, until the noon of the succeeding day. And, indeed, it very seldom happens, that the Indians, on such occasions, indulge in such expressions of hilarity, or even depart in the slightest degree from that silent dignity, until one *sleep* after the council.

On the next day, each one told his dream, beginning at the eldest. Their conversation then turned on the most remarkable occurrences of their lives. As few opportunities ever occur for them to talk honorably of their worthy deeds, they relate, each in his proper turn, everything with the utmost exactness and precision, as to time, season, place, circumstance, &c. whatever they have achieved. He who has the most to speak of, is deemed the greatest "man."

No one of them ever has the mortification of being disappointed, for they have no such thing as being made, or purchasing, the high dignitary of peace-messenger for his nation, by bribery or family influence. His personal achievements must render him the subject of the appointment . . . he looks forward with patient, but ardent wish to enjoy the luxury of having a suitable opportunity of *talking* of himself. I mention this, because, to be talking on ordinary occasions of great actions, bespeaks littleness, and is certain to be neglected or laughed at. Around the council fire in company with chiefs, and especially those of other nations, is the proper place and company to make known their title to high trust. It also, at the same time, puts them on a par, or raises them above their neighboring chiefs [and] lets them know they have bravery and skill to defend their hunting grounds, women, and little ones.

One of the chiefs, Mal-a-heek, observed, with much self-importance, he had killed so many of his enemies, that he could swim in their blood. Kas-ka-he-ga, who sat next to him, looked around with much earnestness on all the persons present, and then observed, "he had killed so many of his enemies, that all present could swim in their blood."

They exchanged presents of belts, tomahawks, flints, &c. in token of friendship, and relaxed into more sociability. The young women presented them with the choicest parts of roasted buffalo meat, and marrowbones of the same animal, which, when well roasted in the fire, are a great delicacy.

When they had all slaked their thirst again at the same spring, each gave the whoop of his nation three times, left his peacepipe and belt with their former enemies, but now friends, and took their leave.

Colonel Boone related the following anecdote to me during the spring of 1819. A Frenchman who was in the habit of trading among the Indians, took, among other articles, a quantity of gunpowder; but the Indians were supplied by the disposal of most of their furs to other traders, and reserved their remaining stock for the purpose of purchasing other necessaries with them. The Frenchman having sold mostly all his goods except this powder, however, and fearing lest it should remain on his hands, had tried every artifice to induce them to barter with him for it, but without succeeding, until Indian curiosity afforded him the opportunity of selling it.

Among other ingenious questions they asked him, was how the white people made powder. The hopes of finding a ready market for the "black dust," at an advantageous price, immediately set to work his powers of invention. He told them, "The white people sowed it in fields like they did wheat or tobacco seeds, and were enabled thereby to raise large crops from a few pounds of seed." The Indians were highly pleased. Everyone who could raise a beaver skin, purchased, at an exorbitant price, as far as his pelting would go. In a little time the Frenchman found himself freed of all his powder, in possession of great booty, and made the best of his way as soon as he could. The delighted Indians directly set to work in preparing a choice spot of ground for the reception of their new crop. Having cleared the land by removing the timber, rubbish, and brushwood, and having loosened the soil, they followed the Frenchman's directions in sowing the powder. They enclosed it, to prevent their horses and wild animals from injuring it. They went from time to time to see if it had come up. After some weeks had elapsed, and finding all their hopes at an end, one old chief, wiser than the rest, wittily observed "he was a Frenchman," of whom they had purchased the powder. This hint was enough; they understood him. They now all believed it was a fraud: they determined to revenge it the first opportunity. It should be kept in mind that when any individual injures an Indian, he entertains the most bitter enmity, not only against him and his relations, but against his nation.

Not long after, another Frenchman went among the same tribe, with a cargo of dry goods. It should be also remembered, that an Indian seldom forgets an injury. The Frenchman obtained permission from the chief to sell his goods among his people. The chief gave up his own wigwam. The industrious peddler opened his bales, and when the goods were all spread out for inspection, as it were, the young warriors, and all that had been fooled by the former Frenchman, rushed on him, and took all the poor man's goods. He laid his bitter complaint before the chief, and demanded satisfaction. The chief very gravely replied, "He certainly should be paid, but for that he must wait until the next gunpowder harvest." This was all the remuneration the disappointed Frenchman could obtain. He left them, but without being loaded with furs as he had anticipated.

The Indians do not have many serious differences among their families, though petty broils sometimes occur. Then they often end seriously. While I was among the Kansas, however, I witnessed several contests among the women, as well as among the children. An Indian woman went out to get wood; during her absence she left her child in a cradle made of the bark of a tree, girdled and peeled while the sap is up, split in two equal parts, and bound round with a belt. The child was cross. When the mother returned, her next neighbor, who was not on very friendly terms with her, told her if she did not move from that part of the village, or strangle her squalling brat, she should not stay any longer. Some other words followed, which did not amount to many. However, they soon began to more serious business: They beat each other heavily for a few rounds, and then seized each other, scratched each other's faces, tore each other's eyes, and pulled one another's hair, to a desperate degree. Ho-keeh, "the clouds," made Shes-ka's nose bleed most dreadfully.

This contest caused no difference between their husbands that I knew of. They were both out on a war expedition at the time this happened. I witnessed the conflict. Although many were near, no one interfered either to urge hostilities or to prevent discord, but let them "fight out their quarrels," as they say, "and when they get tired they will stop themselves."

One of the greatest insults an Indian woman can offer another, is to say her child is an "ugly cross brat"; or, if it be a boy, to call him "a young squaw." Such language is never used, unless where they intend the greatest insult. And the offended woman is very apt to resent the insult with blows, in order to convince her enemy, by a tangible demonstration, that her son's mother does not deserve the epithet.

Of all the traits which distinguish the Indian character, that of nice discrimination is perhaps the most remarkable. Accustomed from his earliest life to no other guide to conduct him, and no other means to satisfy his wants than those with which Nature has supplied him, the Indian follows her footsteps in all his walks, and minutely watches her most secret haunts. Hence, that peculiar faculty so much observed in their deportment by travelers who have witnessed their actions, when any matter of much importance was the subject of their attention. Hence, the accuracy with which they travel through strange woods in the darkest night.* Hence, the swiftness with which they pursue the blind trail of a flying enemy, where a white person would scarcely suspect anyone to have traveled. And hence their ability to detect the resorts of animals, and their success in taking them.

A trader from the state of Kentucky went among the Osages a few years since, with many articles of show, but of little value, such as blue and red beads, glass buttons, toys, &c. The chiefs were not much inclined to favor his views. He pretended much friendship to procure their patronage, saying, he had always been a friend to the Indians, though the greater part of white people had been their enemies. An aged and experienced Indian, who listened with much attention to the trader, looked suddenly up, fixing his eyes steadfast on those of the trader, and replied, "his friendship should not pass unrewarded." He ordered his women to prepare some jerked buffalo for his repast, thanked him kindly for his friendly disposition towards him, and insisted on his keeping his goods, for they were "too fine for us poor Indians." The man, however, insisted on it, that the Indians deserved to have "fine things" as much as any other people; and he declared, he was not willing to leave them without leaving some of his nice beads with his red brothers and sisters. With the same earnestness and seriousness as before, the Indian sage expressed his grateful obligations to his "white brother" for his favorable opinion of his tribe. He then asked the trader how many squaws he had. How many children and relations? The man gave some answer; to which the Indian replied in broken English, "Why didn't give fine things to him? He got no beaver, to give for fine things. White man mouth full honey, talk sweet, say many good things. This please foolish Indians. He then cheat him. He no fool Shoma-cassa." The whole of the bystanders joined in the ridicule of the trader, who, mortified at not being able to impose his worthless trinkets on them, left them to try his fortune at the expense of some more ignorant tribe. . . .

The old men and chiefs, though sometimes as much pleased with such things as any of their tribe, look with indifference, for the most part, and frequently with contempt on them. They are much better pleased with those traders, who carry blankets, knives, firearms, gunpowder, flints, and such articles of utility as they stand in need of, and they never refuse to give a fair, and most usually an exorbitant price for them.

It will cease to surprise my readers, that they are tired of showy trifles, when it is shown how egregiously they have been cheated, especially in those articles whose worth is not easily reduced to a pecuniary standard. I have known a strand of blue beads to sell for a beaver skin, and a few colored glass buttons to sell for twice that amount.

I well recollect the first looking glass I ever saw. A trader came among the Kansas Indians while I was with them. He brought among other trifles a number of small pocket looking glasses, not larger than a man's hand. Nothing can exceed the pleasure of the old, and the astonishment and ecstasy of the women and young Indians, when seeing their likeness reflected in the glassy mirror. Some thought it altogether enchantment, others were frightened, but the most were highly pleased, and thought the trader a supernatural being. The chief gave him up the use of his house to open his goods in, and in a few days he was master of all the valuable furs and peltry in their tribe. Some few of the warriors and counsellors, who had been to St. Louis, had seen looking glasses. By far the major part had never before seen or heard of the like. Some of the glasses were sold for two beavers' skins apiece.

Another trader came among the same tribe, sometime after, and had a considerable supply of clothing, which was of a quality that did not very much suit the taste and means of the Indians. Of course he found but poor market for his goods. In order, however, that he might get in favor with the tribe, he told them how shamefully the man with the looking glasses had cheated them. The Indians hate to hear their judgment derided, and gave the poor man very little thanks for his information. Besides, they did not believe him to be much better.

The same man who had sold them the glasses, went among them the next trading season, and took a number of very useful articles, such as tin cups, knives, &c. When he arrived among the people, with whom he thought himself a favorite, he ventured up to the same house, which was so much at his service the year before, and which was as freely given up to him now. But to his surprise none offered as before to assist him in with his baggage. None brought him wood to kindle his fire. Nor did the chief order his women to prepare him food; nor invite him to "smoke the calamut of peace with his red brothers round the council fire." Several times the young warriors were on the eve of rushing upon him by surprise, but were prevented by the aged. Having the use of the wigwam so freely offered to his service, although his reception was "cold" to what it had been the last year, he was not without hopes of making a profitable disposal of his goods. After they were all opened and ready to sell, the chief went up to the door, and holding the same glass in his hand, he held it up before the trader's eyes, and asked him if he saw himself. The trader said, Yes, and asked the Indian if it was not a very pretty thing? But Mee-ka-a and his tribe were now not in a humor to be fooled with. He asked the man if he did not see "woman's face, when he saw his own in the glass?" "Man, brave man, no cheat Indian. Indian no cheat white man." He then gave the signal whoop. Hoo-Hoop-Roh-Noh! The whole of the assembled tribe, who had concealed themselves a few paces from the house, behind some fallen logs, rushed in and seized as much of his property as they thought would make up for the fraud he had practiced on them the year before. He was forced to leave them without beaver this time, and was glad to get off with his life. . . .

Indian Diseases   11

The Indians are subject to but few diseases, and those are generally simple, and easily cured. Cases, however, of a different character sometimes occur, and assume all the various and complicated symptoms which are experienced in civilized society. They are not, comparatively, so frequent, but, from want of skill in their treatment, prove more fatal. . . .

The diseases most common among them are rheumatism, asthma, fevers, pleurisy, and bowel complaints. These with some others that prevail less frequently . . . I shall consider in the chapter on their Materia Medica.

With the Indians generally, medicinal barks, roots, and herbs are thought essentials in their household contents. Even in their journeys, such are most likely to be wanted as part of their necessary outfits.

Almost every family has its medicine or sacred bag, which consists of a beaver or otter skin curiously ornamented, and generally contains both their medicinal and small sacred articles.

The application of these pouches, however, varies in different tribes. Sometimes they are devoted to a single purpose, at others, from the variety of their contents, they may be denominated catchalls, but they are always esteemed sacred. I do not recollect a single instance in which their privacy has been violated by unhallowed hands.

The shak-kee,* or rattlesnake's master, a plant which is thought to secure its possessor against injury from that reptile, [along with] anise root, eel's liver, tobacco, and small consecrated articles, supposed to neutralize the agency of evil spirits, are generally among the contents of this holy receptacle. They commonly wear it, in order to derive all the advantages which they suppose it is capable of affording. Should any accident befall them while without it, they always ascribe it to their own negligence. To suggest its inefficiency, would give offense. When its possession fails to benefit, the Indian finds a ready apology for it in his own wickedness, and will not rest, until by fastings and prayer he has, as he supposes, canceled his offenses.

The Indians are far from being ignorant of the treatment of their diseases. They have a rich variety of remedies, from the simple to those which are very active; and experience has given them skill, on most occasions, how best to apply them. Nevertheless, among them, as among civilized people, though from totally different causes, new diseases sometimes appear, which baffle the curative powers of their most skillful physicians; such, for instance, have been the smallpox and syphilis. . . .

Syphilis, the Indians say, was entirely unknown among them until they contracted it from the whites.* It prevails among several of the tribes with which I am acquainted, and proves one of their most troublesome and virulent disorders. Those who go among the populous white settlements on the Missouri and Mississippi, where the disease prevails in its most inveterate forms among the traders and boatmen who navigate the river to New Orleans, frequently return to their families and tribes infected with it. It often assumes a most distressing train of symptoms before the emaciated sufferer is aware of his situation. In the treatment of this disorder, they usually begin with teas and warm diuretic infusions. They drink decoctions of the roots of rushes, sumac leaves, and golden root, as the frontier settlers call it, and which I suspect to be the sarsaparilla of the shops. They also use a little creeping vine, which bears a great number of small white blossoms and seed, with cups of a triangular shape, about the size of buckwheat. This plant grows in rich places near watercourses, and supports itself by running on the shrubbery and bushes within its reach. I am persuaded it deserves a distinguished place in the Materia Medica [see p. 191–91]. Its medicinal effects are profusely diuretic without producing nausea, or any unpleasant sensation, except a feeling of fullness somewhat similar to that after partaking too freely of watermelons. From its bitterness and other sensible properties, I have no doubt that its action extends generally to the whole system.

Another plant, which is in considerable repute among the Indians for the cure of the malady in question, is the white plantain. This they give in infusion. Whether it deserves the character they give it or not, I cannot say. I believe it has some virtue as a diuretic. They give the warm tea three or four times a day, in large drafts. I do not say it has any antisyphilitic properties. I merely know that they give it in such cases, and mention that fact without remark.

Wild licorice tea, and a tea of the anise root, are also given as a part of the diet of the patient. Great abstinence is imposed on the Indians in the cure of all their diseases, but especially in this. If they have a strong desire or craving for any particular article of diet, however, it is viewed as a favorable symptom, and is always indulged. The friends of the sufferer will spare no pains to procure it for him. They often travel many days' journey for this purpose.

[Though syphilis and other new diseases challenge their best physicians], we seldom meet with an Indian who has not a sufficient knowledge of their medicine to prescribe on all ordinary occasions. Some are so much more skillful than others, however, as to justly merit and obtain the distinctive title of doctor. In some tribes, this distinction is confined to the men; in others, it is given to both the men and women, according to the success which attends individual practice. In all cases, however, the women are permitted to prescribe for their own peculiar diseases. Where the men are tenacious of titles, it is done quietly, and without ostentation.

Among the more enlightened tribes, the practice of medicine is not confined to particular individuals. All the old men and women know how to manage the generality of their complaints, and the patient usually makes choice of the one he prefers.

Quackery, or unskillful and unsuccessful practice, is in most of the tribes followed by loss of character, and sometimes, when life is supposed to have been sacrificed, by the banishment, and even the death of the pretended physician.

In general, however, no one undertakes the practice of medicine, unless invited to by those suffering under disease, or by the spontaneous call of the tribe. This is not commonly uttered, except from a conviction, arising from results, that the subject is possessed of superior talents. But, among the more ignorant tribes, no regard is had to real qualifications, and the treatment of their sick has no claim to the distinctive quality of being rational. Their physicians resort chiefly to juggling, charms, and conjurations, as curative processes: a course, in most cases, far inferior to that which Nature, when left to herself, most commonly observes.

When practitioners found their claim on real merit, they observe no distinction in dress from the rest of the nation.* When otherwise, they frequently array themselves in the most grotesque habiliments, and, instead of giving their medicine to their patients, take it themselves. They wrap themselves in the skins of some animal, to which are fastened, according to their whims, buffaloes' horns, bears' claws, tortoise shells, &c., in order to frighten away the evil spirit, which, they say, is the cause of their patient's disease. They take drugs to inspire in themselves a power superior to that of the supposed afflicting supernatural agents. They sometimes assume great authority, and, after having prayed, and sweated profusely, tell their patients that they have accomplished their cures by driving away their tormentors. I have known an instance in which the physician became offended, because the sick would not appear better, and charged it to obstinacy.

To question their skill on such occasions would give great offense. I have no doubt that the effect of this kind of practice on the imagination has wrought some cures, and helped to establish the influence and authority they generally exercise.* These pretenders, however, occasionally fail, not only in effecting cures, but in securing their reputations against opprobrium. Even then the more timorous do not withhold outward respect for them, for fear of being made sufferers, on the score of retaliation, through their influence with evil spirits. Nevertheless, their impostures sometimes become so glaring, as to even forfeit this restraint, and they are obliged to fly for self-preservation. I have heard of instances in which their lives have been made to atone for their abuse of sacred things and the public credulity. However, among those tribes, where the choice of a physician is left to the patient or his friends, their claims in general are founded on merit; and, though they should prove unsuccessful in practice, the public opinion is usually indulgent and charitable towards them, and appears to be guided by a just view of the constant liability of all mankind to death.

The Indian physicians are commonly honorable, humane, and experienced men. They are not tempted to follow the profession from the hope of gain. Frequently the title is awarded them from their having relieved a sufferer, when no regular doctor could be procured. Sometimes the character originates from remarkable dreams; as, for instance, if remedies which have been prescribed and have proved successful, seem to them to have been pointed out by some good spirit, through an uncommonly pure channel, and for the benefit of the sufferer. On these occasions, therefore, they are not backward in awarding honors. In general, however, age, acute observation, good judgment, and experience, constitute the qualifications of their most popular and reputable physicians.

The dangerously sick occupy separate lodges, which none but the attendant physician and nurse are allowed to enter. When their disease is less violent, the family do not remove, but remain and nurse the patient. In their villages they uniformly occupy skin cots, elevated something above the ground. When traveling, they are disposed of as circumstances will permit.

The physician, on entering the apartment of the sick, takes his patient by the arm, examines his tongue, feels his hands, feet, and breast; regards him for some time with the most profound attention and silence; and then, in a low voice, inquires into the nature of his sufferings. This ascertained, he continues for a much longer period than before in silent thoughtfulness, and, after having given some general instructions to the nurse, retires to prepare his medicines. On returning, he is guided in their administration by the violence of the disease, as indicated by the symptoms. But, in nearly all their practice, their doses are too large, and often of too active a nature. When their patients are bad, they say, the enemy within is strong, and it requires great force to drive him out. This, whether successful or not, is always the apology for their energetic practice.

The treatment of their women and children, during sickness, is precisely the same as is observed towards the men, so far as there is a conformity in their diseases. In the treatment of those peculiar to their sex, the female practice is rational, and seldom fails to relieve. Indeed, it may justly be said to be attended with great success and the same observations will apply equally well, in regard to the general practice of medicine by the men among the Osages and Kansas.

The women always officiate as nurses to the sick, in their villages, and also in their hunting excursions, when any happen to be of their party, which, to be prepared for an exigency of this kind, more than for any other purpose, is frequently the case.

However, when without them, either in the chase or in war, those best skilled in medicine act both in the capacity of physician and nurse. Should more assistance be required, the young and inexperienced are detached on the service. The Indians say that good nursing is as essential to the recovery of the sick, as are the attendance of a skillful physician, and the kind operation of the prescribed medicine. In consequence, the elderly, most experienced, and most respectable are selected for this duty. The preference is however commonly given to relations or friends. Where the case requires extraordinary attention, these circumstances are overlooked; the most respectable women in the tribe feel themselves honored by being chosen, and particularly so, should their charge be a highly respectable character.

When the danger is great, they have one, and sometimes two adjuncts, who, with the principal, continue alternately with the sick, and promptly administer such medicines and nutritive broths and teas as they may require.

No one presumes to interfere with their duties. They praise or criticize the attending physician, according to the success which results from his practice. The physician calls frequently on the sick; often attends to the operation of his medicine; hears the reports of the nurses, to whom he is generally obliging in his conduct; takes a little rest; and discovers great anxiety till his patient is out of danger. They receive nothing in consideration for all their services, deprivations, and sufferings. Those who have experienced the benefit of their skill, however, sometimes present them with robes, caps, or moccasins, or with some redundant consecrated article, as mementos, or rather acknowledgments of their obligations. A present, tendered in any other form, would be regarded with disdain, and the offer itself considered as an insult.

The friends of the deceased often make presents of a similar nature, in order to testify their satisfaction, in regard to zeal and efforts in his behalf. Such testimonials uniformly impart cheerfulness to the physician, serve to dispel his distress, and, if anything, to increase his reputation. But this is more particularly the case, when they come from the nurses, who, in this way, often approbate his skill.

When the patients have a particular desire for anything, physicians indulge it with moderation, except the crisis be alarming, in which case they impose a rigid abstinence, and say, a contrary course would be feeding the disease. Experience has taught them that full eating increases fever. During the prevalence and the convalescent state, therefore, they are careful in dieting their patients; nor do they suffer them to sleep long at a time, nor in close apartments. Long sleep, they believe, disposes to a return of the fever. In most instances, the recovery of the sick from acute diseases is rapid. But they do not return to severe exercise until they have sufficiently regained their health and strength, which is indicated by a recurrence to smoking their pipes. These occasions call forth rejoicings, feasts, and thanksgivings to the Great Spirit, in which all their friends and relations join.

When all natural means fail, the physicians do not abandon their patients. On the contrary, they cling to them till their last gasp, but substitute, instead of their prescriptions, fastings and prayers to the Great Spirit. "So long as there is life," say they, "there is room for hope; and to despair of effecting good, and to neglect means that appear remote and almost foreign to the disease, bespeak a careless and unskillful practice." When their hopes fail, they seldom inform their patients of their danger, but are very cautious that their last moments may be calm and undisturbed.

In general, patients look upon sickness and affliction as chastisements for their offenses against the Great Spirit, and commonly bear them with great resignation and fortitude. When they become peevish and fretful, as sometimes happens, their doctors then say, that the abatement of their disease permits their minds to be idle or unoccupied, and the danger is past.

Whenever death unfortunately succeeds, they appear deeply afflicted; are foremost to attend to the obsequies of the dead; and afterwards retire in gloomy silence to their lodges, or sacred places, to appease by their supplications the evil spirit, to whose wrath they are wont to ascribe their ill success.

As soon as a physician looks upon the condition of his patient as desperate, he permits the relatives and particular friends to visit his bedside. I have myself been a spectator at such assemblages; witnessed some lingering and painful deaths; particularly noticed their conduct at the closing scene; and can truly declare that they, for the most part, manifest as much firmness and resignation as any people of which I have ever heard.

There is seldom any conversation between them and their relations. All present remain silent, and engaged in inward devotion. Sometimes, however, the sick avail themselves of these affecting occasions, to inculcate on the minds of their audience the sage lessons of age and experience. I have already remarked, that the sayings of the aged are received and attended to, in common, as almost oracular. It may be readily supposed, particularly in respect to youth, that those emanating from a deathbed make much deeper and more lasting impressions.

The Indians, in general, collect much valuable information during the experience of long lives, which is permanently retained in their memories till the period of their dissolution, when it, together with counsels and prayers, is dealt out to their surviving connections and friends as the last and most important legacy they have to bestow. And the respect which is always inculcated, and, on all common occasions, awarded as a proper and just homage to the aged, amounts . . . almost to veneration. The closing scene witnesses a nation overwhelmed with wailings and sorrow.

While on a visit to the Great Osage village, at the time Tecumseh was there, a very aged and respectable Indian died from natural decay. He was sensible his race was nearly run, and met the King of Terrors with a presence of mind, fortitude, and resignation, seldom if ever witnessed in civilized life. His conduct and feelings did not arise from a want of sensibility, or ignorance of the important change he was about to suffer. On the contrary, he appeared to comprehend them in all their bearings, and talked of them, and of the duties of life, connected with present and future happiness, with the calmness and wisdom of a Socrates. At times, his discourses were preceptorial and admonitory; at others, they were persuasive and pathetic, and related to example. And he was listened to, day after day, till his speech failed him, by both young and old, with great solicitude and interest.

In general they manifest no anxiety about the future, but leave the world with an apparent satisfaction, under a belief, provided their conduct has been in consonance with the precepts which they have been taught, that their title to future happiness is unquestionable. When an Indian exhibits fear and weakness, and makes lamentable complaints on his deathbed, it is a source of mortification to his relations and friends, who indulge, though not in his presence, in the most extravagant grief, and, believing him under the influence of some malignant spirit, utter the most fervent prayers to the Great Spirit, for his especial interference in behalf of the suffering.

Entire silence on these occasions is looked upon as a happy omen. It is regarded as a confirmation that the patient has performed all the duties requisite to secure him a future and perpetual residence with the wise and good. His apparent meditations are supposed to be inward devotions, and they doubt not that he is in direct communion with the Good Spirit, which is in waiting to protect him from all injuries and dangers in his journey to the other world.

The attendance of these ministering spirits is thought to be more especial in the night than in the day. The Indians' faith in it is so strong, that their diseased imaginations often give to them forms and presence. They sometimes even pretend to repeat the substance of their discourses. Extraordinary as this may seem to people in civilized life, I am confident this delusion, connected with their lives and death, is to them a source of good. As connected with their moral conduct, it is for them a substitute of that faith which has the Creator of the Universe for its author, and the salvation of souls for its end.

Some Indians believe that death has been inflicted on the human family in consequence of the transgressions they committed against the Great Spirit: indeed, one of their traditions, though I have omitted to mention it, is to this effect.

But, in general, the most observant, judging comparatively from the course of events entailed on all other organized and living beings and things, regard the cessation of the functions of life, and the dissolution of the human body, as a necessary result, conformed to the designed operations of nature. With this view of death, they submit to it, as they do to other circumstances which they cannot avoid, with consistent resignation. But, notwithstanding the exercise of this philosophy, if it may be called such, education avails them of extraordinary reinforcements on these highly important and eventful occasions, for they are taught to believe, that a fearlessness or disregard for death, no matter in what form it may approach, is as essential to the good and perfect character of the warrior, as are bravery and courageous achievements in the deadly fray of battle. Without them, all other externals of dignity are regarded as mere shadows, and cannot secure the respect even of the most humble pretenders.

Observations on the Materia Medica of the Indians

12

I need not anticipate my readers, by telling them the subject offered to their perusal is a dry record of facts. They have my assurance that I have seldom indulged in remarks obtained from a foreign source, but have confined them to such circumstances as came within the sphere of my own immediate notice, or to information from persons whose regard for truth places them above suspicion.

Like their diseases, their remedies are comparatively few, and on that very account seem not to require a systematic arrangement. I shall, nevertheless, discuss them in alphabetical order,* but without attempting to give their technical synonyms, for . . . my acquaintance with these subjects originated under circumstances and views altogether disconnected with their application to the general purposes of civilized life.* Indeed some of the English names are of my own application, but such are conformed either to their Indian meanings, or to their particular qualities or appearance.

[Masterwort; *Angelica atropurpurea*]
La-go-nee-haw—Agreeable taste

Angelica. This plant grows abundantly in high and dry soils, in various parts of the western country. It is held in high repute among the Indians, and always constitutes an ingredient in the medicine bag. It is chiefly valued, however, as an agreeable commodity for smoking, in which way they frequently use it alone, though they prefer it mixed with tobacco. It is often eaten by the Indians while traveling and short of provisions. It is liable, however, to produce heartburn and other symptoms of indigestion. They sometimes give it in the diseases of their children, but it has no great claims as a medicine. It is sometimes mixed with other remedies, to render them more palatable.

*I.e., the first, italicized word of each new entry is alphabetized. (RD)

[Aniseed, anise seed]
Tut-te-see-hau—It expels the wind

Anise grows in great profusion in moist shaded soils. The roots are perennial, and possess a very agreeable taste and aromatic smell. They are frequently eaten in traveling, are considered good to remove flatulency, and are sometimes given in combination with other drugs to render them less disagreeable to the patient.

[Charcoal]
He-ne-pis-ka—Fire gone out

Ashes. The Indians make a lye from water and the ashes obtained from sound wood; it is taken, much diluted, for sourness in the stomach. They digest grains of corn in it, and eat them as a remedy for the same disease. The ashes of tobacco and the mountain laurel are applied with considerable advantage to ill-conditioned ulcers.

Hon-kos-kao-ga-sha—It stops the blood flowing out

Astringent root. This is a shrubby plant, growing in abundance in the edges of the prairies and hillsides through the western country. Its principal virtue consists in its astringent properties, which it possesses in a very high degree. It is one of their favorite remedies in stopping bleeding from wounds; the dried root is powdered and put on the mouths of the bleeding vessel, and a bandage bound over it. The Indians have great confidence in it. They use it very much, both internally in the form of tea, and externally as a wash in female complaints. But by far the most efficacious purpose to which this root is applied, is to stop the spitting of blood; an affection [complaint] which frequently exists amongst them, in consequence of their long and hurried marches. They seldom travel without it; a half teaspoonful in cold water is the dose. I know it to be a highly valuable article in their Materia Medica.

Shes-ka-ne-shu—Washing in the river

Bathing. This, though perhaps not strictly speaking a cure for their diseases, is a very good preventive. It is much practiced, constitutes one of their greatest pleasures, and, I am persuaded, contributes very much to strengthen the body and invigorate the constitution. Men, women, and children, from early infancy, are in the daily habit of bathing during the warm months; and not infrequently after cold weather has set in.*

Was-saw-bape-sha—It scares bears away

Bears' fright. This is a small annual plant, growing in abundance on the hills in the western territories. It has a strong disagreeable smell, on which account the Indians say that the bear will neither approach it, or any one who carries it about them. I should not like to trust its efficacy, particularly with the brown bears of the mountainous regions. The root is given as a sudorific [i.e., sweat-producing], and is also one of their most violent cathartics.

[Bear, OD, *wa-cá-be*]
Was-saw-ba-he-ja—The fat of the bear

Bears' oil. This is used as a medicine, both internally and externally, in combination with many drugs. It is used as a menstruum, for the gall of the earth, yellow root, prickly ash, black root, and several other plants, and with them respectively forms excellent unctions for various cutaneous diseases.* They are in the habit of taking it both for medicine and for food. For colds they seethe the roots of wild licorice in it, which they drink hot as they can well bear it. They also take it for asthma and pleurisy. They esteem it among the most valuable articles of food, especially in their journeys. It is highly nutritive, agrees well with the stomach, and produces no thirst. From the smallness of the quantity necessary to satisfy the appetite, it produces no shortness of breath. The Indians, while travelling, take about four ounces in twenty-four hours, which they continue for days together, with very little other nourishment. An ointment is prepared, by mixing buckeye leaves with it, which, rubbed over the skin, is very good to keep off the mosquitoes; and is much used for that purpose.

[Wild carrot, Queen Anne's lace, "may be
the 'Beaver root'"—Vogel; *Daucus carota;*
beaver, OD, *zhá-be*]
Sha-ba-wa-nem-bra—Beavers eat it

The beaver root very much resembles the common garden carrot, in size and appearance, but in taste it is [dis]agreeably bitter. The top grows to the height of three or four feet, and bears large, broad, and deeply indented leaves. The root is much used by the hunters, as a bait for beavers, which are exceedingly fond of it, and from which circumstances its name is derived.

It is used as a tonic,* and as such deservedly merits the high reputation awarded to it by the Indians.

E-hau-wah—It makes sick

Black locust. The inner bark of this tree is a powerful emetic, and as such is used by the Indians.

[Black snakeroot, black cohosh?
Cimicifuga racemosa? Big Soldier,
Osage brave, *Has-hak-a-tonga*]
Has-hak-a-da-ton-ga—Strong soldier

Black root. The plant rises about one foot in height, has rough serrate leaves, nearly heart-shaped, standing on long foot-stalks. The root, in very small doses, is a drastic cathartic. It commonly produces severe gripping pains, and sometimes the discharge of blood, vertigo, and partial blindness. From its property, which affects vision, some call it Heenee (darkness). It is sometimes taken as an abortive.

He-ne-ska—Dark-colored liquor

Black walnut. The rinds or hulls of the black walnut readily impart their virtues to water, changing its transparency to a deep black. Taken in doses of an ounce, and repeated at proper intervals, it effects a speedy relief in cases of the colic. It is highly reputed among the Indians, and I believe fully merits the character they have given it.

[Horse chestnut]
Tar-ton-ga-on-ba—Eyeball of the buck

Buckeye. There are two varieties of this tree; the medicinal has a most beautiful white soft wood, and is much used by the frontier settlers to make domestic utensils, such as bowls, spoons, &c. The nut is the part used by the Indians as a remedy in diarrhea. Its leaves possess a disagreeable nauseous smell, somewhat similar to the *Datura stramonium,** and, like the nuts, are highly narcotic. The leaves and fruit are both so poisonous as to destroy many of the cattle, which sometimes accidentally eat them; this circumstance has caused the western farmers to cut many of the trees down, in order to prevent similar recurrences. . . .

Chee-za-hau—It seems to fill the belly

Chee-za-hau. The name of this plant in the Indian dialect is indicative of its properties, which are diuretic. It is a small delicate vine, which delights in a rich moist soil, and rising from small fibrous roots, supports itself on the neighboring shrubbery. About the middle of July it produces a great number of small white flowers, which are followed by a profuse crop of small brown-colored seeds, in shape and size resembling the grains of buckwheat. The leaves are heart-shaped, and about the size of a [silver] dollar. It exerts its diuretic properties to an uncommon degree with very little inconvenience to the patient.

A sense of fullness and distention in the abdomen, somewhat similar to that arising from eating freely of watermelons, is the only inconvenience experienced from its use. The Indians employ this plant with good effect in dropsies. They make it into a tea, and give it in large doses, frequently repeated.

The result generally is a profuse discharge of urine, but I have seen them almost faint from the excessive flow of this secretion. The leaves and vine, either in the recent or dried state, and sometimes the whole of the plant, are used. It possesses a slightly bitter taste, from which one might suppose it possessed a tonic power. It is in a small degree narcotic. The Indians sometimes smoke the leaves as a luxury, though they are not so highly esteemed as those of the sumac.

[Columbia-root—Vogel; horse, OD, *ká-wa*]
Kow-o-la-e-ko—Physic for horses

Columbian root. This plant grows in rich southern exposures in great abundance throughout the Arkansas and Missouri countries. It is among the earliest that appear in the spring, rises to three or four feet in height, and sends one large root into the ground, which resembles in size and appearance the common parsnip. It is, in combination with the bark of the wild cherry and snakeroot, a favorite remedy among the Indians in intermittent fever [malaria], general debility, weakness and sickness of the stomach, and in diseases incident to females. When their children are afflicted or supposed to be afflicted with worms, they administer this tonic in mixture with anthelmintic [i.e., worm-expelling] remedies, as they believe it dangerous to purge off the worms when they are much debilitated, without the observance of some such precautionary measure.

[Severely cold, OD, *ni-wa-tse i-gi-ha*]
Ne-wa-sha-ne-wa-sha—Cold as ice

Cooling plant. This grows only in cool, shaded places, where the soil is moist. The stalk is annual, and grows three or four feet high; the leaves are very succulent, of a deep-green color, serrate, oval, and about three inches long. The recent leaves, bruised and applied to swellings and inflammations, give in almost all cases immediate relief. It deserves to be, and is, highly valued by the Indians.

[*Frasera speciosa;* deer, OD, *ta* or *ta-pá*]
Ter-me-a—Like the deer's tongue

Deer's tongue. This is a small plant, producing only a single leaf, which is in the shape of the deer's tongue, from which circumstance it derives its name. It appears early in the spring, and bears a white blossom. It is prized highly in breast complaints, is given in powder, and also in decoction. I do not think it a very active medicine.

[Blazing star; *Chamaelirium luteum;* wolf, OD, *sho-mi-ka-ci*]
Sho-ma-cas-sa-es-sa-rah—It kills wolves

Devil's bit, or *gall of the earth.* This small plant, when applied in its recent state, is capable of exciting inflammation of the skin; it is used in the treatment of ulcers, as an escharotic [i.e., having caustic properties], and also for keeping open tissues, the importance of which in particular constitutional habits the Indians very well understand.

[Disease, etc., OD, *ó-ga-she*]
O-ga-she-ga—Running on the ground

Dewberry root. An infusion of this is given cold in bowel complaints; it is not, however, considered a very active remedy.

[Rabbit, OD, *mon-shtin-ge*]
Mas-tin-jay—Rabbit

Dittany. This is a plant too well known in this country to require any description from me. It is highly esteemed as a sudorific in coughs, colds, and diseases of the febrile order.

They give the hot infusion very freely; the patient being covered up warm. The leaves are much used for smoking and chewing among several tribes. It is entirely free from the narcotic properties of tobacco and is pleasant-tasted, though it produces a slight degree of pungency on the tongue.

[*Cornus* species]
Shen-don-shu-gah—Bitter red berry

Dogwood. They give the bark of this tree, in combination with bitters of various kinds, in fevers of the low type, and when there is great prostration of strength.* I believe, however, they value it mostly in form of poultice, as a corrector of ill-conditioned sores.

E-haw-waw—It pukes

Emetic bean. This vegetable grows in great abundance throughout the countries situated on the Arkansas, Verdigris, and Vermillion [Neosho]. The beans are small and of a red color; two or three of them, chewed and swallowed, prove a pretty active emetic, for which purpose they are employed by the Indians. They are also taken as abortives. They possess something of an intoxicating property, and are taken in small doses as a preparatory regimen for war, and to produce dreams.

Wesh-ke-nah—It relieves hard breathing

The flax weed grows in the fissures of rocks, particularly on cliffs, on the margin of the rivers, to the height of ten or twelve inches; the root sends off many branches, which in July produce numerous small pale-blue flowers. The Indians gather the plant, while in blossom, and prescribe it for asthmas and coughs with the happiest effect. The roots, leaves, and stalks are made into a decoction, and given freely to the patient, as warm as he can conveniently take it. No medicine displays its salutary effects more promptly. I speak thus confidently, because I have witnessed its operations. The Indians sometimes while traveling, or when just returned from long and fatiguing journeys, are seized with the asthma, but are certain to obtain prompt and decided relief from this remedy. I believe it almost uniformly excites a perspiration, on the appearance of which the patient becomes easy.

[Feverwort, horse gentian, American or blue gentian; *Gentiana* family; strong/child, OD, *ton-ga/zhin-gá*]

Ton-ga-shin-ga—It gives strength to a child

Gentian wild. This plant has commonly four or five branching roots, which are about the size of a man's finger. The stalks, to the number of five or six, grow to a height of two or three feet, and bear yellow pulpy seeds or berries, which adhere closely to the stalk, at the junction of the leaves, which are nearly oval-shaped and rough. The Indians make great use of the root in cases of debility, especially when accompanied with affections of the stomach. They most commonly make use of it in decoction, though they sometimes take it in substance. They combine it with dogwood and wild-cherry bark, and give it in cold infusion in intermittents,* while the fever is off. Thus prepared, it is also given for the palpitation of the heart and in dropsies.

[Willow; *Salix* species; river, OD, *ni*]
Sin-des-nes-ni—It grows by the water

Green-twig. This is a shrub very common on the banks of rivers and water-courses. It seldom attains to a height exceeding six or eight feet, and is considered valuable in colds, and asthma; they give a warm infusion at night, with a design to excite perspiration. The roots are used for anthelmintic purposes, and the inner bark as a febrifuge [i.e., fever-reducing] and sudorific.*

[*Corylus americana*]
Shem-ba—Giddiness

Hazelnut. They make poultices of the bark of the hazelnut tree, as an external application for ulcers, tumors, &c.

[Balsam fir; *Abies balsamea*]
Mos-char-ne-wat-char—It causes heat and cold

Indian balsam. This is one of the most valuable articles belonging to the Indian class of remedies. I do not know that it has ever been noticed by any writer; I shall therefore endeavor to give an unmistakable description of it. . . .

The plant seldom attains to a height exceeding four or five inches and has three heart-shaped leaves, about the size of a half dollar, supported on the apex of each stalk. The top is annual, but the root is perennial.

The root separates into four or five branches of from three to five inches in length, are of a very white color, and, when recent, about the size of a goose quill. It is commonly found in an arable fertile soil, completely shaded by other plants. Its other sensible qualities are nearly as follows: the smell is somewhat like that of cedar berries and its taste aromatic and resinous, resembling that of Copaiba balsam—they are both improved by keeping. Chewing it produces a copious flow of saliva, and not infrequently tears.

On swallowing it, a burning sensation is imparted to the throat, which is followed by a sense of coolness that seems to extend over the whole system. It may be described as an agreeable sensation.

It has the remarkable trait of producing an extensive and obvious action on the system, without any inconvenience to the patient. The Indians consider this as one of the most valuable of all their remedies; in colds, coughs, asthmas, and consumptions, they give it in substance or infusion with the most happy effects. In fact such is the reputation of this plant among them, that the physicians settled on their frontiers have introduced it amongst their curatives, and speak highly in its favor. Doctor Kincheloe, near Woodberry, Mississippi, and Doctor Saunderson, near Natchez in Mississippi, have both prescribed it, and declare its effects to have surpassed their expectations. They say its introduction into general practice will constitute a valuable addition to the Materia Medica and is more particularly valuable in pulmonary consumption, during the period of hectic fever.

[American ipecac, Bowman's root; *Gillenia trifoliata;* bowels, intestines, OD, *shú-be*]
Sku-te-na-ja—It makes sick

Indian physic. The emetic and sudorific virtues of this plant are well known to the Indians, and they employ it in the cure of fevers, bowel complaints, &c.

[Jack-in-the-pulpit, wake-robin, dragon root or green dragon, cuckow point; *Arisaema triphyllum*, etc.; thick, OD, *sho-gá*]
E-haw-sho-ga—Bite the mouth

Indian turnip. This is another of the remedies in common use among the Osage and Shawanee Indians. They confine its use, I believe, to coughs and intermitting fevers. For coughs they give it in decoction with spikenard and wild licorice and in intermittents, when the fever is off, in substance combined with snakeroot, and wild cherry-tree bark.

[Copperas; *Ferri sulphas;* black/dark (in color), OD, *çá-be/shá-be*]
Shen-da-saw-ba—Black dye

Iron. From the cliffs of rocks bordering on some streams, mineralized waters much resembling a dilute solution of copperas (sulphate of iron) exude, and especially in very dry weather deposit a substance which I now believe to be the oxide of iron. The Indians collect it, and place much reliance on its vermifuge [i.e., de-worming] powers. They give it as such by simply mixing it with cold water.

But they place more confidence in it as an ingredient in their favorite remedy for dropsy, which is composed of this substance, the leaves of the sourwood [sorrel] tree, and wild cherry bark, without much regard to fixed quantities. They boil them sometimes together; and, when cold, give the patient a draft of it three or four times a day. On the Grand Saline [Cimarron], Vermillion [Neosho], and Blue Earth rivers, this substance is found in considerable quantities.

[Mandrake, Indian apple, wild lemon;
Podophyllum peltatum]
Che-sa-ne-pe-sha—It pains the bowels

May apple. The root of this plant is the part used as a medicine. They give it in powder as a cathartic.* The dose is about the same as that of jalap or rhubarb. They give it as an antidote for poison, and frequently prescribe it in the commencement of fevers. The fruit is esteemed as a delicacy; it is in great abundance in various parts of the western forests.

[1. Silkweed; *Asclepias syriaca*
2. Probably tall milkweed; *Asclepias exaltata*—Gilmore;
white milkweed, Omaha, *ska*]
Ne-pe-sha—Bad luck to touch it

Milkweed. There are two species of the milkweed or silk plant, on the Arkansas River. One is the plant well known in this country by the name of *Asclepias syriaca*. The other is peculiar, I believe, to the western country, at least I have never seen it elsewhere. It is nearly allied to the former in some of its botanical characters; it differs, however, in having its leaves fringed with a white border, and in being less thick and milky. It grows plentifully in open sunny lands, and attains to a height of three or four feet. The Indians use the roots in decoction for the cure of dysentery, dropsy, and asthma. It is also used as an emetic, and held in tolerably high estimation as a medicine in the above cases.*

[Hair/White Hair, OD, *pa-hiú/cka*]
Pa-us-ka—Like hair

Moss. The bark of the shellbark walnut [hickory?], especially on the north side, is frequently covered with moss, in which the Quapaw Indians place the most unshaken confidence in the treatment of catarrhs and asthmas. I know nothing of its value. They give the warm infusion, keeping the patient wrapped up in blankets or buffalo skins.

[*Betula* species]
Ne-lash-kee—(The name of the tree)

Mountain birch. This tree is found on the north sides of mountains and cliffs on western streams in abundance, and attains to fifty or sixty feet in height. The Indians make use of the inner bark as a remedy in colds, coughs, and diseases of the pulmonary organs. They usually administer it in decoction. Many of the frontier settlers in the western territories value it very highly as a table beverage.

[Horse mint? *Monarda punctata?*]
Mos-char—Warming

Mountain tea. This small evergreen thrives only in sterile soils; it is in great repute amongst the Indians, both as a sudorific and anodyne [i.e., pain reliever], in coughs, catarrhs, breast complaints, and fevers.

[*Quercus* species]
Wah-ton-ga

The oak. Several varieties of the oak are used as medicines by the Indians in bowel complaints, and also as a wash for ulcers.*

[Cohosh, blue? *Caulophyllum thalictroides?*]
A-shem-bra—To make sleep

Paint root, blue. The plant connected with this article is found in considerable abundance on the margins of the sterile prairies, and on the hills adjacent to Blue Earth and the healing waters of the Kansas and Arkansas rivers. The stalk is solitary, quadrangularly shaped, of a purple color, and grows to the height of about six inches. The leaves resemble those of the catmint, though they are more rough and of a darker color. It blossoms pale blue in July, and has four or five short radicles of a goose-quill size, which on account of their coloring properties the Indians collect with great industry. It forms a tolerably permanent beautiful blue dye. As such it is highly prized, and applied to partially stain their faces, and to color various articles used in ornamenting their persons. If much rubbed, when applied to the skin, it produces violent itching and inflammation;

if much handled, it induces sleep, and it is sometimes given as an opiate in very minute doses.

Paint root, red. This plant grows on the dry fertile prairies, has rough oval leaves, which alternate, and are of the size of a half dollar. The flowers are of a purple color, set close to the stalk, and appear in July, in the angle formed by the leaf stem. The root is perennial and replete with an intensely red juice, which the Indians use as a cosmetic for their persons and dresses, and also as emblematic of war, the warriors generally coloring their faces with it preceding their hostile operations. It is sometimes used as a vermifuge, but is more esteemed in the furniture of the sacred bag, on account of its supposed protecting influence.

[Prince's pine, wintergreen; *Chimaphila umbellata*]
Ne-was-char-la-go-ne—Good for colds or cough

Pipsisseway. This plant is too generally known among the people of the United States to require any description by me. It is held in considerable esteem by the Indians, and is used as an anodyne and sudorific, especially in diseases of the breast, colds, &c.

[Hercules club, toothache tree; *Zanthoxylum americanum*]
Han-to-la

Prickly ash. This is one of the most valuable remedies the Indians possess in the cure of rheumatism.* The inner bark taken in substance, and the roots boiled in water, to a strong decoction, and drank in large drafts four or five times a day as a sudorific, is a very common internal remedy among them. The inner bark seethed in bears' grease is used externally in form of an embrocation [lotion]. It is also made into poultices, and in powder applied with advantage to ulcers, by the advanced settlers as well as by the Indians. They frequently resort to this remedy, and have great reliance in its efficacy. I can say nothing of its claims to confidence, from my own experience.

[Bloodroot; *Sanguinaria canadensis;*
red, OD, *zhú-dse*]
Shu-jee-hu—Red dye or color

Puccoon. The sanguinaria grows in great abundance in various parts of the western countries, especially in rich and shaded soils. They hold it in high esteem as a remedy in several of their diseases, but more particularly in rheumatism, for which it is taken in the same manner as the prickly ash. I have known them to use the dry powdered root as an escharotic.

Ne-bra-ta-hea—To make drink

Rushes. This plant grows on most of the western waters. It sometimes attains to a height of six feet, though not commonly to more than three or four feet. It is well known to the frontier settlers, who make much use of it in scrubbing and scouring their furniture, rooms, &c. The Indians also use it in making mats, thatching their lodges, and for wicks in their illuminations, for which it answers an exceedingly good purpose. But as a medicine they esteem it more highly. It operates powerfully as a diuretic, and is a very common remedy in dropsies, menstrual and syphilitic diseases.

It produces great thirst, and an increased action throughout the system.

The root is the part used as a medicine. It is given in decoction, in large drafts, three or four times a day.

[*Pinus* species]
Kee-chi-he-ja-ka—Gift of the Great Spirit, Sau-kies

Sap pine, or healing gum tree of the traders. This tree grows on a cold soil to the height of twenty or thirty feet, and sends off long spreading branches. It is an evergreen of the pine family. On its trunk are numerous small protuberances, which contain a medicinal resinous juice, which is somewhat pungent to the taste and smell. It is held in high estimation, in the treatment of breast complaints and coughs; it is also a favorite remedy for gonorrhea and languid ulcers. They give it internally in the three first diseases, and when applied to ulcers, it is spread on thin membranes or skins, and laid over the affected part. It relieves pain, arrests inflammation, reduces the swelling, and disposes the parts to heal. Mr. Spencer, with whom many of my western friends are well acquainted, assured me, that during a trip up the Mississippi to Red Cedar Lake, he contracted, from exposure, an excruciating pain in his limbs and the small of his back, which interrupted his usual avocations. An Indian of the Chippewa tribe prescribed this medicine in doses of about a common teaspoonful, three or four times in the course of the day. He also applied a plaster to his loins. This treatment he declares relieved him in a very short time from all his sufferings. Applied externally to the parts affected, it is said to be an excellent remedy in rheumatism. The Chippewas, Sau-kies and Fox Indians, place so much confidence in this medicine, that they seldom travel without it. I know very little about it myself, though its merit in the above-named diseases is too well established among the Indians, traders, and hunters, to be questioned by me.

[Serviceberry? *Amelanchier?*—Vogel]
Sa-bas-sa—(The name of the tree)

Sarvas tree. The tree which bears this name in the western country is among the earliest, except the dogwood, to adorn the forests with its beautiful white blossoms. Its fruit, which is a small red berry growing in clusters, ripens about the first of June, and is well known in this country.

The bark of the roots is the part used by the Indians with considerable effect, as a remedy in various diseases of the order profluvia [i.e., characterized by a discharge]. Doctor Jones of Kentucky used it, he says, in the form of infusion, with the most decided advantage, in several diseases of that order, and seems to think its reputation among the Indians is justly merited.

[*Sassafras officinalis*]
Shi-kee—(The name of the tree)

Sassafras. The Indians make a drink of the young blossoms and bark from the roots of sassafras in the spring of the year. The bruised leaves are applied as poultices, and are deservedly prized. The pith, or medullary part of the sprouts steeped in cold water, forms a wash for sore eyes, but I know nothing of its merits.* They smoke the dried bark of the root, and prize it very highly.

[Senega, Seneca, milkwort; *Polygala senega*]
Ag-ga-shu—Short crooks

Seneca snakeroot. This plant grows in considerable abundance in various parts of the western territories. It is much used by the Indians, is well known in this country, and therefore requires no description. They make use of it in cold infusions, during the remission of fevers, which are attended with great prostration of strength, and in diseases of the pulmonary organs.

They also give it warm, in combination with various other drugs, with a view to promote the sweating process, or to discharge the collection of mucus from the trachea and lungs.

They esteem it very highly in their female complaints, and also in diseases of their children when there is great difficulty of breathing.*

[Red elm; *Ulmus fulva*]
Hon-kos-kao-ga-sha—It won't go down

Slippery elm. This tree is too well known in this country, to require any description from me. It grows in considerable abundance on the western waters and in other rich lands. The inner bark is the part used. In colds and bowel complaints its properties as a demulcent [i.e., soothing to mucous tissues] are considered valuable; it is also much used as a cataplasm [i.e., a poultice] or emollient [i.e., a soothing lotion] in ulcers and swellings. But though it may deserve some reputation as an article of medicine, its greatest value consists in its nutritive qualities. I have subsisted for days on it, while traveling through the country of unfriendly tribes. The elm bark will support life for a great length of time.* Uncombined with animal food it produces sourness in the stomach and eructations [belchings].

[Button snakeroot? *Eryngium yuccifolium?*]
Sa-wah-ja-ra—Cure for bite of snake

Snake bite of the Indians is an annual plant, grows in hilly countries, attains a height of about two feet, stock single, leaves resembling those of the watermelon, and supported by long foot-stalks; it flowers in July. The whole is made into an infusion, and given warm in large quantities to such as may have been bitten by the rattlesnake.

On such occurrences the Indians frequently suck out the poison, taking care to wash the mouth frequently with water, and to chew tobacco. Excision and subsequent cauterization of the parts is however their most common practice, not only for this, but for obstinate ulcerous affections.

[Sorrel tree; *Oxydendrum arboreum*]
Pin-ne-se-ga—Astringent taste

Sour wood. This tree attains to the height of twenty or thirty feet, and is in diameter about six or eight inches. It never grows on fertile land, but is a certain indication of that of an opposite character. The leaves constitute an ingredient in the celebrated mixture for dropsy.

They seldom, if ever, administer it alone. I suppose its powers, as a remedy, therefore, to be rather feeble. The Quapaw Indians collect the leaves for the use of the pipe, and value the young sprouts for arrows.

[*Aralia racemosa;* obstacles in
the path of life, OD, *ó-ga-she*]
Tu-tus-se-ga-o-ga-she—To expel wind

Spikenard. This spikenard is one of the most luxuriant of the forest plants. It grows in the beds of hollows in hilly districts in great abundance, and if it possesses half the virtues ascribed to it by the Shawanee Indians, it merits a high rank in the Materia Medica. They give it with a view to expel wind from the stomach, to stop coughs, and to relieve pain in the breast and asthma.

[*Trientalis borealis*, Rafinesque?—Vogel; star, OD, *mi-ka-k'e*]
Me-ka-a—The flowers resemble the stars

Starflower. This plant grows in great abundance in the Arkansas, and many other parts of the western country. It spreads from the root into many branches, which rise to two or three feet in height, and expand in August or September into beautiful purple flowers, of a stellated figure; from which circumstance the Indians call it Me-ka-a, or Starweed. The whole plant is sometimes used, but more commonly the leaves and flowers, in form of infusion, as a sweat in acute diseases.

[*Rhus glabra*, etc.]
Kin-ne-ne-kah—(Arbitrary name)

Sumac. The roots and leaves of the sumac are used by the Indians in several of their diseases, but more especially as an ingredient in their favorite composition for the cure of dropsy. They consider it a principal article, next to tobacco, in the stores for the pipe; mixed with about an equal part of tobacco, it forms one of their most fashionable treats.*

Nes-ni-ne-shu-ka-ah—The saltwater runs

Sweating. Among all the various Indian nations with which I am acquainted, sweating constitutes one of their principal remedies, and among some of them, like bathing, it is practiced for the pleasurable sensations which it produces. Various means are resorted to for the attainment of this object. Some effect it by drinking warm infusions. Others assist these means by wrapping themselves in blankets or skins, while a majority have separate apartments prepared for . . . exposure to the steam of water. For this, a house sufficient in size to contain one, two, or more persons, is constructed of sticks or logs. It is commonly on the sloping side of a hill, and convenient to water. An excavation is next made in the earth-flooring, in which they place heated rocks. The bath thus prepared, the patient closes himself in, and pours water on the rocks till the apartment is filled with steam, and the intended effect produced. Herbs and roots of various kinds are placed on the rock, with a view that their virtues may unite and ascend with the vapor. During the process, the patient drinks freely of the infusion of dittany, mountain tea, or other herbs. He remains in as long as the heated rocks retain warmth sufficient to produce vapor. When he leaves it, he wraps himself in a buffalo robe or blanket, and immediately, if able, repairs to his house, and if not, he is assisted and goes to bed. I have frequently known them to remain in until they became quite faint. When this bath is used as a luxury, they frequently, on leaving it, plunge into cold water. I have never witnessed any dangerous or ill effects to arise from the practice.*

Some tribes resort to another expedient to induce sweating. They make a hole in the ground of a size and depth sufficient to contain the body of the person wishing to undergo the operation. They continue a fire in it till it becomes quite heated. The patient, wrapped in his blanket or robe, stands over the excavation, water is poured in it, and the steam rises between his body and its envelope. Others, however, immerse themselves in the water.

They also produce sweating by covering themselves in the hot sands of the barrens, and I believe with much advantage in some cases.

[*Nicotiana* species; tobacco, OD, *no-ní-hi*]
No-ne-aw—Tobacco

Tobacco. The estimation in which this plant is held as a luxury is too generally understood to need any account in this place. The Indians use it in three different ways. They use it in decoction, with the chips of the water oak, as a discutient [i.e., application for swellings], in abscesses, gatherings, and other local inflammations. The leaves are laid warm over the part affected, and kept continually moist by occasionally adding the infusion to them. Second, they apply the dried leaf to ulcers, especially of long standing. Finally, another preparation is to steep the leaves in bears' grease, and use it as an embrocation [lotion] for swellings, cutaneous and eruptive diseases [rashes]. They frequently use it externally in the cure of dropsies, and apply it as a vermifuge to the abdomen of their children. Indeed, I have witnessed some of the most alarming symptoms from its use in this way: nausea, vomiting, vertigo, great prostration of strength, and every appearance of death—though I do not know a case that has terminated in that way.

[Yellow poplar; *Liriodendron tulipifera*]
Es-pe-ton-ga—Poplar tree

Tulip tree. This towering tree is one of the greatest ornaments in the western forests, and frequently attains to a height of one hundred and fifty feet. The bark of the root, and the green seed ball which is extremely bitter, are the parts mostly used by the Indians. An infusion of the root-bark is freely taken as a preventive to fevers of the intermitting type, and the seed balls are given to their children to destroy worms.* I do not know what confidence it deserves in either respect.

[Devil's shoestring, catgut, rabbit's pea;
Tephrosia virginiana; turkey, OD, *çiú-ka*]
Soo-ke-he-ah—Young turkeys' feed

Turkey pea. There are two highly nutritive articles bearing this name, which grow in the western country in great abundance . . . . Graziers on the frontier call one variety the pea vine, which from its great abundance and nutritive properties, constitutes a highly valuable grazing article. The other has a single stock, grows to the height of eight or ten inches, and bears a small pod. It is found in rich loose soils, appears amongst the first plants in the spring, and produces on the root small tubers of the size of a hazelnut, on which the turkeys feed. The Indians are fond of and collect them in considerable quantities. I mention these facts to avoid misunderstanding because these different vegetables bear the same name indiscriminately. But the substance now under notice grows to a foot or foot and a half in height, and adorns the borders of the prairies, where in July it almost uniformly bears a great profusion of beautiful blossoms, which are white, fringed with red on their margins. These are subsequently followed by a luxuriant crop of small peas, of which the wild turkeys are extremely fond, whence their name. The roots are much valued as a medicine by the Osage, Kansas, and Pawnee Indians. They give it in form of tea, and in substance, principally with a view to destroy worms.

[*Schwitzgegreider* or sweat herb;
Aristolochia serpentaria; hair/horse/strong,
OD, *pa-hiu´/ka´-wa/ton-ga*]
Pa-us-ka-ton-ga—Like horse hairs

Virginia snakeroot. The Indians prescribe this article in warm infusion to procure sweating, and in a cold infusion, three or four times a day, as a tonic in cases of debility.

[*Plantago major;* squirrel, OD, *çin-ga*]
Se-in-ja-shu—A little squirrel's ear

White plantain. This is a small evergreen plant, growing abundantly on the southern exposures of gravelly hills, and on poor lands. The Indians have great confidence in it for the cure of coughs, colds, and fevers. With this intention they give it in infusion. They also apply the bruised plant in its recent state externally to inflamed parts.*

[Beaver tree, elk bark, Indian bark, sweet bay;
Magnolia acuminata; finger/little, OD, *sha-ge/zhin-gá*]
Sha-ga-shingah—Little fingers

Wild cucumber tree. This tree grows in the rich valleys in the broken parts of the country situated on the Osage, Kansas, and Missouri rivers. Some Indians call it chawpesha, from its intense bitterness, and the very unpleasant sensation it produces in the mouth. They make use of the fruit and bark in decoction as a vermifuge.

[Canada snakeroot, colic root, colt's root or foot,
Indian ginger; *Asarum canadense*]
E-haw-nes-ni—Water comes in the mouth

Wild ginger is a plant found in all parts of the western territories. The Indian women esteem it highly as an emmenagogue [agent for menstrual discharge]. It is also sometimes taken as an abortive. Taken into the stomach it is apt to produce pyrosis [heartburn], or the water-brash, and nausea. The Indians apply it externally to recent wounds, to prevent their bleeding. But I am unacquainted with its merits in this as well as in other respects.

Non-ja-pe-ga—Light black dust

Wood soot. This is very often given in form of infusion or tea to their children, in cases of griping and bowel complaints.*

[Golden seal, yellow puccoon; *Hydrastic canadensis;* yellow/tenderness, OD, *çi/zhin-gá*]
Se-a-shin-ga—From its extreme tenderness

Yellow root. This is one of the first plants which makes its appearance in the spring. It grows on the alluvions [bottom lands] of the western waters, to the height of six or eight inches, and bears a single rough sinuately lobed leaf, not unlike that of the grapevine. The flower stalk rises simultaneously with the leaf stalk, grows somewhat higher, and resembles that of the puccoon (*Sanguinaria canadensis*), except that its color is of a pale yellow.*

The roots of this plant contain from three to five small tuberous enlargements, about the size of a hazelnut, which are replete with a most brilliant golden-colored acrid juice. They lose nearly three-fourths of their size by drying, and the acidity of their taste becomes very much increased. From its early appearance in the spring, and the utility of this plant, I am persuaded it would be a valuable addition to the gardens of this country.

The yellow root readily imparts its coloring matter to any liquid, forming the most beautiful tincture. I have been tedious in describing this plant, because I have never heard ot its being noticed by any other person. As a generally efficient remedy, the Indians use a cold watery infusion for sore eyes, which is a very common disease in autumn, when from accident or design, the dry leaves of the forests or prairie grass take fire and vitiate the atmosphere with smoke. The powdered root is also used as an escharotic, and I believe with considerable propriety, as it has been in high repute among the Indians for a great length of time, and they seldom retain the use of any remedy which does not prove of manifest advantage.

The Indians use a warm infusion much diluted in dropsy. Hence I suppose it to possess some diuretic properties, though I can say nothing as to the fact. I believe it has some claims as a stimulant or tonic.

Observations on the Indian Practice of Surgery and Medicine   13

The Indians are aware that both respiration and the circulation of the blood are essential to life. They also know that the former is performed by the lungs, and the latter through the heart and blood vessels, though they do not understand the peculiar manner in which these organs perform those functions. And what is of much practical importance to their success in taking game, and aiming at their enemies, they are well acquainted with their situation, and with parts which, if wounded, are likely to prove mortal. They know that the brain is essential to life, and believe that it is the organ of thought. They seldom have any call for the exercise of surgical skill, and when they do, they in general display great want of experience; though I have known them to stop hemorrhages which I am persuaded would otherwise have proved fatal. Spitting of blood is a frequent occurrence in long marches, and more especially when they are pursued by enemies, and their retreat is over districts of country badly supplied with water. In such cases they chew the astringent root and swallow its juice as they run. The warriors usually carry it with them, but when without, they are compelled to seek it. It is an excellent remedy, and generally succeeds in stopping the discharge.

They sometimes experience troublesome bleedings from wounds and other causes, which they manage to arrest by bandaging the fleshy scrapings obtained in dressing skins, moss, or the hair of various animals to the parts affected. They understand the importance of bloodletting in cases of local pains, fevers, and inflammations, and perform the operation in the arm and foot with flintstones, pointed bones, or knives, having previously applied a ligature, as is the common practice amongst the surgeons of the schools. They seldom let blood in any considerable quantity, and never, that I know of, until fainting is induced. When they stop the blood, they secure the orifice with a piece of soft skin, and bind up the part by a bandage. In wounds where matter is collected they suck and spit water into them with the mouth—I believe with very great benefit. They seldom have troublesome or difficult ulcers to heal, except where their constitutions are impaired by intemperance and debauchery, misfortunes which do sometimes occur, since the introduction of ardent spirits among them. They remove the fungous parts either by escharotics or cautery. They say, "that a burn will get well of itself, while an old sore is exceedingly difficult to cure."

They are acquainted with the advantage of relaxing the muscles in dislocations. In cases where they do not readily succeed, they nauseate the patient to a most distressing degree, and then find very little difficulty in replacing a luxated [dislocated] bone.

When a ball simply lodges beneath the integuments, they extract it with the point of the scalping-knife or the handle of their bullet-molds, which, from its shape, is the better qualified of the two. When, however, the ball is lodged more deeply, or has penetrated in a circuitous direction, it is permitted to come out by the slower process of suppuration, or to remain within a sac naturally formed by the surrounding muscular integuments. When it is desirable to extract a ball, they introduce a piece of the slippery-elm bark as far into the wound as is practicable, which is suffered to remain till the sought-for object is obtained, or no danger is likely to result by suffering it to remain.* They also make incisions with the knife on the surface, whenever it heals too fast for the more deep-seated parts of the wound. The slippery-elm bark, beaten to a pulp and applied to the wounded part, is the usual remedy among the Osages for the extraction of a ball, thorn, &c. They sometimes apply the pounded roots of the gall-of-the-earth plant to wounds, inflammation generally follows, and the foreign body is easily extracted.

Plasters of the resin of the sap pine are applied to frosted members, with decided advantage.

They sometimes relieve inward pains by setting a piece of touchwood [punk] on fire, and permitting it to produce a blister over the pained part. They say, "that such treatment draws the enemy from his lurking-place, and exposes him to a direct attack."

I have known several who died from wounds received in battle: they complain of continual thirst. One in particular, a brave warrior of the Osage tribe, named Pau-ton-ga, or the Great Snow, had received a wound in his thigh, in an engagement with the Pawnees. He suffered every symptom of what I now understand by lockjaw, and expired about the seventh day. The attack was slight at first, and excited, as well as I can recollect, very little uneasiness at the time. The physicians applied lye and skins of warm, wet laurel ashes to the part, but were not able to procure much discharge, which they looked upon as essential to effect a cure. Other cases of the kind may have occurred among them, but not within my knowledge.

Having no favorite theories to support, they depend chiefly on experience in the application of their remedies; this being exhausted without procuring the desired relief, they dispute every inch of ground with the grim monster, by resorting to experiments, incantations, charms, dreams, &c.

I once saw an Indian choked. This was from swallowing a plum, which was brought back by efforts to vomit, produced by thrusting a turkey's feather down his throat; a considerable quantity of frothy mucus, tinged with blood, was brought up with it, and the person recovered.

The Indians are not very liable to swellings, tumors, or boils. When they do occur they are generally suffered to come to a crisis, without any application to them. When very much inflamed, they receive cooling plasters of bruised herbs, or fomenting warm poultices. When the color of the parts changes, and the collection of matter is evident, the Indians make an incision, and continue the poultices, to promote a discharge. . . .

Affections of the eyes sometimes occur, but I have never known them to attempt cures by any manual operations. When highly inflamed, they blow decrepitated [roasted] salt into them, but whether this treatment is productive of any benefit I am unable to say. The more mild cases readily yield to their simple applications.

The Indians commence the cure of most of their acute diseases by an emetic, by bleeding, purging, and sweating, the last of which is by far the most common.

In their treatment of ["intermittent"] fevers, they puke the patient at first, and then, while it is on, give him freely of sweating teas, and warm drinks. When the fever is perfectly off, and at no other time, they give bitters, and other tonic medicines, in considerable quantities, to prevent its return.

Pleurisy. They bleed in pleurisy, fill skins with hot ashes, and apply them over the pained parts, and sweat most violently. Whenever the patient begins to sweat freely, the hard breathing and pain in the side abate, and when the discharge of mucus from the mouth commences, they say he is out of danger.

Cholera morbus. In this disease, they resort to the steam bath and cathartics, after which they give copiously of a gruel made from wild rice, and wild licorice tea. They also apply fomentations to the stomach.

Dropsy. The Indians are more subject to this disease since the introduction of ardent spirits amongst them than they formerly were, and also have more remedies for it than for any other disease, probably, from the uncertainty which attends their operation. An infusion of the white flowering vine (Chee-za-hau) is among their most valuable and active remedies. A combination of wild-cherry bark, sumac roots and leaves, black haw, sour-wood leaves, and a mineral substance collected from the banks of rivers in decoction, given in cold, large doses three or four times a day, is also a remedy in high repute amongst them. Powdered shells and burned bones, mixed with bitter barks and herbs, is another remedy. They also apply the leaves of tobacco, steeped in a strong decoction of the chips of water oak (*Quercus lyrata*), warm to the patients, and keep them moist by the infusion. The effects are nausea, vomiting, and great prostration of strength.

Rheumatism. This disease from its frequency and violence has induced the Indians to seek a great variety of remedies, the principal of which are bleeding, steam bathing, warm infusions, fomentings, sweating, frictions, unctions, &c.

They are generally successful in relieving acute cases, and even the chronic ones sometimes yield to their remedies, but they are very liable to return.

Diarrhea. For this disease they puke, sweat, and give astringents. When long continuance has induced great debility, they give frequent and large drafts of bitter infusions. I have frequently known them to cure it by chewing the inner bark of the burr oak.

Consumption [tuberculosis]. This disease but rarely occurs. They generally attempt its cure by giving warm infusions of Indian physic, assisted by large drafts of warm water and herb teas, and not infrequently by the sweat or steam-house bath, their object being to induce sweating and nausea. The cough root or Indian balsam is among their most valuable remedies. Local applications for pain in the breast are also resorted to, as well as many other remedies which are rather harmless than useful. They abstain from animal food, subsisting principally on a gruel prepared from parched corn meal. In fact, abstinence is the Indian's sheet-anchor in the management of this as well as in their febrile diseases. Say they, "while ever the fever is on, to give food is feeding it." They adopt this saying from observing the facts, that eating during the fever increases its violence.

I have known only a few instances of this complaint amongst the Indians, brought on by exposure. Intemperance is the principal cause of its prevalence among them.

Observations on Civilizing the American Indians

14

The propriety of any measure being proved, it may be said that it is absurd to find fault with the means used to effect it, without substituting or pointing at better. We will endeavor to place reasons for the plan proposed before the reader, keeping in view the Indian character, disposition towards the civilization of their tribes, &c., and compare them with the means which have heretofore been pursued.

In the first place, the Indians are acute observers, and look much more deeply into matters than people are commonly willing to believe, and therefore reformers go among them with entirely erroneous views of their character. And the vanity of the attempt to remedy an evil, before anything is accurately understood as to its nature, or the character of the subject, is too apparent to require argument. I have myself known young missionaries, and others also, who were sent among them, and whose correct intentions I do not pretend to question, to deal out long lectures on morality, original sin, vicarious atonement, &c. The disposition of the Indians never to interrupt a talker by a rising, nor even by yawning and other indications of uneasiness, often causes the philanthropist to flatter himself that he has enlisted their whole affections and judgment in the cause, when perhaps they feel themselves insulted! When they are dismissed, and converse among themselves on these subjects, they say, "The white men tell Indian be honest: Indian have no prison; Indian have no jail for unfortunate debtors; Indian have no lock on his doors." And when the preachers make their discourse more evangelical, Indians do not comprehend them, which shows they should become more acquainted with metaphysical disquisitions, before any attempts are made to teach them the mysteries of Christianity.

Secondly, the acuteness of the Indians in prying into the motives of those with whom they are treating, makes them criticize their conduct. They say, "If the white people are so good, why leave their kindred and friends, and go among strangers, of whose mode of living they complain so much?" They look upon it as a poor argument in favor of their doctrine, when they leave their people, and come among those whose language, habits, and pursuits are all so different. And many of them look with pride on the numerous examples of white people, who abandon the habits of civilized life, and adopt those of Indians. These are sometimes men of desperate characters, less able to undergo the hardships of Indian life, or more depraved in morals. The Indians point to them as examples of white men's character, and bless the Great Spirit that they are his red favorites.

Among the white people there are many infidels also, who speak against what the Indians suppose to be their own religion; but among themselves they have no party dissensions—no infidels. It is an insult to an Indian to suppose it necessary to tell him he must believe in a God. There is about as much propriety in such exhortation, as there would be in telling the most accomplished scholar he should learn his letters.

In my tour through the territories of the Choctaw, Cherokee, and Creek nations, I could not avoid observing the difference which exists between them and some other tribes, with whom I had formerly resided, in respect to their modes of life, and their consequent moral tendency. Some of the Indians, it is true, possessed large herds of cattle, horses, and swine, cultivated cotton, corn, and some other necessaries and articles of commerce, and held a number of slaves. But by far the greater portion of them were badly provided, indolent, intemperate, miserably poor, and taken collectively, from their intercourse with the whites, they had become adepts in all their most flagrant and abominable vices, while they continued strangers, at least in practice, to the greatest portion of their virtues. I do not make these remarks from any prejudiced motives or feelings. They are founded on an impartial observation, and from my knowledge of the Indian character.

I am sincerely apprehensive that similar results will follow all similar attempts that may be made to civilize any of the other Indian nations. These fears are strengthened by further observations of my own, and from information which I have received from numerous and highly respectable sources, that the same state of society, somewhat modified by locality, exists among all the tribes bordering on our extensive frontiers. The cause of these unfortunate results or effects, it appears to me, if sought for, cannot be mistaken. The Indians, originally, are accustomed to indulge all their wants, so far as the means are attainable, and seldom restrain themselves except when old, though repeatedly admonished by experience and suffering. Hence, the want of a proper education seems unquestionably to be the radical cause.

The white people, for the most part, who heretofore have had any intercourse with them, have themselves revealed a very doubtful title to the character of civilized beings: they generally are governed in all their transactions by a self-interest which is not in the least scrupulous as to means. [The Indians find that] breach of faith, fraud, and peculation are constantly practiced on them, and that oftentimes too after their appetites for ardent spirits had been purposely indulged to such an extent, as to render them, in the strict sense of the phrase, fit subjects for protection. Added to this, they have suffered severely from various diseases, which have been introduced among them by the whites.

So the general effects of this intercourse on a people, whose very existence depends on the expertness and bravery of its hunters and warriors, are too perceptible in their enervating and destructive consequences, [too] inimical to their habits and morals, to escape their notice. [In fact it] renders them distrustful in their negotiations.

Therefore, before any permanently good effects can result to them, from the beneficent but mistaken efforts of the numerous associations organized for their civilization, in various parts of the world, all their intercourse with this class of people should be broken off. The disposal and use of spirituous liquors should be wholly interdicted. Eminent physicians should be sent amongst them, to teach them to combat with efficiency those diseases to which they were strangers, previous to their acquaintance with the white people. Every practicable means should be employed to regain their confidence and good will. And, finally, as a necessary preparatory measure, they should be enlightened by the same common process that is practiced in respect to infant minds in civilized life. The numeral relations must first be taught, before any aggregated series can be comprehended; and this truism is as justly applicable to the instruction of any other race of people, as of the Indians. Hence the inference is plain: the Indians . . . must be educated before they can comprehend the benefits and advantages to be derived from civilized pursuits, or a change in their religious tenets.

There is, in the Indian mode of life, something peculiarly fascinating: so much so, that scarcely an instance is known of a person, situated like myself—or even with the additional inducements arising from a knowledge of . . . his parents and connections—ever having abandoned it. There are [on the other hand,] numerous instances of persons, who, arriving at a discretionary age, have either been captured, or voluntarily joined them; and who, though subsequently having the option completely at their control, continued with them for the remainder of their lives. This disposition, no doubt, originated in their peculiar mode of education, in their love of ease and indolence, and the almost unrestrained freedom which they enjoy. It is true, their wants force them into action. Otherwise, a more supine and inactive life than they lead, could scarcely be desired even by the disciples of Diogenes themselves.

They live under an implied social compact, have chiefs and other superior officers, and traditionary law for their government, but, nevertheless, surrender comparatively no portion of their personal liberty. They chastise offenses, and revenge insults, regardless of all considerations, and neither yield obedience nor acknowledge fealty to anyone. Their lives are either calms or storms, in which all the passions of their souls are either quiescent or tumultuously excited, and concentrated according to the impelling cause. In fine, all their hopes and desires, whether connected with this or a future life, are completely sensual.

Whether their mode of education can be varied, so long as the means of indulgence are so easily attainable, admits of a doubt only to be resolved by constant, steady, and potent experiments. True Christian charity ought to be extended to them. Although great forbearance and labor may, and probably will, be required from those who undertake the measure, before they can be brought to comprehend and adopt the doctrines and mysteries of revealed religion, they should not on that account be abandoned to their errors.

In extenuation of these difficulties and troubles, it should be remembered with what pertinacity mankind in general adhere to the prejudices and errors derived from custom and early education; and with how much greater force they cling to opinions that have received the adoption and concurrent testimony of immemorial usage, in support of their sanctity and truth. Besides, it should be remembered that there are many individuals in all Christian countries, highly distinguished for their natural and acquired talents, who, though conversant with the Scriptures, profess that they cannot comprehend the doctrines they inculcate.

With what horror and distress would the pious professors of Christianity regard the zealous and unremitted efforts of the followers of Mohammed, to convert them to the Moslem faith. . . . The Indians do not, perhaps, experience the same degree of excitement that the Christians probably would at such attempts to revolutionize their religious opinions. Nevertheless, they look on such efforts as wicked, and upon those who make them, as instruments of the Bad Spirit sent to torment and destroy them. The object of reclaiming them from their present erroneous customs and habits, and of redeeming them from the annihilation with which they are threatened by the encroachment of the white settlers on their hunting grounds, and by a pestilential intercourse with the lowest dregs of civilized life, is of the utmost consequence to their happiness and existence, and highly worthy of the efforts of the enlightened, benevolent, and philanthropic portion of the human family.

Nay, more, it does appear to me, that the American community in particular, which has become great and powerful as it were on the destruction of the Indians, owes the accomplishment of this measure, as far as it is practicable, to its own character, to justice, and to moral right.

Spain, by her cruelty, injustice, and oppression towards the truly unfortunate aborigines of her American dominions, procured for herself a character among the nations which has barred all their sympathies for her, and in some instances caused them to rejoice at her distressing and calamitous trials. Moral reaction has set in and nearly paralyzed the fibers of her heart; and she now feebly struggles, on the brink of anarchy, for a renovated existence.

Although the American people have not trod in the footsteps of Spain, as regards their conduct towards the Indians within their territories, yet they have been guilty of cruelty and injustice to them, in too many instances.

Many proofs might be deduced in support of this assertion; but, on this occasion, I shall only bring forward one, which is mild in its features compared with others of more remote occurrence. I allude to the recent location of the Cherokees in the neighborhood of the Osage nation. These people, till the late treaty was effected between them, had been, it was well known, for a long time past implacable enemies. The least knowledge of their character must have clearly pointed out the consequences that actually did result from the measure, namely, offensive operations, and the death of many warriors belonging to both nations. Now, the powers that be could have effectually prevented this, without endangering the interests of the American people in the slightest degree; they, therefore, as before asserted, have evidently been guilty of cruelty and injustice, to say the least of their conduct, towards both these tribes.

Thousands, perhaps I might say millions of these people, have perished within the boundaries now claimed by the United States, since their intercourse with the first adventurers to this part of our continent. Numerous nations, which before that period were powerful and happy in their pursuits, now cease to exist. Many others have become feeble, and are so rapidly diminishing, that in a short time, unless the proper measures be adopted to prevent it, very little will be known of them except their names. If the past be a criterion for the future, from what is now carrying on in respect to those who still remain as it were, uncorrupted by, and strangers to the cruel policy or effects of an intercourse with the white people . . . it requires no spirit of divination to predict what will ultimately be their fate.

The title of the Indians to the distinctive character of human beings, from their moral and physical endowments, is as good, considering the circumstances in which they are found, as that of any other race of men on the face of the earth. This is so clear to those who are acquainted with them, as not to require any proof. But should there be a doubt on this subject in the minds of any, such are referred to the preceding parts of this work, for a more complete development of their character and capacities.

There are great numbers of pious good people in the United States, who display the greatest solicitude for, and generously contribute to the reclamation of the heathens of foreign countries from the darkness of ignorance of the saving light of wisdom, as promulgated in the gospel, while they overlook the temporal and spiritual welfare of those equally benighted, who live on their very thresholds. I say overlook, because all the measures that have been attempted were so feeble, distracted, and inefficient, as to induce tendencies of a very doubtful, if not of a decidedly injurious nature. The skillful physician is desirous and careful to understand the symptoms and character of his patient's disease, before he prescribes a remedy, but those who would benefit the condition of the Indians, attempted it without scarcely any knowledge of their habits and morals. As might have been expected, [they] have hitherto completely failed.

A plan of education, however, has been recently commenced at the Osage villages, which, if continued on the principles I have ventured to suggest, and agriculture and the mechanic arts be superadded to them, and all religious topics be suppressed till the young minds have been prepared by a sufficient previous education to understand them [—this plan] will, I am well persuaded, after a long time of patient perseverance, result in the happiest consequences.* But "the vineyard is great," and an increase of laborers is absolutely essential to any very beneficial results.

In selecting persons for this labor, those only should be employed who are mild and forbearing in their dispositions; moral and temperate in their habits and lives; and whose regard for the welfare and happiness of the Indians would, on every occasion, show forth eminently superior to everything like self-interest.

The Indians are generally prejudiced against the missionaries, no matter from what denomination or people they come. This feeling also extends to all white people, particularly to those from the United States, excepting only the [Society of] Friends, whose character and disposition towards them are in general well understood by all the frontier tribes, and, in many instances, by those more remotely situated. They are held in the greatest respect and esteem. If they would undertake to revolutionize the habits and opinions of the Indians, they would have the advantage of at least an entire generation of confidence and good will in their favor, over any other religious sect, a circumstance that would almost operate as a miracle in arriving at the measure in view.

Whoever may undertake it, will, if they look for a rich harvest at once, be assuredly disappointed. The opinions and prejudices of nearly all their grown people are so firmly fixed, that it will require much sound policy and good management to obtain permission, in the first place, to interfere with the education of those who are younger. Taught by experience that the white people are sincere in their efforts to serve them, their prejudices will gradually unbend. They will acquire the knowledge of a few facts, that will elicit and confirm a taste for further and more important attainments. And, finally, they will absorb every ray of truth that may be reflected on them, till they become civilized, enlightened, and themselves the teachers of the very truths which they now so much condemn.

Man, without regard to age, color, or endowments, from the circumstance of his reflecting powers, and the constitution of his social feelings, cannot but be discontented and unhappy when removed from his home and connections, comparatively ignorant of the motives which led to the measure, and placed among strangers whose language he knows not, and whose prejudices utterly forbid the formation of any new ties and relations. Precisely such, however, has been the situation of all those Indians who have been brought from, or induced to leave their forests and vagrant pursuits for academic education. Yet, forsooth, some of the philosophers of the day would rank them in their moral and physical endowments and capacities to improve, as intermediates to their own proudly cultivated race, and [to] baboons or apes; because, instructed, though under the above-named circumstances, they prefer their own country, and the society of kindred and friends, to those where their color alone is an insuperable barrier to all social and friendly intercourse. Reverse this state of things: Convey the means of imparting knowledge to them in their native retreats, and enlist them heartily in its pursuit, as readily may be done. I think I am justified, from my knowledge of them, in averring that they will rival the native Mexicans in the development of their mental faculties, of whom so respectful mention has been made by Count Humboldt, in his treatise on the kingdom of New Spain.*

Those who undertake the instruction of the Indians must expect to undergo, at least for a time, some privations, and to suffer some inconveniences. But they need apprehend nothing for their safety, provided they support rigidly just and honorable relations. Their conduct should always be consistent, steady, fearless, and independent, though not stern and authoritative. Any variation from this course will be sure to lessen their respect, or excite their jealousy, either of which would prove exceedingly prejudicial to a successful prosecution of their functions. They are ambitious, and, from the youngest to the oldest, love praise and distinction. [This is a] circumstance of which advantage should be taken, in the distribution of tokens, presents, &c., to smooth down, and render agreeable the irksomeness of their novel studies and pursuits. The teachers should learn the language of the tribes in which they are respectively located and, whenever an appropriate opportunity offers, converse freely, particularly with the older ones, on such subjects only as are agreeable to them. The good opinion of the females will also prove serviceable, and greatly facilitate the education of their children. It should be obtained by kindness and respectful attention. Too great familiarity might excite interests that would lead to disagreeable consequences. Besides, whatever may be their own habits, it would certainly detract from the good opinion of the men.

The climate on the Arkansas, Missouri, and the upper part of the Mississippi rivers, and on their tributary streams, is perhaps among the most healthy in the world. The surface of the country is remarkably even, though in some instances hilly, and the soil is in general easily reclaimable, unusually productive, and; in some parts, well watered. Thus even in temporal or interested views, the inducements which are presented to settlers in this quarter are of a most flattering nature.

I have no doubt that extensive plans may be devised and carried into effect, which would ultimately result in producing great benefits to the Indians. The object is highly important, and no means should be spared in attempting its accomplishment. It will, so far as is consistent with my pursuits, and the state of my affairs, at all times afford me the highest gratification to be instrumental in the education, and consequent preservation, of this neglected, persecuted, and much injured portion of the human family.

Reflections on the Different States and Conditions of Society; with the Outlines of a Plan to Ameliorate the Circumstances of the Indians of North America

Introduction

Mr. J. D. Hunter having published an interesting account of his own life, and of the manners and customs of the Indians in the western territories in North America (of which he had acquired a perfect knowledge by living amongst them for nineteen years), was requested, soon after his arrival in England, by the Company for the Propagation of the Gospel in New England and the Parts adjacent in America, and for civilizing, educating, and instructing the heathen natives—to commit to writing his sentiments on the best means of accomplishing those objects.

He accordingly favored the Company with the manuscript of his plan for educating his "Red Friends," and with permission to print the same. In giving his consent to have it printed, he wished it to be understood that his remarks were local and particular. He added, that although there were some general features in which every tribe of the North American Indians correspond, yet local circumstances, the disposal of their property, various resources as to game, situation, neighboring tribes, &c., all conspired to make them in some respects a different people.

The following is an extract from his letter to the governor of the New England Company:

> This is the reason why I wish my remarks *not* to be made public—so far as they may throw any light upon the benevolent designs of the Company, or contribute to the execution of them, I shall be highly gratified, and submit them to your use with pleasure; but as they are rather applicable to individual tribes of my own acquaintance, than others more remotely situated, I cannot consent to have them published, though they are at the entire service of you, and your friends, who understand my views. With my most hearty wishes for your success in a cause so laudable, I am, with much esteem,
>
> (Signed)
> J. D. HUNTER

Mr. Hunter requested any necessary corrections might be made; but it was thought better to retain his own expressions, than to suggest any alterations beyond a few verbal corrections, and his manuscript is now printed for the *sole use* of the New England Company.*
August, 1823

Reflections on Society

The writer of the following lines has had an opportunity of seeing MAN in almost every condition in which he exists in North America and Great Britain, from the free and high-minded tenants of the forest, to the highest ruler of civil society; and while he has enjoyed the blessings and admired the improvements of civilization, he cannot be blind to the evils, and the affecting miseries, which accompany its purest age, and which upon a superficial examination seem to be unavoidably connected therewith. On a more thorough inspection, however, those impressions are removed, and the evils ascribed to their real and true cause—which will be noticed in its proper place.

On contrasting the condition of that man or that society of men, who occupy a respectable station in a civil community, where the highest intellectual improvement and the deepest sense of moral obligation are united, yet free from the fetters of superstition, and above the tyrannic power of avarice—[on contrasting this condition] with that [of native] man or society, whose vices and virtues are mostly under the dominion of passion, whose virtues are rather the momentary effusions of a generous sympathy than the sound maxims of morality necessary to the greatest happiness of life, and whose vices, which, though few, are sometimes flagrant, and frequently disproportioned to their cause—[in such a contrast of civilized and native man] we find a considerable balance in favor of the former or in that society in which intellectual improvement has proved the handmaid to virtue, and has added purity of heart to the embellishments of the mind.*

To extend these blessings to as many of the human family as it is in our power to do, seems to the writer worthy the exertions of the greatest mind, and the approbation of all the wise and good. The virtues of the heart appear to be all of a social character, which produce a strong desire to extend to others the blessings we enjoy. We can go nowhere in society that we do not find objects, if not destitute, yet lamentably deficient in some moral feature indispensable to the finest symmetry of moral perfection. But evils existing equally in different places, and under various circumstances, do not admit uniform redress by the application of the same remedies.

The philanthropist's first duty is, therefore, to seek the most proper objects for his benevolence. He should be careful that he "cast not his pearls before swine." Counsels which would fail to reclaim, or perhaps be repaid with abuse by an accomplished villain in civilized life, might stimulate the high-minded warrior or the gray-headed chief of the grove to virtuous emulation, and be repaid with kindness and gratitude ever after, by the simplest children of the Western wilds.

The friend of humanity will have much to contend with wherever he may commence his labors. Ignorance is not the only evil he is attempting to remedy. Were the human capacity like an empty vessel into which the owner pours as much as he pleases, the case would be much altered. But, like the prolific soil which is crowded with noxious weeds and briars, he will have much labor to perform before he can work to advantage. Even when the warring passions are subdued, and obstinate prejudices removed, habit, inclination, and mistaken pleasures, will often call the most zealous pupil from the path of instruction. Many loiter long before they return to "wisdom's ways."

Among the various people with whose character I have any acquaintance, either by personal intercourse, by books, or by travelers, there are several tribes of the North American Indians who, in my opinion, deserve the first regard among those of our race whom civilized people call savages. For the character of those tribes an accurate account will be found in several recent publications on the Indians of North America. . . .

The OSAGE tribe, which consists of about five thousand seven or eight hundred *persons*, inhabit a country situated on the waters of Missouri, and those flowing into the Arkansas, extending from the thirty-fifth to the thirty-seventh degree north latitude. Their country abounds with game during a great part of the year. As all animals in a state of nature are migratory some months in every year, however, their country is deserted, from some unknown cause some years. The buffalo (their chief dependence) then leave the country entirely and seek the mountainous regions. This may perhaps be accounted for by the events only happening during the most rainy years.

This causes a great increase of flies in the grassy flats near the waters, which are a great annoyance to the grazing herds, and especially to the calves. This perhaps makes them retreat to the higher regions, where they are less annoyed by the flies and mosquitoes. This rambling disposition of the Indians' chief dependence for support compels the hunters to follow their wanderings, frequently among other tribes' hunting grounds or territories. It is one of the most frequent causes of those destructive wars which have so long diminished their numbers, and destroyed their confidence and friendship.

This source of destruction is greatly augmented by several causes now existing in accumulated force:

In the *first* place, the rapid approach of the white settlements on the Indian borders, and purchase of their lands, throw the tribe farther back among others, who dispute their right to settle near them. The tribe, now between two enemies, the whites on the one side, and the hostile tribes on the other, either perish contending against superior powers, or gradually decline into insignificance, and finally into oblivion, by the enervating vices and luxuries of their white neighbors.

In the *second* place, the incredible destruction of their game since the whites have entered their country, only for the sake of the skins, threatens a great blow to their staff of support, and causes humanity to lament the wantonness of civilized man. The Indians themselves never kill game, which they always look upon as the gift of the Great Spirit, except to supply themselves with provisions. On the other hand, independent of the avaricious motives which prompt the white hunters to destroy this bountiful provision of nature, they wish to have it said, that they have killed so many buffalo, deer, &c. Many have I seen shot down from mere wantonness, when the circumstances of the party did not permit them even to take off the skin.

Thirdly, loss of national pride of character, from being duped out of their lands, is another cause of destruction among the Indians. They have all the ardor of patriotism from earliest life, and no country can they call their own. The consequence is that they fall into all manner of dissipation and vice, disease and poverty follow in their train, and wretchedness and ignominy close the melancholy scene. Witness the Natchez, the Choctaws, the Kickapoos, and a hundred more tribes, once the glory of their race, and pride of the West, to whom history has scarcely given a name in her pages!!

Fourth [is] the introduction of ardent spirits among them. Here, what a gloomy picture is before us! how dismal the scene, how glowing the colors, how affecting the whole! For all other evils some plan for a remedy may be devised; but for this I see but a sickly prospect. The law may interpose its prohibitory voice. The friends of humanity may exert their influence, and expose the fraudulent practice to public execration. But does the well-known thief lose in society by being called dishonest? or what loss does the drunkard's character sustain by its being said among his acquaintances, that he is intemperate? As well may this demoralizing traffic be cut off from among the Indians, by appealing to the sense of shame, honor, or humanity of those who make money their idol—to whom they sacrifice their all, without regard to consequences.

The native, unpolluted, unsophisticated Indian of Western America possesses many estimable qualities. His situation in life makes him from infancy familiar with danger. His passion is glory; his whole soul is bent on war, or taking the bounding game; he pants for distinction; he seeks opportunity; he disdains everything little; and despises the mean soul that can stoop to perpetrate an unprincipled action. To a soul thus elevated in all its attributes; taught by experience to endure pain and fatigue without betraying its pangs, to bear privation and hunger without a murmur; and to prefer even the king of terrors, in his most horrid shape, to loss of bravery; and to look with indifference upon fiery tortures, to preserve his fame—[to such a soul] dishonesty, petty fraud, and all that motley train of vices which are daily practiced behind the counters, and in too many of the walks of refined life—to such a mind how contemptible, how despicable!! He prefers liberty to glittering trash. When his heart beats joy, it is because he is free; when the beams of pleasure glow upon his bosom, or shine in his face, it is this celestial goddess who gives it zest. How pleasing the task to teach such minds the peaceful arts of civilized society—to reclaim such prolific soil to the choicest productions, to transform the fertile forest to a blooming garden!

I look forward with pleasure to the task I have undertaken voluntarily. The motives are no less than the preservation of a high-minded, noble race of the human family, who have been debased, cheated, and slandered, from a destruction which inevitably awaits them, unless some kind arm be interposed to arrest the causes which are rapidly hurrying them to oblivion. The very thought that such a people, inheriting such distinguished gifts from nature, should eventually become extinct, without records even to tell their melancholy fate, must be truly affecting to those who think seriously on the subject. To me, whose liveliest associations and earliest impressions were derived amongst them, it is indescribably painful. I cannot reconcile it to my feelings to believe it. Independent of the encroachments of the white population, their present mode of life exposes them to a great source of destruction. I mean their being dependent on the precarious supply of nature for subsistence. Compelled to follow the roving herds into distant regions, they arrive in an enemy's country sometimes almost famished with hunger, worn down with fatigue, and frequently tortured with disease. This is almost a perpetual cause of war with one or more tribes. Fix the roving native at home, a home he can call his own. Even if he only half cultivates his corn, and but a little spot, under the nurturing influence of a genial sun, in the bosom of a productive soil, his little field will afford bread in abundance, while the towering forests, from the abundance of nuts which they produce, will amply supply him with the pork which they are well known to support in vast numbers, and the fine grazing of the plains and prairies will always supply him with beef, and the blessings of the dairy. Yes! once teach the mountain-minded warrior to unbend his lofty notions of fame, the glory of tearing off the scalp of his enemy; show him living examples of social excellence, moral rectitude of domestic comfort; excite his ambition (not extinguish it) on the side of virtue, the useful and peaceful arts; and enlist his zeal in support of mental and intellectual improvement —succeed thus far, I venture to say the benevolent will have the pleasure to find them as proper objects of their goodness, as any to whom they ever extended it. They will find their labors repaid by their rapid and useful improvement, their time rewarded by a large bounty of valuable land, and for their every charitable action, a warm return of heartfelt gratitude.

My plan to extend the benefits of civil life to the Indians is to settle in the vicinity of the Quapaws. They have a brave and manly chief.* He is a man of talent: His glory is fallen, but his spirit not sunk; his lofty mind, still elastic, rises under pressure, and lifts him above the frowns of misfortune. His influence is felt beyond the little remnant of his tribe, and is felt by the neighboring whites. They have not yet assumed the habits of civilized life; their country yet abounds in game, but it is fast disappearing before the ravages of the white man. I own a tract of land near them. I wish to let them see my improvement, my comfortable house, my rich meadows, my full barn, my fine stock—in short, every comfort which industry, seconded by art, can afford. [I want to] invite them frequently to see me, show them my independence, and let them see that I have not to run after the game, expose my health in the wet and cold, and [lay bare] my life and liberty to my enemies. This will be an appeal to his pride, and his honor, on which points they are extremely sensitive. Emulation would be the consequence, for they hate to be outdone.

I would not wholly abandon their habits. I would frequently amuse myself at shooting, especially when they called to see me: they think it a great mark of worth to excel in the use of the rifle. I would indulge in many of their rural sports. I would use the pipe as a sign of hospitality: I have experienced it, and I know the habits which are hardest to part with or adopt, on entering the civilized life.

The Indian, as well as the white man, clings with ardor to early habits, and commonly resigns them at the expense of his peace. But example can do much, when we are in earnest and feel what we are about. The great object will be to convert the rambler over the forest to a domestic character. Nature has given him a soul which disdains the chains of tyranny: convert his independence from the ardor of war to the cultivation of peace with mankind. Nature has taught his bosom to glow with the flame of love to the softer sex: let domestic education turn that ardor into kindness and attention, an attention which shall elevate his burdened squaw to his equal in society, to a companion of his toils and partner of his joys. Nature has kindled the fires of parental solicitude in his breast: let him teach his children industry, duty to their mother, and all the innocent sports and amusements of life.

It is easy to conceive what would be the result: the Indian wigwam would be soon supplied by a lasting dwelling, and the bountiful fruits of the field supply the exertions of the chase. The roaming tenant of the woods would soon be the ornament of civil society. I have no assistant to accompany me with my designs, though I have many friends in my country. I have much to perform, and but little beyond personal exertion with which to accomplish it. The object alone is of sufficient importance to call forth all the exertions of an individual who feels a lively regard for everything which concerns their happiness: one who will not consider his time wholly thrown away, but feel himself amply rewarded if his labors should result in the improvement and happiness of this truly interesting portion of the human family.

June 27, 1823

Addition

In the preceding pages I had occasion to observe, that the pleasures which the improvements of civilization produced in my mind, were not unmixed with pain at seeing the miseries which its purest community affords, and which, upon a superficial view of it, seem to be the natural result of such a state of society. I am not of that opinion [i.e., that they are a natural result of civilization]. Those countries in which the arts and sciences have been most successfully cultivated, and where civilized man has received his highest polish, have all, so far as my acquaintance extends, been enjoyed at the expense of some other nation. Those who took possession would naturally be haunted by fear of invasion; and the employment of a portion of those people, instead of adding to the general stock of wealth and improvement in their country, has not only proved a heavy tax, but an evil example to the community. The plan of settling any country by conquest is attended with many other evils too tedious to name. It causes a feudal system in the distribution of rewards. While some are made the wealthy lords of whole territories, others are left destitute. The resulting consequences are too obvious to mention.*

Many other remediable evils might be pointed out, which might be entirely kept out of a young community of adventurers. In the choice of amusements much may be done to prevent vicious habits. To the young and the gay I would recommend such amusements as are calculated to exercise the whole frame, and cause a disposition to rest. Others would be capable of choosing for themselves. Man is the creature of motives. As he always obeys the most powerful motive, I would frequently appeal more by actions than by words to the leading and master passions of the Indian's character. That is, after obtaining his confidence and friendship, which is never hard for a good man to do, I would let them see the preferences of my plan, by directing their attention to the great results of virtuous improvement.

The present juncture is more favorable than former times on another account. Not until within a very few years, have the brave Indians believed that all the powers on earth combined could conquer them. The brave and gallant Tecumseh was of that opinion. His fall has damped the ardor and crushed the hopes of many; and now, the wise and experienced are conscious they must either become tenants of the soil, or be soon lost in the sea of forgetfulness! No idea is more affecting to the brave Indian warrior, than that his very tribe and nation shall perish from the face of the earth. The love he bears to his tribe, to his aged parents, his wife and little ones, has caused him to traverse the trackless forest for days without food, to risk his life in battle, and determined him to defend them to the last, or die in the attempt.

Here then is another strong passion to appeal to. If he will suffer so much for his people, destroy his comfort, endanger his life, why not do much more for them by burying the tomahawk at the roots of the tree of peace, and take the handles of the plough and other useful utensils? Preserve his people from annihilation by making them happy by increasing their comforts, by causing the hearts of his aged parents to bless their industrious son; make his wife feel that she has a companion and protector in her husband, and his little ones rioting in all the pleasures of health and plenty, rapidly approaching the meridian splendor of manhood, wise and useful members of civil life. I know of no stronger appeal that can be made to the Indian. He is affectionate; he is fraternal; he is patriotic. Such a people are not likely to neglect the only means of arresting the blow which threatens their destruction. . . .

On the banks of the St. Francis, or White, rivers, in a delightful climate, and prolific soil, where their habits are simple, where nature has lavished her favors, and emptied the horn of abundance, where, with little exertion, the tenant may reap abundant plenty—[there] I propose to lay the plan of a settlement. By selecting such a spot,

I include many advantages. On the one hand, I am on the highway to one of the best markets in the world. Although eight hundred miles from New Orleans, I am a near neighbor by the rapidity of steamboat navigation. Even Pittsburgh and New Orleans are now shaking hands, and exchanging civilities every day.

This immense river is supported by streams issuing from sources from all directions, forming an area of several thousand miles. It commands the resources of all the immeasurable track of fruitful country included in that circle. Thus we can have ample intercourse with the civilized world, and at any time. More than two hundred steamboats, some seven hundred and fifty tons, now navigate the "mother of waters," and its tributaries!!

It is to many beyond belief, and to others a great wonder, to see a hardy band of settlers so far in the interior, bartering for all the necessaries and many of the luxuries of art, brought as it were to their doors, in traveling palaces; for the steamboats in America surpass beyond comparison anything of the kind on this [English] side of the Atlantic.

On the other hand, after enjoying free intercourse with all the commercial world, our situation in the interior gives us all the advantages of an almost interminable wild country, containing all the delights and beauties of bountiful nature, penetrated by streams navigable from seven to nine hundred miles without a settler—save some hunter's temporary camp—smiling with all the splendid gifts of Providence. My Indian friends can enjoy in perfect security what they formerly hardly enjoyed with the risk of their lives.* Hunting, which was formerly an indispensable labor, now becomes a source of amusement, and relaxation from domestic duties. They will have plenty of the necessaries and most of the comforts of life at home; they have boundless tracks to roam upon for sport. Such a country will soon become a point of emigration.

Its attractions are too powerful for avarice to resist, and its happy seclusion will invite the pious and the benevolent from more vicious abodes. The rise of property will be immense. And the Indians, who have formerly been fooled out of their lands, being now more sensible of their value, may become the rightful owners of wealth and power, and occupy that dignified station in society, which all should be ambitious to attain, and which I am certain none more richly deserve than they do.

Many of my friends, who have been acquainted with my design, have endeavored to dissuade me from it, as a task disproportioned to my power to perform. I know of nothing which would cause me to relax, much less to desist from my purpose. I see no way in which I could be any way serviceable in a society highly refined, and deep skilled in accomplishments in which I am almost a novice. I think there is no vanity in saying that I am capable of being in some degree useful among a people whose character I well understand, and among whom I can take information which the wisdom of ages has declared to be essential to the comfort of society. I have in my mind hewed out many plans, but having seen most of the social compacts of that character in the United States, I shall add to the information derived from them what I can collect from those of a similar character in England. I shall therefore defer entering into the minutiae until I shall have finished my journey in this country. In hopes of being useful, I shall cheerfully perform the task I undertake, resting the event with the Arbiter of the universe and Parent of Indians and white people.

August 2, 1823

Notes

(Complete references appear only with the first citation of an article or book.)

Introduction

page xiv
By the twentieth century the list had grown with the addition of four hundred titles: Clara A. Smith, *Narratives of Indian Captivity* (Chicago; Newberry Library, 1928). Dorothy M. F. Behen, "The Captivity Story in American Literature, 1577–1826" (unpubl. Ph.D. diss., University of Chicago, 1951), is a full-scale treatment of the genre in the period of immediate interest here. For a useful survey, see Roy H. Pearce, "The Significances of the Captivity Narrative," *American Literature*, XIX (March 1947), 1–20.

page xv
The appeal of Indian life has continued to haunt white writers, as Fenimore Cooper's novels attest. The possibility that Indian society was in some ways superior was abhorrent to Francis Parkman, yet in his *Conspiracy of Pontiac* (Boston: Little, Brown, 1926) he discussed with ambivalence those former captives who resented being forced "to abandon the wild license of the forest for the irksome restraints of society" (II, 251–56). Thomas Berger's painful *Little Big Man* (New York: Dial, 1964) is one of the more recent fictional treatments of the topic. In a much better book, *The Light in the Forest* (New York: Knopf, 1953)—a title which turned Cotton Mather on his head, so to speak—the late Conrad Richter attempted to account for the fact that such an extraordinary number of white "captives" preferred to stay with the Indians. Though Richter came down on the side of the constraints of white "civilization," he frankly admitted that "the American Indian once enjoyed far more than we. Already two hundred years ago, when restrictions were comparatively few with us, our ideals and restrained manner of existence repelled the Indians." His hero, John Cameron Butler, was allowed a reasoned rejection of white ways, and though a captive of the Delawares and with other differences in background, he might almost have been modeled on the life of John Dunn Hunter. We know Richter

was indebted to the missionary John Heckewelder and others, but the novelist's death unfortunately forecloses pursuing his possible indebtedness to the writer of our narrative. At all events, the captivity story lives on!

page xvi
The full title of the Philadelphia edition was *Manners and Customs of Several Indian Tribes Located West of the Mississippi; Including Some Account of the Soil, Climate, and Vegetable Productions, and the Indian Materia Medica: To Which Is Prefixed the History of the Author's Life During a Residence of Several Years among Them* (J[ames] Maxwell, 1823). The full title of the London edition is reproduced at the head of this volume. All the London editions contained three additional chapters: "Observations on Civilizing the American Indians"; "Indian Anecdotes"; and "A Short Description of the Practice of Physic among Several Tribes. . . ." The third or 1824 edition, whence comes this new edition, also included Hunter's important "Reflections on the Different States and Conditions of Society," which had originally been published in 1823 as a pamphlet by J. R. Lake of London. The narrative was published in German in 1824 at Dresden, in Dutch the same year at Dordrecht, and in Swedish in 1826 at Mariefred.

page xviii
The freshness of Hunter's conviction of the humanity of the Indians can hardly be exaggerated in the context of the 1820s. It was not the core assumption of any of the comparable works with which I am familiar, except for John Heckewelder's justly acclaimed *History, Manners, and Customs of the Indian Nations Who Once Inhabited Pennsylvania* . . . (Philadelphia: Abraham Small, 1819). It was central to John Halkett's *Historical Notes Respecting the Indians of North America* (Edinburgh: Archibald Constable, 1825), one of the first and best histories of Indian–white relations, but Halkett made clear how deeply indebted he was to Hunter for ideas and data. James Buchanan's less important *Sketches of the History, Manners, and Customs of the North American Indians* (London: Black, Young, & Young, 1824) also leaned heavily on Hunter.

page xxi
The article which led to the imbroglio was Anon. (George Procter), "The North American Indians," *Quarterly Review*, XXXI (December 1824), 76–111. Cass counterattacked with "Indians of North America," *North American Review*, XXII (January 1826), 53–119. In response Elias Norgate wrote his pamphlet, *Mr. John Dunn Hunter Defended* (London: John Miller, 1826). Then John Neal entered the lists with "Mr. John Dunn Hunter," *London Magazine*, V (May–August 1826), 317–43.

page xxii
In "Part Two" of *White Savage: The Case of John Dunn Hunter* (New York: Schocken Books, 1972), I deal with the charges of Henry Rowe Schoolcraft,

William Clark, John Neal, Peter Stephen Duponceau, et al. For Cass, see pp. 61–94 et passim. The "Bibliographical Essay," pp. 259–65, should prove helpful to students who wish to pursue their own inquiries into the charges and countercharges.

page xxx
"Of all the many narratives written by white people who have been captured by Indians," wrote Paul Radin, "that of John Tanner easily takes first place"—see his "Introduction" to John Tanner, *An Indian Captivity, 1789–1822*, ed. Edwin James (San Francisco: California State Library, 1940; orig. publ. 1830). To my mind Tanner lacks the depth and reach of Hunter and certainly does not take us as far into Indian–white relations, but this is not the place for such counterclaims or even for, *à la* Veblen, noninvidious comparisons. Tanner's narrative is valuable for the customs of the Ottawas and Ojibwas and for insights into how a man standing between Indian and white cultures could become increasingly embittered and find himself on the way to being destroyed by the crossfire. For a contemporary evaluation of the two narratives, to the disadvantage of Hunter, see "Tanner's Indian Narrative," *American Quarterly Review*, VIII (September 1830), 108–34.

page xxxi
It is instructive to compare our situation with the predicament faced by Bernard DeVoto in preparing a modern edition of T. D. Bonner, ed., *The Life and Adventures of James P. Beckwourth* (New York: Alfred A. Knopf, 1931). A fascinating figure, Beckwourth was a mulatto who became a mountain man and a chief of the Crow Indians; he also became, according to some, a notorious old "lier." DeVoto was unable to identify his editor beyond saying Bonner was probably a newspaper man; in struggling to separate actual happenings from preposterous fables, DeVoto had to conclude rather lamely that the "skeleton of events" related by Beckwourth was true, even though many incidents were not. By contrast the Dripping Fork incident and other problems in our text seem insignificant: We know who editor Edward Clark was, have a relatively large body of evidence on Hunter's last years, and can be quite precise in dealing with most of the charges against him.

page xxxii
The major excisions include the following chapters and chapter fragments from the English edition of 1824: I, "Physical Character of the Missouri and Arkansas Country," pp. 137–53; II, "Observations on the Mountains, Lakes, and Rivers," pp. 154–63; III, "Animals, Plants, and Minerals," pp. 164–76; V, "Statistical Remarks," pp. 209–13; XI, "Manner of Counting Time, Traditions, Tumuli, Monuments, &c.," pp. 304–10; XIX, "Practice of Physic among the Indians," pp. 436–47. There are two major and one minor transpositions: one section (orig. pp. 342–54) has been moved down to become "Indian Diseases," a new chapter (11) which also contains the minor transposition, Hunter's discussion of syphilis (orig. pp. 442–43). The other major transposi-

tion brought "Observations on Civilizing the American Indians" (orig. pp. 360–73) down to precede the final section containing Hunter's "Reflections." I should add that obvious typographical errors have been corrected, British orthography changed to American, and synonyms substituted for rare or archaic words—e.g., *revealed* takes the place of *discovered* when the context clearly indicates Hunter meant the former. When known, modern spellings of rivers and tribes have been inserted following the first appearance of the name. But for the most part I have tried to stay out of the way so the reader can enjoy a good book.

Letter to Longman and Co.

A writer in the *Eclectic Review*, XX (July–December 1823), 174, 180, had asked how the narrative got to the publishers and who the Edward Clark was Hunter had named in his "Preface." Col. Thomas Aspinwall was who Hunter said he was—incidentally, his *Catalogue of Books Relating to America in the Collection of Colonel Aspinwall* (British Museum Shelf No. 619.d.43) showed that it contained a copy of Hunter's *Memoirs* (1823). Charles Toppan was an engraver. Robert Walsh was the editor of the *National Gazette*, a professor of English at the University of Pennsylvania, and one of Hunter's patrons. Hunter misspelled the name of Col. William Duane, the Jeffersonian editor of the *Aurora*. Dr. David Hosack was vice-president of the College of Physicians and Surgeons in New York City, a patron of learning, and one of Hunter's staunchest supporters. It is probable that the Mr. Silliman mentioned was the noted Prof. Benjamin Silliman of Yale. Hunter misspelled the name of Prof. Granville Sharp Pattison, who held the chair of anatomy at the University of Maryland. Prof. Nathaniel Potter was currently serving on the same faculty.

To be sure, Hunter still had not answered the question. But he had never tried to keep Clark's name secret, as you will see on the first page of his preface. And, since they maintained friendly relations, Hunter could have had no devious reason for not further identifying his "assistant." Instead he seems to have believed he had already sufficiently identified Clark; in his letter he obligingly furnished the names of others who could testify to his authenticity.

Preface

page 2
The final prefatory papagraph was slightly different in the American edition, with no reference to "the British Public," of course, and with a differently formulated plea for the reader's indulgence, since "these details have been written from a recollective comparison between the information I have acquired since my assumption of literary habits, and the cursory and accidental observations of youth and immature manhood. . . ."

Memoirs

page 14
In December 1812 Col. John B. Campbell and a force of Americans attacked, captured, and burned four of the Miami Indian villages in what was called the battle of Mississinua or Mississinewa towns.

page 17
By the Ottowas Hunter meant the tribe today called the Otoes or Otos. Hunter's usage was one of those then current and is cited as such by Frederick Webb Hodge, "Handbook of the American Indians North of Mexico," *Bulletin 30 of the Bureau of American Ethnology* (Washington: Government Printing Office [hereafter, GPO], 1912), II, 166. This Platte River tribe should not be confused with the Great Lakes Ottawas.

page 22
The Vermillion Hunter and the party of Kansas crossed was possibly Vermillion Creek, a branch of the Osage River, also variously called Coal Camp or Cole Camp Creek. It was more likely the headwaters of the Verdigris or the Neosho, both of which were sometimes called the Vermillion, just as the latter was also called the Grand, the Cottonwood, and the Six Bull River. The name Vermillion spread far and wide, like the rouge used by the ladies of the streets or, as Elliott Coues complained of rivers named Red, like the paint cowboys used to liven up a town.

page 27
As stated, this was perhaps Hunter's most serious error: He switched the Osage villages around, incorrectly placing White Hair's on the Arkansas and Clermont's on the banks of the Osage in present-day Missouri. But it was just close enough to the facts to make it perplexing. At the instigation of Pierre Chouteau—the fur trader who wanted the tribe out of the trading territory of his rival, Manuel Lisa—shortly after the turn of the century, about half the Great Osages moved to the Three Forks of the Arkansas. This exodus was led by Cashesegra or Big Track, who was apparently accompanied by Clermont, while White Hair remained behind. Why Hunter placed White Hair on the Arkansas is a mystery, unless his final attempt at an explanation offers us a clue. In his chapter "Brief Statistical Remarks on the Kickapoo, Kansas, and Osage Indians," which has not been reprinted in this edition, Hunter wrote that the breakaways were "under the ostensible direction of Big Track, though White Hair instigated the measure and virtually exercised the duties of chief." So much hinges on what Hunter meant by "ostensible": Did he mean that White Hair—said to be, like Big Track, "a chief of Chouteau's creating"—exercised his duties as chief from the old location on the Osage, though Big Track was ostensibly running things on the Arkansas? This would account for White Hair's remaining behind in

the territory of Manuel Lisa: he could look after Chouteau's interests in both villages. And it would account for Hunter's thinking of those who broke away as really White Hair's people and for his continuing to regard Clermont as the true chief of the Great Osages. At all events, even if this is a possibly valid reading of the evidence, what Hunter really meant remains obscure. What can be said with certainty is that editor Edward Clark did little to help clear away the confusion and may even have contributed to it.

page 31
Tecumseh's reference to the Great Spirit speaking "in thunder, and the earth swallows up villages" was to the earthquake mentioned by Hunter above. It did occur in 1811, created havoc along the Mississippi, and swallowed up part of New Madrid. The eschatological vision here, incidentally, was a direct anticipation of the Ghost Dance religion decades later—for Tecumseh's role in the tradition leading up to Wovoka and Sitting Bull, see James Mooney, "The Ghost-Dance Religion and the Sioux Outbreak of 1890," *Fourteenth Annual Report of the Bureau of American Ethnology* (Washington: GPO, 1896). For an able discussion of the great Shawnee statesman and of Hunter's account of his speech, see Glen Tucker, *Tecumseh: Vision of Glory* (Cincinnati: Bobbs-Merrill, 1956).

page 37
Amid all this luxuriance of flora and fauna (the influence of Hunter's "assumption of literary habits" run riot?) the reader should note an interesting fact: Unlike explorers Pike, Long, and others, Hunter clearly believed that this vast extent of country would one day be settled and "civilized." He did not share the general belief, that is, in the myth of the "Great American Desert."

page 38
By some tribes the Pawnees were known as "the wolf people." Their confederacy had four tribes: Grand, Republican, Tapage, and Skidi or Wolf Pawnee. The last lived on the Loup River in present-day Nebraska.

page 39
In 1804 Captains Lewis and Clark referred to the "Staitan or Kite Indians" as one of the small tribes who lived at the head of the Platte and about whom little more was known than their name. Frederick Webb Hodge, "Handbook of the American Indians," II, 632, thought the reference was to the Sutaio, a formerly distinct tribe which had since incorporated with the Cheyenne. Hodge listed Hunter's "Sta-he-tah" as one spelling of the name.

page 40
"Pash-e-quah": It is tempting to think that Hunter's reference was to the *camas*, which was a staple root food for the Western Indians and which

was used most extensively in the valleys of the upper Columbia. But his observation that the root was "not a bad substitute for bread, particularly when roasted," suggests he may have had the *kouse* in mind. Second only to the camas in importance, the kouse roots were pounded into loaves of bread a foot wide and three feet long and then laid on poles over a fire to bake.

page 43
Hunter seemed to contradict himself. On the one hand was the tradition handed down by "our old men, that the great waters divide the residence of the Great Spirit, from the temporary abodes of his red children." On the other was his assertion that "we had ever been taught to believe, that the Great Spirit resided on the western side of the Rocky Mountains, and this idea continued throughout the journey, notwithstanding the more specific water boundary assigned to him by our traditionary dogmas." Were "the delightful hunting grounds" on the other side of the great waters, then, or on the other side of the great mountains? Here a bit of knowledge of Osage cosmology helps: in their thought the West "meant" Water and was associated as well with the setting sun, night, mystery, death, and, as Hunter pointed out, Spiritland. Though he obviously had difficulty stating this clearly, his seeming contradiction disappears once we understand that, for the Osages, the western side of the Rocky Mountains and "the more specific water boundary" were one and the same. Incidentally, Hunter's reference to "our old men" echoed the Osage veneration of the "Little Old Men," those founding fathers who first discovered the silent, invisible creative power that gives life to the sun and moon and stars and earth. The power that Hunter called *"the Great Spirit" was sometimes called Wa-kon -da. "Mysterious Power," and sometimes E-á-*wa-won *-aka.* "The Causer of Our Being" (Francis La Flesche, "The Osage Tribe: Two Versions of the Child-Naming Rite," *Forty-third Annual Report of the Bureau of American Ethnology* [Washington: GPO, 1928], pp. 29–30).

page 44
In 1805 William Clark had called this tribe "Clap-sott." Hodge, "Handbook of the American Indians," I, 305, listed Hunter's "Calt-sops" as a variant. Hunter's ethnological data on these transmontane Indians are generally accurate but read much like that in the so-called Biddle edition of the report of Lewis and Clark—see Paul Allen, ed., *History of the Expedition under the Command of Captains Lewis and Clark* . . . (Philadelphia: Bradford & Inskeep, 1814), II, 32, 125–39. As you will note, moreover, Hunter did not mention Astoria at the mouth of the Columbia or in fact any buildings or parties of whites. Yet this was not necessarily damning, for he rarely mentioned forts in areas he knew very well; and, since he kept no journal, he or his editor might very well have turned to the Lewis and Clark report to flesh out skeletal recollections. Finally, rejection of this Pacific trip as another Dripping Fork incident, added for the titillation of readers, presents

almost insuperable problems in accounting for what Hunter demonstrably knew about the country through which he said his party passed. In short, I find more compelling reasons for believing the trip genuine than for believing it spurious. The reader should be aware, however, that this section presents problems.

page 44
In 1806 Lewis and Clark referred to the principal southern tributary of the Columbia as the Multnomah; their map showed the sources of the present-day Willamette rising in the vicinity of what is now known as Great Salt Lake. Two decades later Clark's famous map, which he constantly revised as it hung on the wall of his office in St. Louis, showed the Great Salt Lake as the source of the Multnomah (Willamette). No one then or since seemed to realize that Hunter's narrative called this erroneous geography into question. As you will note, Hunter did not place the headwaters of the river so far to the south and certainly not at a saltwater lake. The Multnomah Indians were a Chinookan tribe that formerly lived on the upper end of Sauvies Island in the Columbia. The name also referred to all the tribes living near the mouth of the Willamette. Hunter's translation of the name to mean "River of much game" is a puzzle. Franz Boas translated it in 1905 as "Down river."

page 45
"Lesh-te-losh": Hodge, "Handbook of the American Indians," I, 762, cited Hunter for the name, noting they were "probably a Kalapooian band, said to have lived near the headwaters of Willamette r., Oreg."

page 50
"Tetau": The Teton was the western and principal division of the Sioux. The name was a contraction of "Titon wan" and meant "dwellers on the prairie." Hodge, "Handbook of the American Indians," II, 736, listed Hunter's "Tetaus" as one variant.

page 50
Elliott Coues, ed., *The Expeditions of Zebulon Montgomery Pike* (New York: Francis P. Harper, 1895), II, 400n, pointed out that the river was referred to alternatively as the Vermillion or the Verdigris. From the context it appears that Hunter had the latter in mind, though on other occasions he seems to have thought of the Neosho (Grand) as the Vermillion. The confusion about rivers in this area was well-nigh universal, with geographers and others constantly misapplying their names (see Coues's note, II, 552–54). But since the Verdigris and the Neosho empty into the Arkansas within a few miles of each other, which Hunter had in mind is of little consequence here.

page 51
The sixteen moons were from the early spring of 1813 or, more probably,

1814, to the autumn of the following year. Given the sparseness of Hunter's details, any attempt to lay out the route of his party must remain conjectural. But hypothetically: they started up the Arkansas, crossed to the Kansas and the Platte, ascended the latter nearly to its source, crossed the Rockies, and descended the Columbia to the Pacific. They returned up the Columbia, ascended the Willamette, took the Salt Creek Pass through the Cascades, crossed over Oregon via the headwaters of the Deschutes, and found in Malheur their very large lake. Hunter's discussion of hot springs near their winter camp suggests that it was somewhere near the area of thermal waters in present-day Yellowstone Park, perhaps not far from the route Astorian Robert Stuart followed in 1812–13. Their ease in crossing the Continental Divide suggests that they too, like Stuart, "discovered" the South Pass. Then, after some confusion, they hit the Arkansas and followed it home. Tare-heem, the leader of the expedition, incidentally, may have been the "Tarehem" or "Yellow Skin Deer" Pike reported as one of the principal Little Osages (*Expeditions*, II, 591).

page 51
In 1819 Thomas Nuttall reported a man of this name running a house of entertainment on the Mississippi at a place called "M'Lane's Landing"—Reuben Gold Thwaites, ed., *Early Western Travels* (Cleveland, Ohio: Arthur H. Clark, 1905), XIII, 96.

page 53
In his *Travels in the Interior of America in the Years 1809, 1810, and 1811*, the botanist John Bradbury discussed a trip up the Missouri with Lisa and also commented on how the hunters aimlessly killed buffalo. He tried to restrain them, "but they scarcely ever lose an opportunity of killing, if it offers, even although not in want of food"—see *Early Western Travels*, V, 148–49.

page 54
Hunter's account of this expedition with Manuel Lisa was notable for its perceptiveness in detailing the trader's operating techniques, quarrelsomeness, treachery. In *Three Years among the Indians and Mexicans* (Waterloo, Ill.: War Eagle Press, 1846), Thomas James, who had been one of Lisa's *engagés* on an earlier trip (1809), corroborated every significant circumstance Hunter had related. Moreover, Hunter provided here the only known evidence on Lisa's activities in the winter and spring of 1816. Conceding that Hunter's "fanciful tale" was the sole source for his subject's whereabouts then, Richard Edward Oglesby drew on it for indispensable evidence and then attacked its general validity in a footnote: "Like all of these fictions, this one may contain a germ of truth. Hunter claimed to have gone on an expedition in or about 1816. His description tallies very closely with that of Thomas James, and he may have gotten his information from that source" (*Manuel Lisa* [Norman: Univ. of Oklahoma Press, 1963], pp. 160–61).

A curious corner to paint oneself into: this possibility was truly "fanciful," if not absurd, since James's *Three Years* was first published twenty-three years after Hunter's *Memoirs*.

page 55
"Tun-gah": This was probably a misprint or misspelling of To^n-ga´, which meant big, by implication strong, and, as a ritual name, The Great (Francis La Flesche, "A Dictionary of the Osage Language [hereafter "Osage Dictionary"]," *Bulletin 109 of the Bureau of American Ethnology* (Washington: GPO, 1932). As you will note, in his "Observations on the Materia Medica of the Indians" Hunter correctly translated Has-hak-a-da-ton-gah as meaning "Strong Soldier." And in fact there was a leading Osage brave, who may have been the "Tun-gah" named here, called Has-hak-a-tonga or, in an alternative translation, "Big Soldier" (*Niles Weekly Register*, Sept. 14, 1822).

page 69
On Zebulon Pike's "Chart of the Internal Part of Louisiana" (1810) this settlement on the White River appeared as "Flee's."

page 75
Among the documents collected by General Cass and incorporated in his *North American Review* article, the most damaging was a letter from John Dunn, identified as "a member of the Missouri Legislature." The writer stated that he had never known a "John Dunn Hunter," that in the preceding twenty years he had never heard of anyone "bearing the same name with myself in this country," and that therefore the "reputed author" had to be an impostor, "most probably . . . an individual who has never seen the various tribes of Indians of whom he speaks." But internal evidence makes quite clear that this John Dunn had never read Hunter's *Memoirs* and therefore had no personal knowledge of *how* Hunter spoke of the various tribes of Indians nor of *what* he said. Besides, how could this John Dunn have possibly known what the unknown writer (of an unread work) had seen? Moreover, how could this unknown individual have possibly fabricated his own name and address, namely that of John Dunn, Cape Girardeau County, state of Missouri? Now, in fact there was no such person as John Dunn, "a member of the Missouri Legislature." Perhaps Cass meant *former* member, for there had been a John Dunn in the third Territorial Assembly of 1816. But hard evidence that there was another John Dunn "in this country," and almost certainly at least two others, destroyed what was left of the credibility of Cass's star witness—for a detailed discussion of Dunn's testimony, see *White Savage*, pp. 77–78, 88–90.

page 79
After the wave of denunciations against Hunter, why George P. Watkins never stepped forth to defend his rescuer is unknown. Perhaps he was dead or beyond the reach of the press. At all events, we do know that Thomas

Jefferson believed Hunter genuine. As Elliott Cresson, scion of the Philadelphia family of merchants, wrote, "the opinion of our late President, Thomas Jefferson, Esq. as expressed to myself was certainly free from all doubt" (letter reproduced in Elias Norgate, *Mr. John Dunn Hunter Defended* [London: John Miller, 1826]). And we know that Jefferson almost certainly considered the Watkins letter genuine, though we do not know precisely what evidence he had to go on. Dr. David Hosack, Hunter's New York patron, wrote Peter Stephen Duponceau, the philologist, on January 28, 1826, that the letter had weighed heavily in his own evaluations of Hunter and that "Mr. Jefferson as you know is also among his friends and I believe considered the deliverance of Watkins to be an ascertained truth" (Duponceau Papers, American Philosophical Society).

Chapter 1: Physical and Moral Condition of the Indians

page 83
The ellipsis indicates a cross-reference Hunter made to a preceding chapter, omitted here, in which he had attempted to give "a very imperfect description" of this extensive country. The boundaries he then established, from the spaced periods to my bracketed interpolation, also delimit his reference and come from pp. 137–38 of the London edition of 1824.

page 86
Like Jefferson, Hunter was of course correct about the great number of radically different Indian languages. Peter Stephen Duponceau, John Pickering, and other philologists of the day saw in this a threat to the received Mosaic chronology, since sharp differences would indicate the passage of an immense course of time since the languages had commenced to recede from their common origin. Duponceau, whose contributions to linguistics made him justly acclaimed, thought he had overcome this threat with his discovery that native languages were one in the way they interwove words and various parts of speech. Ironically enough, it turned out that *all* Indian languages did not exhibit this "wonderful organization" and that the relatively unlettered Hunter, whom Duponceau accused of being "an arrant impostor," had a better idea of their real diversity.

page 90
For some reason—a sense of liberation from local taboos, a growing impatience with the arguments of compatriots, or whatever—once across the Atlantic Hunter added sections to the American edition which showed he had come to believe that it indeed "belonged" to him to take sides on the question of many races or one. As you will see, he openly expressed scorn for those "philosophers of the day" who ranked Indians, "in their moral and physical endowments and capabilities to improve, as intermediates to their own proudly cultivated race, and [to] baboons or apes" (see below, page 218).

page 91
Hunter was disabusing his readers here of the vagaries of the French naturalist Buffon, of William Robertson, whom I have discussed as Cass's mentor, and of others who contended the Indians had no body hair, had no or virtually no sex drive, and so on.

page 93
Planned Parenthood: Others agreed that Indian women seldom raised more than three or four children, but no one seemed to know quite how they limited their offspring. As the reader will see, in his "Materia Medica" Hunter mentioned wild ginger and an unidentified "Black root" as two of the abortives sometimes resorted to. But he makes clear here that by prolonging the suckling period to two or three years, "under the belief that it promotes sterility," some Indian women were "spacing" their children and deliberately practicing what came to be known as birth control—and this considerably in advance of the publication of the *Fruits of Philosophy* (1832) by Charles Knowlton, the "American Father of Birth Control."

page 95
Field investigations, contemporary accounts, and modern experiments all show, says Virgil Vogel, "that dental ills were more common among sedentary tribes who subsisted largely on corn than they were among the nomadic hunters. It is further evident that the incidence of tooth decay was far less frequent among aboriginal Americans than among contemporary Americans" (*American Indian Medicine* [Norman: Univ. of Oklahoma Press, 1970], p. 245). And one of his sources traces the greater incidence of tooth caries to use of "the foods of modern commerce." Hunter's paragraph would have slipped smoothly into these more recent findings.

Chapter 2: Religion, Good and Bad Spirits, &c.

page 101
The Great Spirit as also "the Giver of Life" was an exact equivalent of the translation I have already mentioned: "The Causer of Our Being." Whether this Spirit had corporeal form was the subject of speculation and discussion among the Osages. In one tradition an Ancient Man, whom the Little Ones had called Wa-kon-da, objected to being so named and instructed the people that the Great Spirit had no bodily form. Here, as though white readers were too much on his mind, Hunter wrote of the Osage origin myth with distinctly Christian overtones. Elsewhere in an otherwise relatively unimportant chapter which I have cut from this edition, Hunter mentioned other versions of the myth:

> Some relate, that the whole human family, and every living thing, like vegetables, sprang out of the earth many hundred snows ago; others . . . that the Great Spirit created at first only one of each sex, and placed them on an

island in the midst of the great waters, which, in the process of time, became too small for their accommodation, and threatened them with great calamities. In this distress, the woman, who was remarkable for her piety and goodness, prayed to the Great Father, who took compassion on them and sent the beavers, muskrats, and turtles to enlarge it with materials from the bottom of the ocean, which they collected in such great quantities, as to give to the island the present extent of our earth [1824 edn., p. 306].

Though Hunter was more than a little apologetic about recounting these traditions, they were in fact more authentic than his red version of the Adam and Eve story. The deluge myth above has parallels with the Great Elk and other Osage songs. And, according to one version of the Osage genesis myth, the Little Ones indeed "sprang out of the earth many hundred snows ago": see J. O. Dorsey, "Osage Traditions," *Sixth Annual Report of the Bureau of American Ethnology* (Washington: GPO, 1888).

page 106
"Tut-tus-sug-geh": This may have been the Little Osage Chief whom Pike called "Tuttasuggy, or Wind" (*Expeditions*, II, 371). And you will recall the Kansas warrior, a member of the same Sioux language family, whom Hunter called Tut-tes-se-gau, which he translated in like fashion as "the Rushing Wind" (see above, p. 16).

page 108
"Tecumseh and Francis, the celebrated Shawanee prophets": This is one of Hunter's most interesting errors. As you will recall, he had already said that Tecumseh made his memorable visit to the Osages "in company with Francis the prophet." Here he showed he thought Francis a Shawnee. But Francis was in fact a Creek and a most remarkable man in his own right. He had a white father who had settled among the Indians and married a Creek woman. The son was known to the traders as Josiah Francis and to the Creeks as Hillis Hadjo. On his visit to the South, Tecumseh had created him "the great prophet of the Creeks." Later Francis visited England, was commissioned a brigadier general, and, like Hunter, received by George IV. During the Seminole War, General Andrew Jackson had him hanged. (See Carolyn Thomas Foreman, *Indians Abroad, 1493–1938* [Norman: Univ. of Oklahoma Press, 1943], pp. 114–16.) But Hunter's error is interesting primarily because Glen Tucker has established that Francis did indeed accompany Tecumseh on the trip that included the appearance Hunter recounted (*Tecumseh*, pp. 214–17). Hunter may have understandably assumed that, since Francis was called the prophet, that he was The Prophet, Tenskwatawa, Tecumseh's brother, and hence a Shawnee. Now, unless he was precisely where he said he was, how could Hunter possibly have known that a prophet named Francis traveled with Tecumseh to the Osage country?

Chapter 3: Courtship, Marriage and Families

page 113
Hunter's insistence that Indian sexual customs were sensible and decent

was as rare as his conviction that they were human beings. His views were not shared, for instance, by Mr. Requa, a teacher in the United Foreign Missionary school near the Great Osage village. Writing at about the same time, Mr. Requa held that Indian life was one of "defilement and uncleanliness. The half has not been told. I could give you an account of their lewd and immodest conduct. Let it suffice to say, that chastity and modesty are not known, or very little regarded by them. They have little sense of shame" (quoted in Louis Houck, *History of Missouri* [Chicago: R. R. Donnelley, 1908], I, 191). The half had not and would never be told about the orgies in the bushes, just across the frontier: Hunter was understandably impatient with all the Mr. Requas "who pretend to be well acquainted with the subject."

Chapter 5: Hunting, Agriculture and Crafts

page 144
This paragraph on buffalo-hair blankets has a remarkable ethnohistory. In "Prehistoric Textile Art of the Eastern United States," *Thirteenth Annual Report of the Bureau of American Ethnology* (Washington: GPO, 1896), William H. Holmes used it for his description of native weaving. In "The Various Uses of Buffalo Hair by the North American Indians," *American Anthropologist*, XI (1909), David I. Bushnell, Jr., drew on it as the most graphic and detailed account of how the Indians wove blankets from buffalo hair. Finally, in his authoritative *Navaho Weaving* (Albuquerque: Univ. of New Mexico Press, 1949), Charles Avery Amsden quoted it and noted that the process described therein was somewhat similar to the archaeological evidence on "the loom of early Tiahuanaco times in Peru. . . . But Hunter's description fits Pima weaving more closely still." In his reference to "a long flattened wooden needle," Hunter was discussing, Amsden added, part of what was close to the true loom, the "only machine aboriginal America ever produced."

Chapter 6: Crime and Punishment

page 151
As of 1897 the sixteen "families," or gentes, of the Kansas did not include the Wolf and the Panther. But the tribe was by then dissolving: between 1850 and 1905 they declined from 1700 to 209 souls. There may have been more and other gentes at the beginning of the century.

Chapter 8: Patriotism and War

page 159
"Kut-che-nau": I regret having been unable to trace this fascinating reference. It was not to peyote, probably, though there are reports from the early eighteenth century of its use by the Indians in the Southwest and we know the Osages were ranging far into that region. In any event, Hunter mentioned only "a plant," not a cactus. And there were, of course, a considerable number of narcotic plants known to aboriginal America.

page 160
"Shin-ga-was-sa": When George Catlin was at Fort Gibson in 1834, he painted a portrait of "Shin-ga-wás-sa, the Handsome Bird; a splendid-looking fellow, 6 feet 8 inches high; with war club and quiver" (Thomas Donaldson, "The George Catlin Indian Gallery," *Smithsonian Report of 1885* [Washington: GPO, 1887], II, 44).

Chapter 9: Residence, Dress, Painting, Mournings, &c.

page 167
By now, after the buffalo-hair blankets, painted posts, planned parenthood, skin canoes, sound teeth, death songs, his insistence on the importance of dreams—in the same spirit as the "Stand Awake or Vigil Song" I use as an epigraph—after all this, the reader may need no further persuasion that Hunter was a splendid field observer. But if you do, simply compare these paragraphs with those in Francis La Flesche, "War Ceremony and Peace Ceremony of the Osage Indians," *Bulletin 101 of the Bureau of American Ethnology* (Washington: GPO, 1939), p. 54. La Flesche's data on Osage body-painting read almost as if they came directly from Hunter.

page 170
As Hunter tried to straighten out this matter of their early-morning "lamentations or howlings," Dr. Pixley, who also taught at the United Foreign Missionary school, was reporting that the Osages "pray, indeed if it may be called prayer, as we are told; and even now as the day dawns whilst I am writing in my house I can hear their orgies, where their lodges are set up, more than a mile from me. They begin very high in a sing-song note, as loud as they can halloo, and then run their voice, as long as they can carry breath, to the lowest key. Thus they continue the strain, until they are wrought to a pitch, wherein you will hear them sob and cry as though their hearts would break. . . . In such a case they put mud on their faces and heads, which I understand they do not wash off till their desire is in some measure answered" (quoted in Houck, *History of Missouri*, I, 198–99). Our "Stand Awake or Vigil Song" suggests that the "mud" with which the Little Ones darkened their faces was really "the sacred soil of the earth." But such orgies were hard for whites to understand. Botanist John Bradbury had reported their mournings and passed on the information "that the loss of a horse or a dog was as powerful a stimulus to their lamentations as that of a relative or friend" (*Early Western Travels*, V, 63). Geographer Henry Marie Brackenridge recorded that he had been awakened at daylight

> by the most hideous howlings I ever heard. They proceeded from the Osages, among whom this is a prevailing custom. On inquiry, I found they were unable to give any satisfactory reason for it; I could only learn, that it was partly devotional, and if it be true, as is supposed by some, that they offer worship only to the evil spirit, the orison was certainly not unworthy of him. I much doubt whether any more lugubrious and infernal wailings ever issued from

Pandamonium itself. I was also informed that it proceeded from another cause; when anyone, on awaking in the morning, happens to think of a departed friend, or even of some lost dog or horse, which has been prized by the owner, he instantly begins this doleful howl. . . . (*Early Western Travels*, VI, 61–62)

These were the travelers' accounts Hunter had in mind, accounts which made his red friends seem ridiculous wildmen, horse and dog mourners, if not devil worshipers—shades of Cotton Mather! Of the sincerity of the mournings and the depth of the affliction Hunter reported there can of course be no doubt. As late as 1874, long after they had been "removed," Osages used to return to their village in Missouri to cry over the dead they had left behind.

Chapter 10: Indian Anecdotes

page 173
"Mu-kea": As you will see, Hunter translated the *starflower* in his "Materia Medica" as *me-ka-a*. The word for "star" in La Flesche's "Osage Dictionary" is *mi-ká-k'e*. Perhaps *mu-kea* was a misprint or misspelling or, still more likely, the Kansas word for "star"—though like the Osages the Kansas Indians were in the Dhegiha subdivision of the Siouan language group—was slightly different.

page 177
In his important *Historical Notes Respecting the Indians of North America* (Edinburgh: Archibald Constable, 1825), p. 324n, John Halkett related he had asked Hunter how the Indians were able to travel at night: "I was informed by Mr. Hunter that the Indians can march at night in a direct line through the forests, when they cannot see even a star to guide them, merely by feeling the bark of the trees as they move along." Henry David Thoreau was copying this passage into his "Indian Notebooks," when he broke off the quotation at the "I was informed by Mr. Hunter. . . ," to exclaim in his own voice: "So he had seen such a person!" Thoreau was understandably excited, for Hunter's life illustrated his own abiding conviction that man lived best with a mixture of "civilization" and "wildness."

Chapter 11: Indian Diseases

page 180
"Shak-kee": La Flesche, "Osage Dictionary," translates rattlesnake as "shé-ki."

page 181
It is likely that the Indians were right in saying, as reported by Hunter, that syphilis was unknown among them until they contracted it from whites. Whites have liked to believe the opposite, of course, contending that they

got rather than *brought* the dread disease. But the evidence indicates that syphilis was present in Europe during the Middle Ages, known under a variety of names, especially "leprosy," while a single case has never been established in the pre-Columbian Americas. Hunter's discussion of syphilis, from the spaced periods to my bracketed interpolation two paragraphs later, was originally on pp. 442–43 of the London edition of 1824.

page 182
To white ears the term "medicine man" usually sounds like conjurer, shaman, or "witch doctor." Knowing this, Hunter took pains to distinguish what may be termed the "bad magic" of the charlatan, the fakir, the self-server, with his grotesque garb and exclusive access to the occult, from the "good magic" of the genuine healer, with his common dress and shared tribal lore. (For Hunter's word-sketch of the former, in this instance of the Arikara priest who calls to mind George Catlin's famous "Mandan Medicine Man," turn back to p. 107.) His purpose was worthwhile: He wanted his reader to know that the practice of medicine was not peculiar to whites, that the Indians had physicians who were "honorable, humane, and experienced men," and that the body of knowledge and techniques they had accumulated were relevant to general human needs—that it was not, in short, simply a matter of "science" versus "magic." In fact, according to contemporary white accounts, the Osages were particularly "skillful in medicine." Hunter's obvious enthusiasm for their medicinal practices argues powerfully that he had internalized the culture of this tribe.

page 183
Hunter showed a surprising awareness of the importance of shared cultural expectations and of the essentially therapeutic role of medicine men in such cures. Compare his assessment, almost in psychosomatic terms, "of this kind of practice on the imagination," with that of E. Bradford Torrey, a modern psychiatrist and anthropologist who has worked with doctor-healers in other cultures: "Witchdoctors and psychiatrists perform essentially the same function in their respective cultures," Torrey writes. "They are both therapists; both treat patients, using similar techniques; and both get similar results" (*Guardian* [London], August 2, 1972). A hundred and fifty years ago Hunter entered a comparable protest against white ethno-arrogance.

Chapter 12: Materia Medica of the Indians

page 188
Hunter cross-referred here to an earlier chapter in which he had explained why he was not using technical terms: his explanation, from the spaced periods to the end of the sentence, comes from p. 137 of the London edition of 1824.

"A dry record of facts" this chapter is not. It is instead Hunter's monument to the intelligent concern of tribal peoples to lessen human distress and pain, to clear away what the Osages called *ó-ga-she,* obstacles in the path of life such as the diseases and accidents which interfere with well-being. This concern created the aboriginal materia medica which he could draw on to help the fever-ridden whites at Flees' Settlement. They not unsurprisingly welcomed him with open arms for a very good reason: what medicine there was on the frontier came mainly from the Indians—I find Hunter's "great astonishment" at their ignorance of "the treatment of diseases" one of the most singular and quietly funny passages in the narrative (*supra,* p. 69). Across the Atlantic his knowledge of North American medical flora was of great interest to his friends in the Royal Society and no doubt especially so to Sir James Smith, author of the great *English Botany* and one of his most enthusiastic supporters. And this aspect of Hunter's work has interested other naturalists down through the decades, including Thoreau and the entomologist W. J. Holland.

Yet waves of the future have washed over naturalists, making them seem like "herbalists," curiosities out of a pre-strip-mining past. "The people of the European race in coming into the New World have not really sought to make friends of the native population," observed the ethnobotanist Melvin Gilmore, "or to make adequate use of the plants, or the animals indigenous to this continent, but rather to exterminate everything they found here and to supplant it with plants and animals to which they were accustomed at home" ("Uses of Plants by Indians of the Missouri River Region," *Thirty-third Annual Report of the Bureau of American Ethnology, 1911–12* [Washington: GPO, 1919], p. 53). To be sure, during wars and other catastrophes white Americans have often had to turn back to native remedies. Now that we have exterminated almost everything we found here, however, we face an ecological crisis which dwarfs all preceding catastrophes and do so at a moment when there is not all that much to turn back to. Our predicament makes Hunter's materia medica suddenly relevant again, especially for the young who are engaged in their own experiments in survival. With such potential readers in mind, I have tried to edit Hunter's version of the Indian pharmacopeia so that it can speak directly to them and still be of some interest to the specialist.

How to help without hurting is, as always, a problem. I try to deal with it here with bracketed interpolations. First appear other common names of remedies, when known and better known than some of those which, as Hunter said, "are of my own application." Second appear the Latin names, when known, since of the sixty-one remedies Hunter discussed, fifty-five are botanical. And third, I occasionally insert Francis La Flesche's rendering (in "Osage Dictionary" [herein, OD]) of an Indian term or part of a term, on the assumption that a chance to compare Hunter's Osage names may prove of interest to some and not a nuisance to others.

These bracketed identifications are supplemented by data that I hope will make the materia still more understandable and useful. To my mind the real test of the drugs Hunter discussed is whether they worked for other tribes. References to comparable usages therefore appear in these endnotes—here listed by remedies rather than page numbers, but with asterisks continuing to indicate the existence of a particular note. (The reader who wants to pursue this topic on his own might well start with, notwithstanding differences in tribe and region, Gladys Tantaquidgeon, "Mohegan Medicinal Practices. . . ," *Forty-third Annual Report of the Bureau of American Ethnology* [Washington: GPO, 1928], pp. 264–70.) For the names of plants and a knowledgeable discussion of their use, I draw on Melvin R. Gilmore's essay, quoted above, and rely still more heavily on Virgil Vogel's more recent and comprehensive *American Indian Medicine* (hereafter, AIM), which—not incidentally—has a mercifully useful index containing some three dozen items on Hunter.

Bathing: Even the northern Indians, Vogel points out, practiced year-round bathing, and this at a time when, as Dr. Daniel Drake observed (1850), "an overwhelming majority of our population seldom bathe at all" (AIM, pp. 253–54).

Bears' oil: Hundreds of miles to the east and a century earlier, Robert Beverley of Virginia had also reported the Indians anointing their skin with bears' oil mixed with herbs (Vogel, AIM, p. 218).

Beaver root: Or wild carrot was listed as a tonic/stimulant in the *Pharmacopeia of the United States of America* (hereafter, USP) from 1820 to 1882.

Datura stramonium (p. 191): Jimson weed, angel's trumpet, Jamestown lily. Hunter correctly used the Latin name of this narcotic plant, known to Cotton Mather as the "Jamestown weed, whereof some having eaten plentifully became fools for several days; one would blow up a feather in the air; a third sit naked, like a monkey grinning at the rest" (Vogel, AIM, pp. 326–27).

Dogwood: A number of tribes used the bark as a febrifuge. It has since been discovered to contain properties like that of the cinchona, from which quinine was extracted, and thus was quite appropriate for "fevers of the low type." USP, 1820–94; *National Formulary* (hereafter, NF), 1916–36.

Gentian wild: A recognized febrifuge, mixed with dogwood bark it may have proved effective against malarial fevers or, as they were called in the nineteenth century, "intermittents." USP, 1820–82.

Green-twig: The willow proved useful to other tribes (Pima, Houma, Creek, Alabama, and Natchez) against fevers, and well it might, for it contains *salicin*, the now well-known painkiller. (Vogel, AIM, pp. 392–93.) USP, 1882–1926; NF, 1936–55.

May apple was one of the best known of the Indian laxatives which whites adopted. USP, 1820–1942; 1955—.

Milkweed: Gilmore noted that this white or tall variety was called *ska* by the Omaha Ponca: "The root was eaten raw as a remedy for stomach trouble" ("Uses of Plants," p. 110). USP (dwarf sp.), 1820–63, 1873–82.

The oak: "Many Indian tribes were cognizant of the properties of oak bark, which was widely used in maladies calling for an astringent or antiseptic remedy" (Vogel, AIM, p. 145). USP, 1820–1916; NF, 1916–36.

Prickly ash: After learning its uses from the Indians, settlers adopted the bark as a folk remedy for rheumatism. USP, 1820–1926; NF, 1916–47.

Sassafras: As you will recall, Hunter observed above that the lodges and tepees of the Plains tribes were intolerably smoky except to the Indians who were used to the discomfort. But even they suffered "sore eyes" (opthalmia) for which they had several remedies, including "the cold watery infusion for sore eyes," made from the yellow root or golden seal Hunter discussed below, and the sassafras-sprout eyewash he mentioned here. Sassafras was in addition, of course, the proverbial spring tonic and blood cleanser. USP, 1820–1955; NF, 1926–65.

Seneca snakeroot: The Chippewas also used this root for coughs, sore throats, colds. Vogel reports it became so sought after, "the Menominees almost exterminated the plant in their district by collecting it for the drug trade" (AIM, p. 372). Hunter's discussion of it as an expectorant, as a remedy for colds and respiratory problems, was exactly what it came to be used for by white practitioners. USP, 1820–1936; NF, 1936–60.

Slippery elm: Gilmore also said the inner bark was used ("Uses of Plants," p. 76). The Pillager Chippewas or Ojibwas, for example, used the inner bark as a remedy for sore throats. White practitioners have used it for precisely the purposes listed by Hunter, as a substance capable of soothing inflamed mucuous membrane and as a soothing application. USP, 1820–1936; NF, 1936–60. As for its nutritive qualities or at least its aid to such, let me quote from a package of THOMPSON'S SLIPPERY ELM FOOD just purchased at the local Boots pharmacy here in London: "In the forest glades of the Americas there grows a tree, the Slippery Elm, from the lining of whose bark is obtained a remarkable demulcent factor. . . ."

Sumac: "In the fall when the leaves turned red they were gathered and dried for smoking by all the tribes" (Gilmore, "Uses of Plants," p. 99).

Sweating: The sweat bath was another hygenic practice of these not-so-filthy savages. (In speaking of this and of bathing as "remedies," Hunter came close to using the terms of preventive medicine—indeed, he referred to bathing as a "preventive.") As he observes, sweat baths were enormously popular among all the Plains Indians for reasons of health and pleasure. But, though he may never have personally witnessed any ill effects from the after-plunge into cold water, it apparently killed many during smallpox epidemics. (Vogel, AIM, p. 256.)

Tulip tree: Like the dogwood, the bark of the yellow poplar has properties similar to the cinchona and thus probably was effective against malaria. The Catawbas used it as a worm medicine. USP, 1820–82.

White plantain: Gilmore reported that a Ponca told him that "a bunch of leaves of this plant made hot, and applied to the foot is good to draw out a thorn or splinter" ("Uses of Plants," p. 115). Hundreds of miles away to the east tribes also used the large plantain as a fever remedy (Vogel, AIM, p. 175).

Wood soot: This is one of Hunter's nonbotanical remedies, the other five being the two measures of body hygiene, bathing and sweating, the bears' oil already discussed, iron, and ashes. Iron or ferrous sulphate still appears, Vogel observes, in pharmaceutical preparations (AIM, p. 402). Ashes and this "light black dust" were obviously of the same order as the wood charcoal used for bowel and other complaints. USP, 1820–1936.

Yellow root: Vogel notes that, "undoubtedly, *Hydrastis* [or golden seal] was the 'yellow root' described by Hunter" (AIM, p. 311). (The problem of sorting out names is never-ending, for this particular plant had almost a score of common names, some of which were applied to other plants, one of which has come to be known as "yellow root.") Other Indians used the *Hydrastis* for inflamed eyes, as a diuretic, and for dropsy. Settlers made use of it for some of the same purposes, and the drug became important in all the pharmacopeias. USP, 1831–42, 1863–1936; NF, 1936–60.

In 1827 the secretary of war asked General Lewis Cass to seek out an Indian snakebite remedy, since, he reasoned, aborigines might be expected to know what Nature had in her "vast storehouse of remedies." Coming as they did just a year after Cass had dismissed Hunter's materia medica as "trash," these instructions carried their own special irony: Hunter had already placed before the general and his white associates a long list of precious items from the warehouse they were so blindly plundering.

Chapter 13: Indian Practice of Surgery and Medicine

page 209
Writing in the mid-nineteenth century about the Michigan Indians, Dr. Zina Pitcher also said they took care to keep gunshot wounds open so they would suppurate. To this end they introduced a "tent" of slippery elm bark. As Vogel observes, it is remarkable that the elm bark was used in these precisely parallel ways by Indians a thousand miles from each other. His

research indicates that in the treatment of internal ailments and the practice of surgery, the methods Hunter discussed were similar among widely separated tribes. (See AIM, pp. 107, 197, 226–29.)

Chapter 14: Observations on Civilizing the Indians

page 217
The "plan of education" was no doubt the United Foreign Missionary school, established in 1821 on the Marais des Cygnes River at a place called Harmony, about fifteen miles from the Great Osage village in Missouri. Had Hunter known what Mr. Requa and Dr. Pixley were saying about the "idolatrous race" to which they had been called to minister, he would have been less sure about the happy consequences of their labors.

page 218
The reference was to *Political Essay on the Kingdom of New Spain,* trans. John Black (London, 1811), the two-volume study by Alexander von Humboldt (who was, incidentally, a baron). The reader will have noted in this paragraph and in earlier passages Hunter's extraordinary sensitivity to the issue of skin color and its role, for both Indians and whites, in determining the relationships of their respective societies.

Reflections on the Different States, &c.

page 221
Longman and others apparently persuaded Hunter to give his remarks wider public circulation, for there follows the pamphlet which was first published by J. R. Lake and then reprinted in the London edition of 1824.

page 221
Like a centipede, Hunter's tortuous sentence marched—or did not march—on many legs. The "sound maxims" of his more pious teachers probably had something to do with its locomotor ataxia. What he tried to say, apparently, was that in the contrast between civilized intellectuality and primitive passion, the balance of value swung toward the former. I have inserted bracketed interpolations, without much confidence, in an attempt to help the reader past a narrow spot in the trail.

page 225
It is not clear whether Hunter is referring here to Heckaton or to Saracen, the principal chiefs of the Quapaws.

page 226
Between his "Reflections" proper and this "Addition," Hunter had met Robert Owen, who had been warring against Christianity and the churches for years. Owen may well have influenced this afterword, for, as you will observe,

Hunter said no more about the desirability of educating the Indians to understand the mysteries of revealed religion. Instead he advanced a radical, secular interpretation of what was wrong with man and society: it was not man's nature, but the nature of imperialistic societies. Hunter was a quick student.

page 228
By the time Hunter reached his Quapaw friends, they had been induced, probably through generous gifts of spirits, to part with the land of their fathers. When Hunter arrived, he probably urged Heckaton and Saracen to try to undo the treaty they had marked by throwing themselves on the mercy of the Arkansas authorities. His sanguine hopes, as with the steamboats, were misplaced. Governor George Izard told the chiefs that he realized that it was always hard to give up a land "where the bones of one's ancestors repose," but added he could do nothing for them. Like his red friends, Hunter was soon to become a displaced person, driven from river to river to the City of Mexico and on to an end outlined above in the introduction.